DIRTY WORD

The Vulgar, Offensive Language of the Kingdom of God

Jim Walker

DISCIPLESHIP RESOURCES

PO BOX 340003 • NASHVILLE, TN 37203-0003
www.discipleshipresources.org

Cover design by Denman Rooke
Interior design by PerfecType, Nashville, TN
Author's photograph by Julie Petrick

ISBN 13: 978-0-88177-539-6

Library of Congress Cataloging-in-Publication Data

Walker, James Perry.
  Dirty word : the vulgar, offensive language of the kingdom of God /
Jim Walker.
      p. cm.
  ISBN 978-0-88177-539-6
  1. Christianity--21st century. 2. Postmodernism--Religious
aspects--Christianity. I. Title.
  BR121.3.W35 2008
  277.3'083--dc22
                                                    2008015793
Scripture quotations, unless otherwise indicated, are from the New Revised Standard
Version Bible, copyright © 1989, Division of Christian Education of the National
Council of the Churches of Christ in the United States of America. Used by permis-
sion. All rights reserved.

For Brenda,
The love of my life.

For Carly and Daniel,
You guys rock and I'm proud of you.

CONTENTS

ACKNOWLEDGEMENTS

As I began thinking about writing a book, I decided I wanted to make it as communal an experience as possible. I cleared a bulletin board in a room of our office space, made note cards available, and invited the folks in our faith community to write down a story, thought, or a suggestion. At the same time, I started to find myself in some deep conversations in coffee shops and bars about faith and God and life and church. It was out of those discussions that this book was born. If you were part of any those discussions you will recognize most of the content of this book. I want to thank, primarily, all of those friends who have taken the time to sit wrestled with me over what it means to be a follower of Jesus in our world today. To the guys that have gathered for our unsponsored, unadvertised community event 'pint night', thank you. To the people who have found themselves in the basement of a tattoo shop fighting about the theology of baptism, thanks. To all those who have sat with me, late at night, at a coffee shop, struggling over what it means to "exist," thanks. And for those who have stuck around even though you had to endure yet another one of Pastor Jim's manic sermons about koinonia, thanks. In all these ways, I believe the writing of this book has been a communal experience, and for those who have experienced it with me, I'm in your debt.

The second thing I wanted this book to be was honest. I made every effort to tell the truth, even when I thought it might make the reader uncomfortable or angry. So, I guess, in this time of acknowledgements I need to be honest and tell you that this book would be two pages long if it were not for the now Rev. Jeff Eddings. This is really his book. I just put it down in ink. It was Jeff who quit his job without any real certainty of where his next paycheck would come from, packed up his family and moved to the South Side in an effort to get this church going. It is probably Jeff more than myself, who actually lives out what is offered in these pages. I need to thank Jeff for the use of many of his stories, metaphors and talk points. And to be even more honest, there actually would be no stories at all if it were not for some very important people in our lives. Special thanks to Bishop Thomas Bickerton, who had the guts to give his thumbs up to our crazy little 'not by the book' church plant, and to Don Scandrol, Martha Orphe and everyone else in the Western Pennsylvania Annual Conference who helped make the dream of Hot Metal Bridge a reality. Vera White and Don Dawson from the Pittsburgh Presbytery are certainly not innocent bystanders. They believed in us when no one else did- including ourselves! Thanks. I also want to thank the professors at the Pittsburgh Theological Seminary. Whether they like it or not, the material in this book is a product of their teaching. Many thanks. Thanks, too, to Tony Norman, of the Pittsburgh Post-Gazette, who came to visit Hot Metal one Sunday morning with the intention of just staying a few minutes and has never left. Tony ended up looking over this manuscript and giving me some key pointers. Thanks Tony.

Lastly, this would be the most boring book on the planet if it weren't for the gathering of friends at the Hot Metal Bridge Faith Community. We've created some wonderfully memorable moments together, worthy of a book evidently. Thanks, one and all, for loving Jesus,, loving each other, and loving me with reckless abandoned. Thanks to Denman Rooke, a talented young artist, who did the completely awesome artwork on the cover. In addition, thanks to Doug Brunner, a gifted artist himself, for holding the bread and cup and shouting into the sky. I hope that this book blesses all of you as much as the experiences that created it have blessed me. I love you all.

DIRTY WORD

INTRODUCTION

In the early morning hours of March 24, 2002, I had a waking dream, a flash of a vision that has ended up changing my whole life. It was one of those dreams where things are vivid and it seems that you have a little bit of control over the events and the choices. It was almost as if I knew that I was dreaming and I wanted the dream to go my way. Maybe it was the fact that I had spent the entire month of March thinking and dreaming about what church should be and what I thought it maybe could be. Or maybe it was something else, maybe something more spiritual, like the Holy Spirit moving in my life. I like to think it was the latter. The realist in me thinks that maybe it was the former. Either way, I had a dream, a vision, of a bridge. The bridge in my dream wasn't the typical bridge. In fact, I can remember thinking that I had never quite seen a bridge like this one. It had the look of a railroad trestle bridge with big, black, crisscrossing steel beams. It was the kind of bridge that we have a lot of here in Pittsburgh. What made this bridge different was it wasn't a bridge that carried trains. This bridge had a road on it, a kind of lit pathway.

In my dream, I was with Jeff. Jeff Eddings and I met years ago, 1987 to be exact, when we were both theater arts students at Point Park College. Since then, Jeff and I have worked together in ministry as performers, as youth pastors, and as journeyers in the Way. We've been through a lot of ups and downs together, but somehow we have remained good friends, if not brothers. If it's true that God intends for ministers to be sent out in pairs, Jeff and I are meant to be sent out together. We have done ministry, many times in the form of drama, in shopping malls, in people's living rooms, in retirement homes, and in the most humiliating of venues. Now, in my vision, we were running across this railroad bridge that wasn't really a railroad bridge. It seems like a simple vision. One that's not all that exciting. What has made it one of the most motivating events of my life is that in my dream there was a person at the end of the bridge calling us to "come over and help."

And that is the whole dream. I never made it to the other side to see who was calling us. I don't think I needed to. Now, six years later or so, it's obvious who it was. Anyway, I woke up and rolled out of bed, contemplating the vision that had been conjured up in my sleep. I showered, wondering what it all meant in relation to the things I had been thinking lately. At the beginning of that March in 2002, Jeff and I had met for breakfast, as was our habit, and we had begun to talk about what it would be like to plant a church. Of course, we had no clue what it meant to plant a church. If we had known, we would have run screaming out of the Bob Evans, never to talk with one another ever again. But we had started to dream about planting a church, and now I had this weird vision of a bridge. At the time, I wasn't quite sure what it meant or where all of these thoughts were leading.

The same morning of the vision, I met up with Jeff. For years, we have been writing and performing plays for churches and churchy events. We met at a Presbyterian Church in Beaver, Pennsylvania, to do a play we had written, ironically or appropriately maybe, about doubting Thomas. The play is entitled "Blind Faith"—which makes this whole story sound made up, but it's not. We met at the church and unloaded our set and props for the play, cup of coffee in one hand, backdrop in the other. As we set up, I told Jeff about the dream I had had earlier that morning. I knew I could share the dream with Jeff and he wouldn't think I was nuts or self-serving, although sharing a dream always comes off a bit egocentric.

When I finished telling him the vision, which of course didn't take very long, he said:

"Oh, I know a bridge like the one you're talking about. It goes over the Mon (the Monongahela, for you non-Pittsburghers) down near the city."

"No, I don't mean the Birmingham or the Liberty Bridge. This was a railroad bridge that we could run on," I replied.

"Yeah, I know," he said. "There is a new bridge down there now. I think it used to be a railroad bridge, but now it's used for traffic."

The next thing I remember is sitting at the stoplight at the end of that very bridge looking up at the brand-new street sign. The white words on blue background read "Hot Metal Bridge." I turned onto the bridge and drove over it, all the while wondering, "What is this? What does all this mean? Is this anything?" On the other side of the bridge, I found myself on the South Side. For me, this was a new world. I drove a few blocks and found a pay phone (I don't know why I didn't have a cell phone). I called my wife Brenda, and I called Jeff. Both conversations were the same. They each answered the phone, said "Hello," and I excitedly shouted into their ears about how there was a new bridge and a new community and a new world and there had to be a new church and blah, blah, blah. They thought I had lost it. Later that week, I dragged them down to see. As they crossed the bridge, they asked the same questions I had asked:

"What is this? What does this mean? Is this anything?"

Six years have passed and we have not stopped asking those same three questions. We ended up using the local Goodwill building to meet and to worship in. It's two blocks from the Hot Metal Bridge. So, of course, the church was eventually named the Hot Metal Bridge Faith Community. There is an elevator in the Goodwill building that takes you to the third floor where we meet in a rather large cafeteria space. I can remember many mornings going up to the third floor in that elevator with Jeff, cup of coffee in one hand, backdrop in the other, with a look on both of our faces that said, "What is this? What does this mean? Is this anything?"

This book is written in the same spirit of wonderment. This book isn't written in an effort to provide any answers at all. It is simply meant to be a voice in the already ongoing conversation. The experiences that Jeff and I have had in the past six years have brought us to some awkward and sometimes offensive theological conclusions. Jeff likes to call himself a theological mutt. I like to say I'm a recovering evangelical. Neither one of us has had a clue as to what this is, or what all this means, or even if this is anything at all. But it is always fun and always worthwhile to try and find out. So, this book isn't written in an effort to get any quick fixes or big answers. I write in an effort to share what we've seen and then ask, "What is this? What does this mean? Is this anything?"

When the Presbyterian Church was considering sponsoring us as church planters, we had to undergo psychological evaluations to see if we had what it took to plant a church. At that time, we had been gathering as a small worshipping community using our own energy, free time, and our own money. The presbytery brought in a psychologist who specializes in determining whether someone is church-planter material or not. He spent a whole day interviewing each of us. The outcome? "Ambiguous." There were certain assets and certain liabilities. According to the results of the examination, I had one church-planter asset and that was "spousal cooperation," and that has little to do with me. So I had nothing to offer. All I had was that I had happened to marry an awesome woman.

When the results came in and we sat down with the committee from the presbytery, we were totally expecting them to tell us to hit the bricks. Instead, they told us in the meeting that they had decided to commit fully and to sponsor fully the Hot Metal Bridge Faith Community. Stunned, we daringly asked why.

"We don't get it," we said. "We clearly don't have the gifts, we don't have a clue as to what we're doing, neither one of us has graduated from seminary yet, and neither one of us is even Presbyterian. Why on earth would you want to sponsor this church?"

I'll never forget Don Dawson's reply. Don was the chairperson of the committee. He simply said, "The Holy Spirit. We need to factor in the Holy Spirit. And we think the Holy Spirit is up to something here."

I think that phrase sums up our church: "The Holy Spirit is up to something here." Sometimes we're not really sure what the Spirit is up to, but it sure is up to something. The growth and the blessing and the adventure and the community that have been experienced at Hot Metal has had nothing to do with Jim or Jeff. The Holy Spirit has been involved here somehow. It is my hope that the stories and the lessons that we've learned will become seeds for other communities like Hot

Metal. What we offer doesn't come from our expertise or from some committee but from the work of the Holy Spirit, being up to something, touching and transforming lives. If I were to sum up this book, it would be, "Look out. The Holy Spirit is up to something here. Get out of the way and let the Spirit move."

It seems that all of my life I have been on a quest for God. Not to just learn about, read about, or talk about God, but really to meet God. You know, face to face. I'm still unsure of the depth of my motivations, but it's always been there. At a very young age, maybe four or five years old, I scattered my army men on the floor of our basement in Carlisle and challenged God: "If you exist, if you're really there, put these men back in the bucket." The next day, I woke up and ran down to the basement. To my amazement, the army men had returned to the bucket. Well, most of them had returned. One regiment was still lined up as if they were marching into the bucket. There it was—proof! The army men were in the bucket. This evidence was enough for me. There was a God.

Of course, it wasn't until I was teenager that I realized that my mother had gone down and cleaned up the army men. But my quest has continued. In my high-school years, I did the youth-group thing; I walked down to the altar to "give my life to Jesus." I spent my twenties trying to find ways to use my gifts for God's service. I tried many venues, from Christian theater companies to Christian television to Christian camps, retreats, conferences, etc. I eventually got a job in youth ministry at a local church. Still, my quest, my search went on. I've spent countless hours and days finding prayer closets and big rocks in the woods and starry nights, and candlelight services and all those places where I was convinced God could be found. In my thirties, I went off to seminary, taking the search to deeper, more complicated places. I read Athanasius, Anselm, Augustine and all those theologians whose names start with "A" . . . and "B" . . . and "C" . . . . Surely, I would find God in their books. I could meet God in their words.

All of those experiences, from church camp to seminary, were good, and I do not regret one moment of the journey, but nothing has prepared me for what has happened in my journey in recent years. Nothing has prepared me for where I finally met God face to face. It has brought me to my knees. For all the candlelight services, all the starry nights, all of the books in the world cannot prepare you for the moment when you find the kingdom of God in the basement of a tattoo shop. I believe I have gotten the great blessing of meeting God face to face, but it wasn't where I expected to find God. Strangely enough, God has shown up in my life in the form of spiky-haired punks, idealistic dreamers, and starving artists whose spirits inspire me. God has shown up in the form of a couple of homeless people who live under Birmingham Bridge. God has shown up in the form of a punk-rock band with members who scare the crap out of me when they're on stage, but off-stage like to "cuddle" with Pastor Jim. The most hardened-looking street kids have melted my heart. God has shown up, but it wasn't where I expected to find God.

That's why this book is called *Dirty Word*. Well, it's called *Dirty Word* for a few reasons, really. First, I have become more and more convinced that the gospel, God's message and mission, is completely offensive. Much like a dirty word, the gospel should actually be censored. It is subversive, counter-cultural, and totally punk-rock. It is grimy and wild-haired and, well, kind of dirty. Second, I think that things "dirty" are usually inspiring, as God's Word is. Think about it. Which is more inspiring, watching the Steelers trot off the field at half-time in the Superdome, their jerseys nice, clean, and unscathed, or watching the Steelers trot off the field in rainy, dreary Pittsburgh, their jerseys muddy and grass-stained, covered with blood. Now that's inspiring. And that's the way of Jesus. Jesus doesn't ever trot off the field with a clean jersey. He gets dirty. Jesus gets in the grime and muck of life. And that's the third reason: if we follow Christ, we too are going to have to get dirty. And I mean really dirty. All the time. Not just on the special, once-a-year mission trip to Central America, where we get to eat exotic food and touch a lizard. I mean the kingdom of God is found in the dirty, unclean places of this world. That's where Jesus found it. That's where we'll find it.

I've been putting off writing this book for some time. One reason is that it seems kind of hypocritical to write a book about practicing communion. It seems to me that the best way to promote the idea of communion is just to do it, to actually be in communion and shut up, right? And through the relationships I have made on the South Side, through Hot Metal Bridge, I have gotten small glimpses of the kingdom of God. I feel as if I found what I had been looking for, and it is enough. So, I had little motivation for writing a book. But as I have experienced what I have experienced on the streets of this city, and as I have sat in silence with the scriptures, and as I have read other books that Christian America seems to go bananas over, I have sensed a kind of dissonance. A mixed message. What I've seen on the streets, what I'm reading in scripture, and what I'm reading from the Christian bookstore don't seem to match. At first, I thought I'd be a man of grace and let it ride. When we were told that God wants "to expand our territory," I smiled politely. When the Left Behind video game came out, depicting weapon-wielding Christians, I grimaced and whistled into the air like I'd been hit on the toe. And when I found myself standing in front of an entire bookshelf filled floor to ceiling with books urging me to have "my best life now," I doubled over, thinking I might vomit. But I continued to remind myself that we should have grace for one another. "But for the grace of God go I, right? I'm certainly no saint. Who am I to criticize how other people should live out their faith?" And so, I was still unmotivated to write a book.

Then one day I walked into the bookstore, and I came face to face with Your Best Life Now, the Game. Friends, I couldn't believe it. It was a game, blast it, a game, based on the book that proclaims that life is about being successful, being "blessed." How many ways can these people find to make money?! I didn't smile. I didn't whistle. I didn't double over. I stood frozen, box in my hand, reading the rules to the game, and uttered the dirtiest swear word I know, "Jiminy Crickets!"

To win Your Best Life Now, the Game, the player has to be the first to pass Level Seven, choose to be happy, and begin living at his or her full potential. Essentially, this wildly fun game reinforces the warped cultural value that to have worth and to be happy, one has to be a winner. Sure enough, when I bought the game, took it home, and opened it, I found that one of the main game pieces is a mirror. A mirror! Evidently, to get past Level 2 on the rise to their best life now, players must look into the mirror as they make positive statements about themselves.

Look, Jesus is for loser, folks. Being a Christian doesn't mean you get to have it all; it means you get to follow the Sufferer. It's not a game where the winners are living to their full potential. It's not a quest to be happy. It's a life of surrender and sacrifice, which means sometimes you might *not* be happy. You might actually find the most precious gift of all through your own brokenness.

When I finally got over the initial shock and horror of this insanely screwed-up game, I took some time to be quiet, and it broke my heart. It broke my heart to the point of getting me in front of a keyboard to start typing. I mean, is this really what Christians in America believe? Do we really believe that life is like a game where we have to say nice things about ourselves in a mirror to find joy? What are the consequences of such selfishness? What are the ramifications of such spiritual blindness? And how in the world do you begin to show people who already consider themselves Christians what it really means to follow Christ? Following Jesus isn't about having your best life now, that's for sure. It's not about me at all. It's about denying myself, picking up my cross, and following the Sufferer all the way. The way is rough, the way is narrow, and the way is very, very dirty. The time for being friendly is over. I have had enough. And I know I'm not alone. There are others of us out here who have stood by long enough and said nothing because we don't want to offend or hurt someone's feelings. Hey man, maybe there's a place in this world for a dirty word or two. I'm sure the prophet Jeremiah didn't always keep it clean. Why should we? Enough is enough.

So, as you read this book, I hope you get a little dirty yourself. Maybe you'll find yourself running off the field all muddy and bloody, arms raised in a "V," a few teeth missing. Certainly, I don't pretend to have all the answers, and most likely, in many places I am dead wrong. No doubt this book will get a raised eyebrow from at least one of my former seminary professors. God, I hope so. My prayer isn't that you might find any answers here. My prayer is that by hearing our story—the story of Hot Metal Bridge Faith Community and our struggle to find a way to follow the call of Jesus in this screwed-up world—you will become so offended that your face turns red, you throw this book across the room, and hopefully you even say a dirty word or two. But I also hope that you become inspired so much that you end up dreaming about bridges yourself. I hope you also conjure up enough courage to take a risk and get dirty. I hope you decide to become part of the bridge yourself.

DIRTY WORD

PART 1: ENOUGH BULL#@%!

"Would someone please save me from all this bull@#$%?"

This is the horrible thought that ran screaming through my head like a cage-fighter with a metal, folding chair.

"Good God! I can't take it anymore! Could someone please get me out of this?! I'm up to my neck here. Save me from this bizarre church thing! Save me from Christianity! Please! Save me from all this bull#@%!"

I hate church. I really do.

Church. Do We Really Need It?

It had been an especially good worship service that morning, or so I thought. You know, pastors spend more time evaluating and criticizing their ministry than being and living and loving and caring. So, of course, instead of actually worshipping God, I was, as usual, constantly evaluating everything. "Boy, the band nailed that song . . . ;" "That was a thought-provoking drama. I wonder what people are thinking?" It was one of those Sundays where everything seemed to click. The music had been extra loud and passionate. The drama had been one of those intriguing stories that really made you think. The bridge moment (that's what we call the sermon because it's short and sweet and it bridges the drama with communion) had been one with an extra edge to it. The Spirit was moving. As the service came to end and people ate the last of the bread, we held hands and sang the benediction. I wondered if anyone had been touched in a significant way. That's what we pastors do at the end of good worship services. We ask ourselves if it made any difference.

And so when Reagan approached me moments later, my mind raced with the possibilities. Perhaps this will be one of those important conversations. Maybe I'll be able to justify my existence, maybe even pat myself on the back for a job well done.

"Can I talk to you for a minute, Pastor Jim?" Reagan said.
"Sure," I said. "What's up?"

I had seen Reagan once or twice before. She was another young adult who had gotten involved in some of our church activities, if you could call them church activities. We hang out in the basement of the tattoo shop, in the Beehive (a local coffee shop), and help feed the homeless on Saturday afternoon. I could faintly remember someone telling me about Reagan. She was new to our church and she—and here it comes—was not a Christian. Well, of course, that news did more harm than good inside of me as she approached, because I instantly began to chart my course toward bringing her to "saving faith in Jesus." Hey, don't judge. That's how I'd been trained to think in the ways of the "Evangelical Christian Manipulative Arts." Anyway, here was Reagan, a young adult, standing before me after a relatively powerful worship service, wanting to talk, and me plotting to rescue her from hell.

"I don't know quite how to say this, so I'll just say it," she said. "I'm not really a Christian, and I don't know if I'll ever be one. But I like it here, and I think something good is happening here. Is it all right with you if I get involved in this church if I'm not a Christian?"

Her question knocked me off guard in more ways than one. Reagan didn't want to be "led to the Lord." There was no need for me to say the special prayer with her. That was my first thought. But that wasn't the jarring part. It was my second thought that shook me up, and it is the thought that I've had ever since. This thought motivates the writing of this book. As she continued to talk to me about how involved she was with the people in the church and how much she enjoyed it, I thought, "Something's wrong here. It's not that I have something that she doesn't have; it's that she has something that I don't have and I want it. Instead of saying the special prayer with her that gets her into Christianity, why can't she say the special 'un-Christianity' prayer that gets *me* out of it?" But of course I didn't say that out loud. I think I was able to muster something nebulous like, "It's cool, Reagan. We're all on the journey together. Let's keep journeying together and see where this leads."

That thought of being saved from Christianity has rattled my cage and has made me rethink what it all means. What does it all mean? What is church? Why do we do all this stuff? What is Christianity? Why am I so bored with it? Is this Christianity that I practice real, or is it just another mask that I use to hide behind? Why does it seem that this Christianity thing that I try to get people to sign up for is the very thing that alienates me and isolates me from not only others, but also from God? If being a Christian is so good, why does it force me into a place of loneliness? And if alienation, isolation, and loneliness are characteristics of hell, am I living in hell but calling myself a Christian? Is this Christianity actually my hell?

As I've wrestled with these questions over the last few months, I've also observed Reagan's involvement with our church. In worship, she sings with such devotion. She has gotten involved in our compassion ministry. She has helped Linda, a wonderful woman in our community, fix up her house. Whenever I saw Reagan, she seemed to be filled with so much life, so much joy. If this was what it was like *not* to be a Christian, then I was ready to sign up. Conversely, I witness many friends and associates who claim "victory in Jesus," have a Jesus fish on their car's bumper, and walk around angry toward everyone and everything. It all makes one wonder.

I didn't speak with Reagan again until the art show. Some artists in our community decided to have an art show, and I thought I'd bring a piece or two. One of the pieces that I brought was a metal cross that I had welded together. Down the middle, I had splattered the word *grace* using metal slag.

"Grace?" Reagan asked as she helped me set up my installation. "What's that mean—grace?"

"Do you mean the piece of art, or do you mean the word?" I replied.

"I mean the word, or the concept."

Again, for some reason I froze up. I didn't know what to do. Fifteen years of ministry experience and the slow-boat-to-China, one-class-at-a-time, seven years in seminary and I can't describe the idea of grace? I paused, but not for long, because I didn't want her to think that I didn't know what *grace* meant. I was embarrassed. So, without any real thought I blathered out a long, complex explanation of the character of God and Jesus Christ's sacrificial atonement on the cross. It was all theologically correct and even good, and it would have been even better if it had been motivated by my involuntary reflex to evangelize. Suddenly, I was no longer her friend. I was this bizarre, freakish monster. It was weird. We went from having a discussion like two normal people, to Pastor Jim preaching a sermon. I felt less like a pastor, and more like a used-car salesman.

The next week I didn't see Reagan in worship, and I assumed that I had scared her off. "Why can't I just let people be?" I kicked myself. But then, a week later, I noticed Reagan in worship again. I noticed her because, to my surprise, she came forward to share in the Lord's Supper. I couldn't resist. I couldn't leave her be. I had to have another conversation.

"Can I talk to you for a minute, Reagan?" I asked, as I approached her after worship.

"Sure."

"I actually need to apologize to you. When I found out that you were not a Christian, I began treating you differently, like a project or something, like I needed to save you, and I'm sorry about that. I really don't want to be one of those kinds of Christians," I said.

"It's okay. We're good. As a matter of fact, I didn't notice that at all. It's like you said—it's a journey, right?"

She smiled; I was relieved. But then I couldn't leave well enough alone. I took a chance to ask her where she was. "I noticed that you took communion today. . . . What was with that?"

"Well, it's just like you say every week before everyone comes forward. You always say, 'The table is open to anyone who is hungry for the gifts of God, anyone hungry for Jesus.' I'm just as hungry as everyone else, I guess."

And that's when I began to piece some things together. There was no need for Reagan to say the special prayer. Jesus already had a hold of her. That's what really matters. Likewise, Jesus had a hold of me. Jesus was doing the work that he needed to do in each of us. Reagan and I are just like everyone else in the world. We aren't longing for church. We don't deeply desire to be Christians. We don't want to be involved in ministry. We aren't even too excited about praying or reading the Bible. What we do long for, however, is to be in communion with God, the real, living God, to experience life eternal right now. We desire a community of friends where we can belong just as we are. We might not be too excited about doing ministry, but we are interested and even motivated to love and to care for others. If praying and reading the Bible means sharing our lives with God, telling God our stories and listening to the stories of others who have struggled in the faith, then count us in. Christianity is not the problem; it's what we've turned Christianity into that is the problem.

Again: would someone please, get me out of this?

Does Anyone Really Know What Time It Is?

There is something going on in this world that we can no longer ignore. It doesn't take a genius to see that we live in a very different world than the one our parents lived in. With a new world comes a new kind of mission field. First, people who are eighteen to thirty-five are least likely to describe themselves as Christian or religious. Many of the young adults I share community with refuse to use the term Christian and prefer to be called "followers of Jesus Christ" (if anything at all) because of the negative connotation the word Christian has in our culture today. These young people, who hate labels to being with, want to be associated with Jesus Christ, but they are very turned off by

Christianity. As a result, many young people, even those who describe themselves as followers of Christ, are still avoiding church. I mean, come on, there are plenty of better things to do. This absence from church has much to do with these huge ideological gaps we see in our world today. Ask the average young person on the street if he or she believes in God, and you're likely to get a positive response. Ask the same young person how that belief has translated into ethical behavior, knowledge of faith or scripture, and sense of community and belonging, and you'll probably get some head scratches. There is a gap. Something, somewhere along the line, is broken, and it needs to be fixed.

Technology, of course, is playing a big part in this cultural shift and in these gaps that we are experiencing. Just as Gutenberg's printing press changed the world and eventually led to the Reformation, so are technological advances affecting our society and the church. As I look at the iPhone in my hand, I see that same Holy Bible that Gutenberg ripped out in 1455. Think about it: I hold in my hand access to unlimited amounts of information, communication, community, and connection. If a Holy Bible in the hands of the common people in the fifteenth century started a reformation, what on earth is this little gadget going to bring? Are we quickly moving to the days when I can sit in a coffee shop, download a hymn, download my favorite preacher, and share in "church" with people from around the world? If that day is coming, why are so many churches continuing to build, making their empty buildings even bigger?

If you look and listen closely enough, you might get small glimpses of what is to come. A few days after hurricane Katrina hit the Gulf Coast, I read this article in the Pittsburgh *Post-Gazette* about a mother who became a missionary from the comfort of her own home:

> On August 31, our blog, Beenthere-link.com, went from being an average mommy blog to a supplies "clearinghouse" for those in need. . . . Amazingly, thousands of people started coming to our blog from around the world, offering everything from clothes to mobile homes. . . . What we heard from people across the country was that they were aching to give to individuals, person to person, family to family. . . . The other day, a woman said she spent hours trying to find a site

like ours. There's nothing like BeenthereClearinghouse on the Web, allowing individuals to donate to individuals . . ." (*Post-Gazette*, Sept. 9, 2005).

This article fascinated me because this woman was able to do what the government could not. She was able to mobilize a worldwide relief effort, not only from her home, but also on a tribal level. See, although we are becoming people who are hyper-connected technologically and able to connect with one another facelessly, we are still people who deeply desire to share intimate, meaningful, communal relationships. We are living in a culture where people might have six hundred friends on facebook.com but no one to talk to, no one to confide in. Let's face it—people in our frenzied culture simply have less friends. As a result, loneliness, isolation, fear, and alienation seem to be at epidemic levels. Many young people feel cut off from God and from others. They struggle with feelings of meaninglessness and hopelessness. Some experience depression. There is a deep mistrust of everything, and sometimes, especially the church. On top of it all, there is a real distaste for mask-wearing, for superficiality, and for inauthenticity. Unfortunately, mask-wearing, superficiality, and inauthenticity are the modern church's specialties.

A few years ago, I got a chance to go to England to see the John Wesley sites. We toured his boyhood home, we saw his father's tombstone on which he famously preached, and we visited the New Room, the church that he established in Bristol early on in his ministry. We were excited to see the old church. John Wesley was a fiery preacher whose ministry style bordered on militant. John took the gospel right to the people and became a preacher to the miners on their way to work, caring for the poor and needy. As we walked to the New Room, our excitement rose as we traveled down a crowded Bristol street. We imagined how Wesley would have cared and preached to this twenty-first-century flock, as spiky-haired and tattooed punk rockers brushed by us. We could see John hitting these streets with the same passion and energy that helped start the movement he began in the eighteenth century. When we arrived at the New Room, which was nestled smack dab in the middle of a crowded shopping district, we found something quite different from what we imagined. Instead of walking into an eighteenth-century missionary outpost, we stepped into a twentieth-century museum. That's right, a museum—complete with "do not touch" signs, neatly pruned shrubbery, and a gift shop. The fire that John had started had long been extinguished. What remained was an artifact, an exhibit, and—dare I say it—an idol. As I walked through the New Room, I couldn't help thinking of all of those United Methodist churches I had been to over the years. Shoot, there's a United Methodist church in every little town, village, and hamlet in America. I couldn't help wondering if this is what we've become—a church perfectly positioned with a very relevant theology and message, but with a missiology that is archaic, frozen in time.

Is this what the church in America has become today—a museum, an artifact, an idol? If we back up a little and get some historical perspective, we can see clearly that we've become a relic. The church in America is actually a dying elder that was born between 1800-1830 when the Second Great Awakening spread across our land. Through that movement, based on tent-revival evangelism and Sunday school-style discipleship, most of the churches and ministries in this country were built. Hello! That was two hundred years ago! Naturally, these churches and these ministry agencies are coming to the end of their lives. What are we doing about it? Instead of planting new seeds in the ground, instead of birthing new churches so that new ministries can be born, most of us are trying in vain to keep the elder alive. We keep trying to keep the boat afloat. Unfortunately, the boat sits in the middle of a museum with velvet rope draped around it. "Do not touch," reads the sign on the precious silver service. "Come explore our fabulous gift shop," invites the curator.

This may not sound like a big deal to you, but I believe that this is the defining conflict of our day, and the outcome will determine the future of our world. In many towns across America, there is a church on every corner, and yet there are people who still do not have food to eat, a roof over their heads, or someone to listen to them. We have this thing, this little god, this idol called "Christianity," an ideology based on the truth, but meanwhile it seems we do more staying comfortable than following the Sufferer. We do all this stuff called ministry, spending tons of time and money, but rarely is someone actually cared for. Yes, I know that being a Christian and following Jesus are the same thing, but somewhere along the way we've gotten lost, and we've followed something else. I realize that ministry and caring about people are supposed to be synonymous, but let's get real—they aren't. We've turned doing ministry into something very different and, quite frankly, ineffective and un-Christlike. It all makes one wonder if we really need church in its present form, or if we'd all be better off without it. It makes one wonder if this is what Jesus had in mind. Doesn't Jesus' vision of the kingdom of God really match our version of the church?

In Marge We Trust

In my very favorite episode of the Simpsons, *In Marge We Trust*, the Simpson family goes to church and experiences exactly what I'm talking about. Reverend Lovejoy has to use special effects, a loud birdcall, to keep everyone awake during his sermon about constancy. When Homer and the gang get home, they tumble into the house and start shedding their church clothes.

"This is the best part of the week!" Lisa declares. "It's the most possible time until more church!"

Marge chastises her family with her typical Marge groan. "Church is supposed to be meaningful. It should help us in our daily lives." Then, as Homer slides into his old pair of blue pants, he very bluntly tells it like it is: "Marge, it should, but it doesn't. Now who wants to go with me to the dump?"

As Homer and the kids have their own adventure at the dump, Marge goes to volunteer at the church and inadvertently fills a very needed position as "the listen lady." When Marge simply makes herself available to listen to people, she finds herself suddenly swamped with broken person after broken person wanting her to listen to them. She quickly, but very unintentionally, takes over the pastor's job by taking time to listen to people. As a result, Reverend Lovejoy has a mid-life crisis because he finds himself a shepherd without a flock. The whole episode is a sermon. My favorite moment is Reverend Lovejoy's line at the very end, after he has joined forces with Marge to save Ned Flanders from some hungry baboons.

> Ned says, "Thank you, Reverend. You saved me. How can I ever repay you?"
>
> Reverend Lovejoy responds, "Don't thank me. Thank Marge Simpson. She's taught me that there's more to being a minister than not caring about people."

I believe that's exactly where we find ourselves as the church. We seem to be really, really good at not caring about people. We spend so much time chasing after the little gods that we have lost our way. The result is that hurting, broken people, including ourselves, do not get cared for. If we are to get back to being the church, we need to throw down our idols and change our methods of engagement.

New Assumptions

But it isn't so simple. The problem with changing our methods of engagement is that we don't get new methods by simply changing our methods. We have to go deeper. Methods are actually built upon a certain set of assumptions. Change the assumptions, and methods will change. See, it's not just our methods. Many of our assumptions are wrong. As long as those same old assumptions exist in the church, the church will not change. We must question all of our assumptions, keep a few, and get rid of the rest. If we continue to let our modernist assumptions go unquestioned, the church will continue to die. But as we question our old assumptions and begin to embrace new ones, new behaviors and new methods will start to shape the church. Trying a new program or introducing a new contemporary worship service in your church is not going to cut it. That's just creating new idols! We must go deeper if real change is to occur.

I have noticed when I sit in on church visioning and re-visioning committees that there is a tendency, a knee-jerk reaction, to evaluate the current ecclesiology, find the problems, and quickly patch them up. This is the old modern model—the old "we can build a better machine to fix it" approach. We want to slap some duct tape on our current ecclesiology and walk away. We see a broken system, and we continue to try to fix it from the top down. That's not going to work this time. We need to go to the roots. A church's ecclesiology is birthed out of its missiology, not the other way around. You can't define the *hows* until you clearly define the *whats*. And for the church, we can't define the *whats* (what the church's job is), until we define the big *who* (who Jesus is).

You might be thinking, "What's the point here? We've already been through all this. We know who Jesus is and we know what our mission is. Jesus is Lord and we are to make disciples." The last few years in the

Let's take a look at some old assumptions that many of us continue to hold as gospel:

- The church is a building, with signs, advertisements, goods, and services;

- Christians "go" to church, usually 11 am-noon on Sunday;

- The "good" or "right" people are in the church, the "bad" or "wrong" people are out there in the world;

- We need to figure out ways of getting those bad people into our church so that we can change them into us;

- Church is a worship service. The better the church, the bigger the attendance;

- The church has a "frontline" where we send missionaries and people interested in working with the poor;

- Ministry is done by the pastor alone; everyone else assists in his or her mission.

- Ministry is done best in groups of commonality, i.e., youth group, men's group, women's group, mother's group;

- "Saved" means to go to heaven when you die;

- The church's mission is to "make disciples."

United Methodist Church especially, our mission statement has been to "make disciples for the transformation of the world." Sit in on any annual conference and you'll hear this phrase ad nauseam. It's a good statement and I agree that making disciples is the ultimate goal, but I do think it has become an assumption or even a buzzword that we don't call into question. Is making disciples really the mission, or is it more the goal, the desired outcome? Does the conquering and controlling language of "make disciples" really work for the church moving into the postmodern age?

There is something going on in this world that we cannot ignore any longer. As people are drowning in a sea of isolation, brokenness, and desperation, the church continues to cling to the idols that are causing it to sink. We need to change.

Mother Teresa

This story, this weird journey that has led me to the most peculiar of places and to the most peculiar of people, began in February 2002. Don't think it all started with some grandiose vision or scheme or fire from above. This crazy chapter of my story comes out of some bleak and utterly broken moments. It was about a year or so after my dad had died of cancer and five months after 9/11. I was still recovering from the loss of my dad; our country was still recovering from the terrorist attacks. Looking back, I can see that both events affected me in some profound ways. I had already been in seminary for what seemed like an eternity. I was to graduate soon, and the thought of being a pastor simply turned my stomach. It was in that month of February that I struggled in my faith like no other time in my life. I can remember sitting in class at seminary and writing in my notes, "Is there really a God?" as the professor lectured. February in Pittsburgh is already pretty depressing, but add to the grey sky and the muddy snow a deep sense of feeling completely lost, and you've got yourself a recipe for disaster. I honestly felt like quitting seminary and pursuing something else entirely. Papers I should have written went unwritten. Books I should have read went unread. I was tired, burned out, and very indifferent to the concept of God.

However, the concepts, the ideas, the theologies of God are one thing; the reality of God is another. There's talking about God, reading about God, writing about God, and then there's God showing up, setting you down, and shutting you up. It was during the last week of this terrible month that I believe God showed up and turned my life completely upside-down. It was a cold February morning, snow piled high outside, and as I sat down at my desk with my cup of coffee, an old newspaper stuck in a large stack beside my desk caught my eye. I pulled the newspaper out of the pile and read an article entitled, "Mother Teresa's letters, diary tells of her lifelong doubt and despair." As I read the very first sentence, I began to break down.

> "Mother Teresa sometimes felt rejected by God, helpless and tempted to abandon her work caring for the poor and dying, according to her diaries."

A myriad of emotions ran through me all at once as tears fell. I felt liberated, comforted, and free as I read excerpts from Teresa's diary:

"Now, Jesus, I go the wrong way. They say that people in hell suffer eternal pain because of loss of God. In my soul, I feel just the terrible pain of loss, of God not wanting me, of God not being God, of God not really existing" (Mother Teresa, *Come Be My Light, The Private Writings of the Saint of Calcutta* [New York: DoubleDay, 2007], 192-93).

Of course, in no way am I comparing myself with Mother Teresa, but I certainly could relate to her pain. What hit me the most, and what has become a revelation that has deeply affected my ministry, is this: if Mother Teresa can feel lost, lonely, and abandoned by God, then we all can and do, more often than we want to admit. The notion that those folks in the pews have it all together is just a hoax. It is yet another idol. I began to realize that the doubt and struggle that I was experiencing was part of the story. God is a great novelist—the best, really. God doesn't write schmaltzy sitcoms; God specializes in epics. Just like Mother Teresa's story, my story is not without trial, doubt, and pain. Reading those intimate words in Teresa's diary has given me great hope.

Super-Objectives

In the world of drama and theater, actors use a term to help them find their motivation. The term is *super-objective*. In any given play or movie or scene, every character has a super-objective. The super-objective is the thing that the character wants more than anything else. A super-objective can be as simple as getting rent money or as complex as surviving a hurricane. Think about any play or movie you've seen, and you can spot the super-objective pretty quickly, at first. In *Indiana Jones and the Last Crusade*, Indiana Jones wants to find the Holy Grail. In *Castaway*, Tom Hanks wants to stay alive. Look again and you'll see a character with two super-objectives, one external and one internal. Yes, externally Indiana Jones wants the Holy Grail, but internally he wants something else, something deeper. Tom Hanks wants to survive as a castaway, but deeper down inside he wants something bigger. We could try to give a name or names to these deeper somethings, but we might have trouble with our clumsy language. Simply to say that Indiana Jones wants to find his faith or understand God, or that Tom Hanks wants to be rescued and brought back to civilization, is to make light of those wants. Our wants, our super-objectives have such deep, profound effects on our personhood that they become our identity.

God has designed every one of us with a super-objective. Sorry folks, but it's not to be rich, to be privileged, to have our best life now, to be happy, to have it all, to say the special sinner's prayer, to get our ticket into heaven, or to stop smoking. Our super-objective might be too deep to explain or put into words. We need it more than those external wants: money, power, fame, good looks. It's even more precious than air, water, food, and shelter. We have been created to be in perfect union and communion with God and with each other. That's what we want more than anything else.

Describing this inner super-objective, this big want of ours, is not that simple. Actually, I believe this want that motivates us is multifaceted. Our super-objective has four features: assurance, belonging, meaning, and identity. These four things are not four separate objectives, but the same objective with four specific aspects. It's kind of like fire. Fire is fire, but it burns, emanates light, gives off energy, and consumes some sort of fuel. It is one thing with four aspects. In the same way, we don't simply want to be in communion with God; we long for the fire of God. We actually want to burn, to glow, to have heat emanate out of us and ultimately to consume us. We want to have assurance. We want to belong. We want our lives to have meaning. And we want to be known, all through communion with God. We cannot separate or compartmentalize these desires. It is one desire, one want, one super-objective that is fulfilled only when we share in communion with God.

The New Testament describes these same super-objectives in a number of different ways. In John, Jesus talks about life abundant or life eternal. In many places in the Gospels, Jesus emphasizes belonging to this thing he calls the kingdom of God. Jesus offers meaning to his disciples by calling them. He said to the fishermen, "Follow me and I will make you fish for people" (Matthew 4:19). Later on, Jesus explains what following him really means when he says, "If any want to become my followers, let them deny themselves, take up their cross

Our Super-Objectives

- Assurance—We all long to know we are safe, secure;

- Belonging—We all desire to be accepted and part of a family;

- Meaning—We need to know that our lives matter, that we make a difference;

- Identity—We all want to be truly known.

daily and follow me" (Luke 9:23). Then Paul talks about our being adopted sons and daughters of God (Romans 8:14-17). It is clear that Jesus understands the human condition and knows what our super-objective is: we long to have life abundant, to belong to God's kingdom, to find meaning through compassion, and to know God and to be known by God.

In the modern age, the church's apologetic was based on proofs. This made complete sense in a world centered on analysis and critical thinking. During the modern age, we pulled out microscopes and pulled apart the atom, the genome, and every letter of scripture. To evangelize, one only needed to have a convincing argument. This is why Billy Graham and his crew were so successful. Graham's methods of engagement worked for the world he lived in. Those ways won't always work in the world that will soon be here. In the postmodern age, our apologetic must change to meet a changing world. I believe the new apologetic will be found in the sharing in authentic, intimate relationships by experiencing the kingdom of God here on earth. Certainly, this new generation needs to "know we are Christians by our love." I hope this thought excites you as much as it excites me. After all, what better proof do we need, what better apologetic, than the kingdom of God among us?

This poses a big problem for the church today. Authentic, intimate relationships cannot exist by creating a new staff position. The kingdom of God is not conjured up by creating a program. You can't make intimacy magically appear by throwing money around. Love doesn't need a marketing campaign. Lone Rangers can't create caring communities. The kingdom of God doesn't break out into our communities by expecting people to come to our cool thing. And we can't be the body of Christ by putting ourselves above others or being one-up. The problem? This is exactly how the church has handled ministry in the past. Let's do a program. Let's create a staff position. Let's throw some money at it. These tactics are not going to work this time. We need to question our old assumptions and create some new ones. Or perhaps, instead of creating new ones, we simply need to go back to the beginning and revive some ancient truths.

The Meaning of Koinonia

The Greeks had a word for it, κοινωνια (or *koinonia*). Koinonia means "to share in fellowship with." You might have heard of this word before, perhaps used in a sermon about fellowshipping together. But koinonia means more than just fellowshipping. A quick look in a Greek/English lexicon reveals some deeper meanings. Koinonia means:

- to be in communion with;
- to be in close relationship with;
- to be in partnership with;
- to participate in or with;
- to be yoked or bound together;
- to be tightly woven or closely connected with.

This word, for me, has unlocked the whole gospel and my understanding of God. This is what we've been created for: koinonia. I need koinonia to live! To me, what I find even more fascinating is where this word occurs in the New Testament:

Koinonia with Jesus Christ. "God, who has called you into *fellowship* with his Son Jesus Christ our Lord, is faithful" (1 Cor. 1:9, NIV).

Koinonia with the Holy Spirit. "May the grace of the Lord Jesus Christ, and the love of God, and the *fellowship* of the Holy Spirit be with you all" (2 Cor. 13:14, NIV).

Koinonia in the body and blood of Jesus Christ. "Is not the cup of thanksgiving for which we give thanks a *participation* in the blood of Christ? And is not the bread that we break a *participation* in the body of Christ?" (1 Cor. 10:16, NIV).

Koinonia with others. "They devoted themselves to the apostles' teaching and to *fellowship*, to the breaking of bread and the prayers" (Acts 2:42).

Koinonia with the poor through giving. "For Macedonia and Achaia were pleased to make a *contribution* for the poor among the saints in Jerusalem" (Romans 15:26).

Koinonia in Christ's sufferings. "I want to know Christ and the power of his resurrection and the *fellowship of sharing* in his sufferings, becoming like him in his death" (Philippians 3:10).

Koinonia in the good news of God's grace. "I pray that you may be active in *sharing* your faith, so that you will have a full understanding of every good thing we have in Christ" (Philemon 6).

Koinonia in the faith. ". . . because of your *partnership* in the gospel from the first day until now . . ." (Philippians 1:5).

Partnership in the Gospel

God wants us to enjoy koinonia with God and to share in God's love and grace. God wants us to enjoy koinonia with others, to share in Jesus' body and blood, to share in his sufferings, to be in koinonia with the poor, and to be in koinonia with God's mission, or the Missio Dei which means "the mission of God." The early church practiced koinonia. That's how it exploded across Asia and into Europe in less than one hundred years. I'm sure they were all big believers of Matthew 28, and I'm sure they did plenty of baptizing, but their mission statement wasn't "make disciples." They just practiced koinonia and disciples were made.

Check out Acts 2:42: "And they devoted themselves to the apostles' teachings, to the fellowship (koinonia), to the breaking of bread and the prayers."

In the old modern discipleship-oriented church, the *mission* is to "make disciples." This has made perfect sense for the world we lived in. Unfortunately, the mission statement now has a very conquering and controlling ring to it. "Making disciples" reinforces a "one-up" mentality. Think about it. No one wants to be made into anything by anyone else. Young people don't want to be made into anything. Old people don't want to be made into anything. Be honest: YOU don't want to be

Deep Needs	Koinonia (Share in)	Acts 2:42
Assurance	Communion	Prayer
Belonging	Community	Fellowship
Meaning	Compassion (to suffer with)	Breaking of Bread
Identity	God's mission/ the Gospel	Apostles' Teachings

made into anything. If someone tried to make you into something, you would resist, wouldn't you? That's human nature. In a postmodern, *mission*-oriented church, the mission is koinonia. Koinonia becomes the doorway to the kingdom of God. Disciples will be "made" when they see and experience the kingdom of God lived out. "Making disciples" has become such a buzzword that we have no idea what the meaning is or how to go about doing it. Koinonia is not a buzzword. Being in communion with Jesus, with others, with the poor, with suffering, with the broken, with God's mission—we know exactly what that means and choose not to practice it. We'd rather have the buzzword. It's easier.

I have been working in the United Methodist Church for fifteen years now, ten years as a program director/associate pastor in two different churches and now five years at Hot Metal. I have been to many council on ministry meetings, and I know from experience that if you set everyone on the committee down and say, "Okay, folks. We have to make disciples. How are we going to make disciples?" You will get all of these weird, awkward ideas. Each idea will be centered on pulling people in or coaxing people to come to our thing. There will be someone with an idea centered on an event, and that event will have flyers, and music, and a big deal. And then, when push comes to shove, the day of the event comes and no one shows up, not even the person who came up with the idea!

Making disciples is like making people. We have no idea how to make people. Only God knows how to make people. So, if you had to gather your people, sit down, and say, "Okay folks. We're going to make people. How are we going to make people?" Then you would have people trying to connect a big arm to a small torso and a weird looking head with stitches all over it. You get Frankenstein! And that's what we have in the church today: Frankensteinian missiology! We try to cram people into these weird, scary-looking programs and ministries that we saw some guy draw up on a diagram at a conference. These ministries are like big hungry monsters that suck up our time, money, and energy and at the end of the day don't work. The guy who drew it up at the conference won't even come!

How do we make people? Simple. We have sex. And just as people naturally have sex and more people are naturally *made*, when we share in koinonia, more disciples of Christ are made. People aren't made into disciples by going through some sort of weird program. People become disciples by experiencing koinonia through Christ. This means we need to drop the programs and get authentic, intimate, and take time with one another.

What if you sat down with your council of ministries committee and said, "Okay, folks. We're going to practice koinonia. How are we going to share in communion with God? How are we going to share in partnership with Christ's sufferings? How are we going to connect with the poor? How are we going to be part of God's mission?" Suddenly, instead of getting a whole bunch of weird ideas, you get responses like, "Why are we even meeting about this?" Why don't we stop making all of these plans and live this out? Let's stop planning on how're going to do church and be the church." Now your group would be thinking in terms of koinonia rather than "making disciples." And then, strangely enough, disciples would be made. Once everyone has a handle on the clear mission, you will meet the goal of making disciples. This is what the early church did and this is why it exploded so quickly. There was no evangelistic scheme; there was only koinonia.

Hippos and Turtles

I'm sure by this time you've heard the story of Owen the Hippo and Mzee the turtle. Owen was orphaned on December 26, 2004, and adopted by the turtle shortly after that. I imagine Owen's Christmas was peaceful. He probably had spent it the way most hippos spend most Christmases, or most days in general, for that matter. I bet it was a simple affair. No decorations. No tree. No turkey dinner. Owen chewed on a little cud, slept a little, splashed in the water, and wallowed in the mud there on the peaceful river bank in East Africa, all the while nestled close to his mother. Christmas of 2004 was a good day for Owen. The next day, on the other hand, was a terrible day, most likely, the worst day of Owen's short life. You see, December 26, 2004, was the day that a massive earthquake hit the Indian Ocean floor, causing the monster of all tsunamis. A giant wave crashed ashore in Indonesia, India, and Africa, destroying everything in its path. The wall of water hit the eastern coast of the continent of Africa, raced up the river, grabbed many of the animals that lived there, including Owen, the baby hippo, and his mother, and dragged them out to sea. The current was so terribly strong and unyielding that neither Owen nor his mother had a prayer for survival.

But somehow, some way, Owen survived the tsunami. Park rangers found him the next day, moments away from sharing his mother's fate, drowning in the Indian Ocean. Not quite sure what to do with an orphaned hippopotamus, the park rangers took Owen to Haller park preserve in Mombassa, Kenya, and put him in a small animal pen. When they set Owen free in his new home, tired, cold and shaking with fear, he ran to the only thing he could see that even came close to looking like mommy. Poor Owen nuzzled his big, fat hippo body against the giant shell of Mzee, a 120-year-old tortoise. Of course, Mzee (which means "old man" in Swahili) was taken a little off guard at first, not quite sure what kind of beast was using her home as a scratching post. But as time passed, Mzee warmed up to Owen and adopted him as her own.

Owen spent New Year's Day sharing his life with his new friend Mzee, an ancient tortoise. He followed her everywhere she went. What an odd friendship: a fat baby hippo and an ancient tortoise. The hippo is covered in mud; the tortoise is covered with wrinkles. The hippo chews food with his big mouth, and still the food spills out the sides. The tortoise is an old hermit who hides in her hard shell for days at a time. What might be the most amazing thing of all is that the hippo and the turtle have begun to communicate with one another. Mzee, not knowing how to speak hippo, and Owen, not knowing how to speak turtle, have developed a kind of love language. Two completely different creatures sharing in communion with one another, finding ways to bridge their differences. Is this a sermon for us? Is there a way we can share in communion with those who don't quite speak our language?

Amazingly, Owen the hippo found refuge with his new mommy, and Mzee responded as she stuck her head out of her shell and showed the orphan the care and love he needed. For Owen, salvation came in the most unlikely of places. But interestingly enough, salvation came to Mzee as well. Owen was saved. Mzee was saved.

I use the words "salvation" and "saved" here on purpose. In the modern age, the church defined *saved* only as getting into heaven when you die. Is it possible that this is not the complete definition of salvation? In his excellent book *Being as Communion* (St. Vladimirs Seminary Press, 1997) John Zizioulas writes, "The being of God is a relational being: without the concept of communion it would not be possible to speak of the being of God. It is communion which makes beings "be": nothing exists without it, not even God" (17). It is communion with Jesus Christ that saves us, not some special, "magical" prayer. Without communion, we cease to exist, and that non-existence is hell. So, what is this anti-communion that sends us to hell? Selfishness, of course. As Thomas Merton puts it, "To worship our false selves is to worship nothing. And the worship of nothing is hell." (*New Seeds of Contemplation,* [New Your: New Direction Publishing, 1972], 26). As the Apostle Paul puts it, "To set the mind on the flesh is death, but to set the mind on the Spirit is life and peace" (Romans 8:6). Salvation isn't about saying a special prayer and getting a ticket into heaven. Salvation is a present reality available to us here and now, available through communion with Jesus Christ. Salvation is available through koinonia with God, who is Communion, Father, Son, and Holy Spirit, and through koinonia with others, the poor, the suffering, the broken, and the lost. Koinonia with myself is not koinonia at all, but actually hell.

> For those who are according to the flesh set their minds on the things of the flesh, but those who are according to the Spirit, the things of the Spirit. For the mind set on the flesh is death, but the mind set on the Spirit is life and peace (Romans 8:5-6).

The Four Curses

When we live for ourselves, koinonia doesn't rule our lives. Rather, little gods rule our lives. I think you know what I mean. The gods of this world—money, power, fame, image, and success—so heavily influence us. Think about it. Have you ever stopped and evaluated your motivations? What is it that gets you up in the morning? Why are you going to school? Why are you going to work? Why do you treat other people the way you do? The little gods of this culture constantly sway us. It has become so pervasive that our idol worship has invaded the church and has essentially brought it to its knees. The core problem in the church today is not contemporary worship versus traditional worship, or left versus right; it is idolatry. We are guilty of worshipping the little gods. It's time to repent.

We all have four deep needs: assurance, belonging, meaning, and identity. It is actually through koinonia in Christ that these needs are fulfilled. It is only through koinonia, or *communion* with God in Christ, that we can have real *assurance*. It is only through koinonia, or *community* with others in Christ, that we can experience real *belonging*. It is only through koinonia, or sharing in *Christ's sufferings* and connecting with the poor, the outcast, and the broken, that we can find real *meaning* and *hope* that last. And it is only in Christ that we can really be known—by God, by others and by ourselves. We find our true identity through koinonia in Christ.

I use the phrase "in Christ" in conjunction with koinonia on purpose. The fact is, we only experience real koinonia in Jesus Christ. Sitting around the table in the church basement gossiping about other people is not koinonia. Koinonia is where life is found, not death.

As we try to live lives of koinonia, four big obstacles confront us, four curses if you will. If koinonia fulfills our deep needs of assurance, belonging, meaning, and identity, wouldn't it make sense that the four curses, the enemies of koinonia, are fear, rejection, luxury, and superficiality? Certainly, if being bound to God through Christ brings us *assurance*, then a life separated from God would be ruled by *fear*. If sharing community in Christ fulfills our need for *belonging*, then isolation and loneliness are brought on by *rejection*. If sharing in Christ's *sufferings* gives meaning to our lives, then a life lived in all comfort and

Marie are a little different than us supposedly normal people. They don't live in a nice, big house; they don't have a lot of money. Dewey has to walk with a crutch because of a hurt knee. When they first started coming to Hot Metal, they were amazed at how much people loved and accepted them. You see, Dewey and Marie like to sit in the front row at church. People in their churches had told them they had to sit in the back so that the television cameras wouldn't pick them up. Is this an expression of love and acceptance, or is this typical behavior in the church in America today, laying down our lives at the altar of rejection?

Instead of letting ourselves experience the joy of suffering, we have sold out to the god of luxury. I attended a worship service at a local mega-church not so long ago. It was a weekday evening service and they had selected the theme of heroes, which probably would have been very appropriate. Who knows, however, how much money this church spent to hype-up their hero theme? Using the same logo and art as the television show *Heroes*, there were posters, flyers, and brochures. The big projection screen in the church continually flashed hero images and there was a special video that must have cost thousands to produce. Finally, when it came time for the sermon, there were neat slides that reinforced the theme of heroes. Unfortunately, the message was a bit watered-down and generic. This church wasn't interested in actually being heroic, by going against the flow and showing courage. This church was bowing down to the idol called big, linking itself to a popular television show so it could be popular, instead of proclaiming a clear message of heroic self-sacrifice. The sad part is, it was working. It certainly was and is the coolest church in town.

Instead of having the courage to face truth, be honest, and transparent, we have handed our lives over to the masks of fake, fraud, fame, and fallacy. One of the underlying values in our culture today is beauty. Hollywood and Madison Avenue have trained us, like it or not, to value people according to how beautiful they are. Of course this is completely evil and the very opposite of any value Jesus held, but somehow this corrupt value has wormed its way into the church, and it rules with an iron fist. Walk into any church in America, and you will find people making every effort to be beautiful. We have fancy pews, fancy lights, cool video projections, and worship leaders with the prettiest eyes and the whitest teeth. By doing this, we perpetuate the lie that our worth is directly connected to our looks. As a result, we all walk around with masks on, big fake masks, trying to be someone we aren't so that others will value us and so that God will value us. In an effort to find worth, we bow down to the little gods of image, fame, and good looks.

We have made the little gods our super-objective, leading us to the land of Me. When all I care about is me, what I can get, what I can have, and how I can be comfortable, then I have bowed down to the little god, and I am experiencing anti-communion. In short, I am in hell. That is where we find ourselves in America in the early twenty-first century. We find ourselves in hell. We might all be going to church each week, and we might all be singing the hymns and doing the church thing, but in pew after pew after pew, in church after church after church, people who call themselves Christians are actually living in hell. The sad part is, we don't even realize it. We continue to blame the devil and the demons, playing the blame game, as the real enemies— fear, rejection, big masks—rule our lives. To top it off, instead of proclaiming a gospel of koinonia, the church encourages us to worship ourselves. We deserve it, they say. God wants us to have our best lives now. While we focus on ourselves, trying desperately to enjoy koinonia with ourselves, we travel further and further away from communion. How can we claim Jesus as Lord and Savior, how can we call ourselves Christians, when all the while the little gods are our real masters?

Again: would someone please save me from this bull#@%?

How Americans View God

In *USA Today*, there was an article about the way Americans view God and how those views determine the political landscape. A Gallup poll revealed that Americans view God in one of four ways. "Though 91.8% say they believe in God, a higher power, or a cosmic force, they had four distinct views of God's personality and engagement in human affairs. These Four Gods—dubbed by researchers Authoritarian, Benevolent, Critical, or Distant" (*USA Today*, September 11, 2006).

Here are some results of the study:

- The Authoritarian God (31.4 percent of Americans overall, 43.3 percent in the South) is angry at humanity's sins and engaged in every creature's life and world affairs. He is ready to throw the thunderbolt of judgment down on "the unfaithful or ungodly."
- The Benevolent God (23 percent overall, 28.7 percent in the Midwest) still sets absolute standards for mankind in the Bible. More than half (54.8 percent) want the government to advocate Christian values. But this group, which draws more from mainline Protestants, Catholics and Jews, sees primarily a giving God, more like the father who embraces his repentant prodigal son in the Bible.
- The Critical God (16 percent overall, 21.3 percent in the East) has his judgmental eye on the world, but he's not going to intervene, either to punish or to comfort.
- The Distant God (24.4 percent overall, 30.3 percent in the West) is "no bearded old man in the sky raining down his opinions on us," Bader says. Followers of this God see a cosmic force that launched the world, and then left it spinning on its own (*USA Today*, September 11, 2006).

Authoritarian, Benevolent, Critical, or Distant. Those are my choices? If that's it, I'm not interested. I have a question: what if we've got God all wrong? What if God is really none of these? What if we've been blinded by our little gods and have been perceiving a god who is not God at all? It seems kind of fishy to me that we would view God as either a big scary boss, a distant meaningless blob, a rejecting critic, or a fake-friendly Santa Claus figure. These characteristics, these personality types, sound like human traits to me. Could it be that we've been creating God in our own image? Could it be that we've been projecting our insecurities, our own curses onto who God is?

If we've been living in the curse of *fear*, wouldn't it make sense to perceive God as a big mean boss? If we've been living in constant *rejection*, of others, of ourselves, doesn't it make sense to paint God with the same paintbrush, making God a critic? If we've been living distantly, behind the masks of *superficiality*, wouldn't it figure that we'd view God as distant? If we've been living in the lap of *luxury*, wouldn't we assume

Curses	Americans' Views of God
Fear	Authoritarian
Rejection	Critical
Superficiality	Distant
Luxury	Benevolent

that God was a magical genie who grants all of our wishes and who wants us to be rich? It doesn't surprise me to see that Americans perceive God in these ways. This bossy, distant, critical, fake-friendly god is the god who has been ruling over Christian America for some time now. When will we throw down our idols?

The true essence of God's character is not authoritarian, distant, critical, or benevolent. God's true character is communal. God is relational first. Yes, God is the boss, but whatever rules God makes all stem from communion. God is benevolent, but God is communion, and being in communion with Communion is the real gift. All of scripture points to a God who is communal and wants to be in communion with us. Any place where there are laws, God is not being authoritarian, but inviting us toward communion. What we perceive as authoritarian is God warning us to avoid breaking the laws because disobedience is actually anti-communion. Disobedience, breaking the law, is us going our way, doing our own thing, fueled by our selfishness, which breaks our communion with God. Yes, God is distant, but God is also closer than we realize. Yes, God is just (not critical), but God's justice comes from communion-ness. And yes, God is benevolent. But look in the New Testament at the places where Jesus exhibits benevolence. These are actually his reaffirmation of the mission— communion with God. It's like Jesus is saying, "Want to be in communion with God? Don't just say this prayer, *be* this prayer. Want to be in communion with God? Humble yourself, give away everything you have, and follow in the ways of God. Want to be in communion with God? If you're poor in Spirit, you already are, you just don't realize it." Both the Old and New Testament point to a God who is, above all communal, not authoritarian, distant, critical, or benevolent.

DIRTY WORD

When we create a god in our image, we end up with a Christianity that is screwed up, backwards, harmful, and wrong. The way we view God determines everything—our theology, our interpretation of scripture, and the way we do church. For instance, if we see God as authoritarian, then we'll interpret the Sermon on the Mount as a list of rules from the boss instead of an invitation into communion.

If we view God as benevolent, we might believe God wants us to be rich and prosperous and have our best life now. But how can this be? If being a follower of Christ is to live Christ's life, to give it all away, how can it be about getting? When did Jesus have his best life now? When he was living homeless, with one pair of clothes, with Pharisees breathing down his neck? Was it when he was being beaten with a cat-o'-nine-tails? Was Jesus having his best life now when he was hanging from the cross? You could counter that we are not Jesus, but what about Martin Luther King, the Apostle Paul, or Dietrich Bonhoeffer? Were they having their best life now when they were being shot, being beheaded, or hanging from the gallows? Following Jesus is not about getting everything you want; it's about getting everything you need, and, believe it or not, what you need is to be in koinonia with suffering. That is when we have our best life now, when we die as Christ died.

If we perceive God as critical, we might build our ecclesiology around making ourselves feel guilty. But if we can see that God is communion, the scriptures open up and we can see what the writers really meant by "saved" and "kingdom of God." Our churches can become what they're meant to be: bridges to God.

Changing the church in America doesn't start with a contemporary service. It starts with helping people see who God really is and tearing down the idols that we call god. These idols are really just cardboard cutouts and projections of our own insecurities.

Hot Metal Bridge Faith Community—A Head Wound!

One morning I sat across from my best friend Jeff, and we began discussing the idea of planting a new kind of church. Jeff Eddings, whom I met as a freshman in college, has had a journey very similar, if not identical to my own. For almost a decade, Jeff and I had worked together doing a drama ministry called Crosslight Productions while we both worked as youth pastors in separate, but similar suburban churches. We would do dramas at churches, conferences and retreat centers across western Pennsylvania and across the country. We had joked many times about settling down, planting our own church, and using the dramas as the sermons. But this time, as we sat in Bob Evans, dreaming and laughing about what kind of church two doofuses like us would plant, there was an underlying importance to our discussion. I think we both realized that this could be another step in the journey. Somehow, this could bring us closer to our goal.

A few weeks later, we found ourselves standing on a big dirt mound on Pittsburgh's South Side, looking into the surrounding hills of our city. From where we were standing, we could see downtown, the struggling community of the Hill District, Duquesne University, and the University of Pittsburgh. We could see the neighborhoods of Arlington, Hazelwood, and Greenfield, old Pittsburgh neighborhoods with a lot of old, empty churches. On that dirt mound, just a few yards away from the Hot Metal Bridge, we prayed and we wept for this hurting, broken city.

In 2002, the Hot Metal Bridge was brand new. Well, kind of. It was actually a very old bridge connecting J&L Steel with J&L Steel. The mill covered both sides of the river. The steel company used the bridge to carry hot metal and electrical and gas lines. When the closed steel mill was eventually torn down, the bridge remained. For a long time, it was a bridge to nowhere. It was a connector that didn't connect anything. But now, the J&L Steel site is a flourishing urban center with stores and restaurants and the bridge has been restored. The bridge is an important connector in this city, allowing thousands of folks to get where they're going every day. This is why we named our faith community after this bridge. As we stood on that dirt mound and prayed for our city, we asked God to make us into a new kind of bridge.

Later that year, we went with our wives to a church-planting boot camp somewhere in California. Armed with a bunch of ideas, a lot of idealism, and a cool brochure, we spent four days listening to the experts. At the end of the fourth day, we finally conjured up enough courage to share our brochure with the head expert. We were expecting a little advice, secretly hoping that he would be amazed at our

got their religious goods and services. At that point, I'm sure many of them began thinking about what was for lunch.

Then, Jesus throws a curveball. He says, "Surely, you will quote this proverb to me: 'Physician, heal yourself! Do here in your hometown what we have heard that you did in Capernaum'" (Luke 4:23, NIV). Jesus knew what they were thinking. He knew what the people of Nazareth thought of Capernaum. That's the city down by the sea. There's nothing there but a bunch of smelly, dirty fishermen. They had heard of what Jesus had done there; just imagine what he would do in his hometown. Visions of "mega-synagogues" and praise bands danced in their heads. I'm sure someone was already on the way to Kinko's with a new brochure in hand. But what Jesus says next changed everything.

With everyone waiting for the glory of the Lord to be in their midst, with everyone anticipating great blessings and God's favor, Jesus says:

"I tell you the truth . . . no prophet is accepted in his hometown. I assure you that there were many widows in Israel in Elijah's time, when the sky was shut for three and a half years and there was a severe famine. Yet Elijah was not sent to any of them, but to a widow in Zarephath in the region of Sidon. And there were many in Israel with leprosy in the time of Elisha the prophet, yet not one of them was healed—only Naaman the Syrian" (Luke 4:24-27, NIV).

That's all Jesus had to say for the crowd to turn on him completely. They all got up and ran him out of town. They took Jesus to the brow of a hill. They were going to throw him off. They wanted to kill him. But they couldn't. By the power of the Spirit, Jesus walked through the crowd and away.

Wow. What a change of heart, huh? What the heck was it that Jesus said that made everyone so mad? Why does the whole town, his hometown, turn on him because of one small comment? It's because his comment isn't so small. Jesus' comment is completely offensive. It was completely offensive to the people of Nazareth, and it should be completely offensive to us. Jesus is saying that this message, the good news of the kingdom of God, isn't for the healthy; it isn't for those who pretend to have it all together; it isn't for those who are all cleaned up. The message is actually for the foreigner (in Sidon), and for *those* people (in Syria). You know what I mean by "*those* people," right? The message is for *those* people we perceive as unclean. The message is for *those* people we label as dirty.

It's like Jesus going into a suburban church here in America, with Beemers resting in the parking lot. He rushes in with news. He's found the kingdom of God, heaven here on earth. Everyone in the pews smiles at one another. They think he's talking about their lovely sanctuary. Then he says, "Come check it out with me. It's down at the truck stop. It's down at the local bar. It's down at the strip club. It's down in the projects. It's down in the trailer park. I'm heading down there to be part of it. Anyone want to join me?"

You can see why the people went ape. It was as if Jesus said the worst of all things. See, Jesus' message, his whole mission, was for dirty people, and it still is.

People didn't like that back then. His hometown fans tried to kill him over it. People don't like that now either. We'd get rid of Jesus if we could, but we can't. Instead, we'll just clean him up, soften his language, censor him a bit, put a sheep on his back and a big white smile on his face, and put words in his mouth that make us feel better about ourselves. After all, how could the message be for those bad, dirty people when the universe revolves around the good, clean people—us?

Jesus' Kingdom vs. Today's Church

Jesus continued with his ministry after his visit to his hometown. This event was a defining moment, and it conveys to us his mission statement. His mission centered on the kingdom of God. The kingdom of God is like a precious jewel, he said. The kingdom of God is like a wedding banquet. I wonder, if he had heard about Owen and Mzee, would he have said the kingdom of God is like the adoption of an orphaned hippo by a 120-year-old turtle?

Jesus' message and his mission are both tied up in this thing he calls the kingdom of God. In Matthew 4:17 it says, "From that time Jesus began to proclaim, 'Repent, for the kingdom of heaven is near.'"; "The time is fulfilled, and the kingdom of God has come near; repent and believe in the good news" (Mark 1:15); "I must proclaim the good news of the kingdom of God to the other cities also; for I was sent for this purpose" (Luke 4:43); " Very Truly, I tell you, no one can see the kingdom of God without being born from above" (John 3:3). At the beginning of each gospel, Jesus declares his mission statement. He is all about the kingdom of God. But what is it? What is this kingdom of God? Where is it? Is it the bright, shiny place we all go when we die? Or is the kingdom of God something more? Is the kingdom of God near, amongst us, even right now, and we could experience it if we would simply open our eyes?

The kingdom of God and the church should be synonymous, but let's face it, in America at least they are not even close. We insist on looking for God in all the wrong places. Growing up in America I was taught, through culture, through the media, that those things that have beauty—the most beautiful buildings, the most beautiful places, the most beautiful people—are those things that have the most value. A beautiful thing is a worthy thing. This is the most horrible of lies, and yet we have taken this broken value and have brought it into the church. Buildings, programs, worship leaders, worship services, and even our messages reinforce the lie that it's all about looks, it's all about appearances. We connect this lie with our spirituality. We convince ourselves that to be accepted and loved by God and by others we have to have worth and to have worth we must have beauty. In order to be beautiful, however, something must be done with the truth. Somehow, some way, we must cover over dirt.

That's exactly what we do. We cover over our dirt with the masks of artificial beauty. Week after week, Sunday after Sunday, we sit in the pews of our churches, hiding behind a thick veneer of superficiality. The result is isolation. The result is alienation. The result is hell. Could you imagine what that animal pen in Africa would be like if Owen pretended to be proper and well-mannered by covering his muddy body with a cocktail dress? And what if Mzee decided he was too good to be seen with a dirty, smelly baby hippo? The result: church as we've known it. Instead, Owen and Mzee are real, willing to be intimate and willing to bond, even though they are two completely different species.

It was no accident that Jesus made his message and mission the kingdom of God. You see, we long for authentic, intimate relationships.

It's what we need the most. We long for authenticity. We desire intimacy. We need deep, meaningful relationships. These things can only be found once we take off our masks and begin living in grace.

Jesus' word, his message, was the good news of the kingdom of God. His mission was to see this kingdom break out into this dark world. How he carried out this mission is quite intriguing. Jesus took his message and mission to some smelly fishermen, some unclean lepers, some dishonest tax-collectors, some immoral prostitutes, and to all of those in the world he encountered whom the Pharisees considered unclean. Jesus, in short, went to those who were dirty. Could it be that what we've been calling church and what Jesus meant by the kingdom of God are two different things? Could it even be that they are actually complete opposites? If Jesus were to walk the streets of America today, would he venture into one of our houses of worship, where things are slick, clean, and the people are all dressed up nice? Or would you find him in the bars, in the tattoo shops, at the bowling alleys, where the paint is chipping off the walls, the smell is less than pleasant, and the people (the hippos and turtles of this world) have gathered simply to hang out and be themselves?

Look at the characteristics of the kingdom of God. Authenticity. Intimacy. Tightly-knit relationships. Do we find these things in the church today? Or are we more likely to find superficiality, isolation, and an individualism that reinforces an already pervasive spirit of selfishness in our culture? Where the kingdom of God is about communion with God, the church seems to be about religion. Where we should be about community, we're about politics. Where there should be a heart for the suffering and the poor, we bow down to the idols of big, bigger, and biggest. Where the Word of God should be, our cultural values of beauty, fame, and wealth have flourished.

Koinonia is a dirty word. Or it should be. To experience koinonia, to experience life, we must be willing to share in communion with Jesus Christ, his sufferings, the poor, the broken, the lost, the overlooked, the authentic, the real. Jesus had a message—a word—and that word was the good news of the kingdom of God. It is not a clean word. It is a dirty word. It is a dirty word for dirty people. It's time to proclaim it.

The Kingdom of God and the church: one and the same?

The Kingdom of God	"Church"
Authenticity	Superficiality
Assurance	Fear
Belonging	Rejection
Meaning/compassion	Luxury
Intimacy	Isolation
Tightly-knit relationships	Individualism
We	Me
Communion with God	Religion
Sharing in Community	Advancing Politics
Heart for the suffering/poor	The idol of "big, bigger, biggest"
The Word of God	Cultural values of beauty, fame, and wealth

A Lonely Man and His Sign

Not too long ago, I was with a group of guys at a local pub on Pittsburgh's South Side. We were all sitting at the window, laughing, talking about theology, and enjoying each other's company. Walking along the sidewalk was a middle-aged man, all by himself, with an angry look on his face and carrying a sign. The sign read, written in dark, black ink, "Unless you repent and accept Jesus Christ as your Lord and Savior, you will surely burn in hell for all eternity." The man walked up to the window where we were sitting. Without changing expression, the man stood outside the bar, holding the sign up to the window so everyone could read about their eternal reward for such debauchery. The man looked so lonely, so miserable. I couldn't help wondering, "Who's really in hell here?" Not knowing what else to do, one of the guys in our group motioned for the man to come inside and join us. The man shook his head and made an even angrier face, if that was possible. "Come on, join us," one of us shouted. "You don't have to drink. Order a Coke! I'm buying!" But the man scowled at us, turned and continued down the street. All by himself. Just him and his sign. As he walked away, he turned around one last time to look at us. I think I saw myself, I think I saw one of those people sitting in the pew in Nazareth, I think I saw yet another Christian trapped in Christianity. Maybe it was my imagination, but I could have sworn that as he turned away, he mouthed this phrase to me:

"Would someone please save me from this bull#@%?"

PART 2: WHAT THE HELL?

Texas Hold 'Em and the Kingdom of God

Could it be that I found the kingdom of God over a game of Texas hold 'em?

John was an amazing person and a good friend. He was a member of our church's congregation—whatever all that means. John had a servant's heart, volunteering for many different organizations and ministries in Pittsburgh. He also liked to cut hair in his living room for extra dough. Getting your hair cut by John was always nourishing. John had this way of going deeper with people, not as a gossip, but as a caring friend. He had a gift of helping people feel beautiful, both inside and out, as they walked out of his house after getting their hair done. John considered his hair-cutting business a ministry. I agreed with him. John's thoughtful, humble nature reminded me of Christ. Getting my hair cut and connecting with John in so many ways through our community saved me. My friendship with John was another one of those hippo/turtle things that I have shared with more than a few people on the South Side.

On one particular Saturday night, John invited me and five other guys in our faith community over to his house to play poker. Being a pastor and all, I don't get a lot of opportunities to lose a few bucks playing poker, so I went. We had a great time, stuffing our faces, watching the hockey game, and trying to con each other into thinking we actually had a good hand. I hadn't laughed so hard in a long time.

The Monday night following the poker game, we had a meeting in the church office to begin planning a new healing service. John was there, as well as six or seven other interested leaders. I began the meeting with prayer and then led the discussion with this question: "When I say the word 'healing,' what comes to mind?" As we went around the room, everyone shared their experiences, from watching Benny Hinn in confusion, to experiencing healing in their own lives. When it came to John, the mood in the room quickly got serious. With tears in his eyes, John said, "When I think of healing, I think of Saturday night's poker game. Never in my life have I experienced such love and acceptance. You have to know, I have never had any friends who were heterosexual males. Saturday's poker game was a healing moment for me."

If you haven't guessed already, John was gay. For most of his life he had to endure all kinds of rejection from his family, from his friends, and from the church. No group had been more hateful to him than heterosexual males. To have five guys hang out and play poker with him showed more than friendship; it showed him Jesus. While playing poker, we connected; we shared in koinonia. As I listened to John share about the importance of a dumb poker game in his life, I began to wonder some things. Is it possible that we experienced the kingdom of God at that poker table? If that is possible, is it possible that we all, including John, experienced the saving love of Christ?

Now, you need to know that John and I didn't see eye-to-eye when it comes to issues surrounding homosexuality. John believed that homosexual behavior should not be considered sinful. I disagreed with him. I contend that homosexual behavior is a result of human brokenness, and to consider it not sinful would be to justify ourselves. I believe we should be justified by the crucified Christ. To say that a certain sin is not a sin is to deny one's brokenness. Even though John and I did not agree, we continued to be good friends and John continued to be an active participant in our faith community. What blew my mind during that healing ministry meeting was this question: what if the saving love of God in Christ isn't bound by our little minds? What if, even though John and I believe differently, we both found koinonia through a poker game? What if that experience, through the power of the Spirit, led John to find salvation?

I know what you're thinking. What? This is heresy! How could it be that John and I both experienced salvation when we don't share the same belief? I suppose before we go any further, we need to look at what we mean by the kingdom of God. To do that, we need to explore who we believe Jesus is and what exactly he saves us from.

What the Hell Do We Believe about Hell?

To start off, let's get some terms straight.

First we have the word *ecclesiology*. This word refers to *how* the church does its job. When we are arguing about which is better, traditional worship or contemporary worship, it is an ecclesiological argument.

Next, we have the word *missiology*. This word refers to the church's mission, or *what* the church's job is. When we begin thinking about what it means to be the church in America in the twenty-first century, we are thinking missiologically.

Third, we have the word *Christology*. This word refers to *who* we believe God is or, more specifically, who Jesus Christ is. When we are talking about the atonement or resurrection, we're talking in terms of Christology.

Finally, we have this ugly word *hell*. I believe this word refers to that which Jesus Christ saves us from. If we're talking atonement, what is it that we are being atoned from?

I propose that each one of these realms of thinking is connected to the other. In other words, how can we begin talking about Christology, before we have at least gotten a glimpse of the human condition? This was John Wesley's take on repentance, really. He defined repentance as that moment when the Holy Spirit revealed for a person his or her own human condition in the light of Christ. Isn't it natural and even important to understand what we need saving from before we consider the savior? Similarly, how can we begin to think about what the church's job is, our ecclesiology, if we do not fully understand who Jesus is? Isn't Jesus Christ the total motivation of the church? In a way, isn't the church and Jesus Christ synonymous? Are we not the body of Christ? How can the body of Christ operate if we do not understand who Christ is? And likewise, how can we begin to do the job of the church if we don't have a clue what that job is?

You see, the question of hell is so interconnected and intertwined with who we are as a church that it forms everything the church does, from worship, to missions, to discipleship, to bake sales. Look and see what I mean. . .

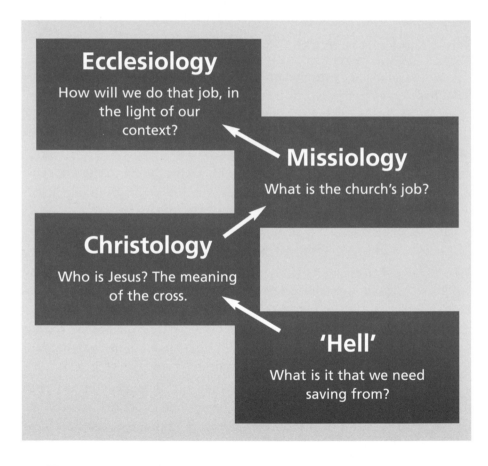

Ecclesiology
How will we do that job, in the light of our context?

Missiology
What is the church's job?

Christology
Who is Jesus? The meaning of the cross.

'Hell'
What is it that we need saving from?

How we answer the question of hell affects everything.

The Turn or Burn Church

Hell—"Where sinners burn in a lake of fire forever."

Jesus—"You must repent and believe in Jesus to escape hell."

Missiology—"Saving people from hell by getting them to be saved."

Ecclesiology—"Turn or burn evangelism crusades and campaigns."

The Cookie-cutter Church

Hell—"A horrible place where people look and act different from us."

Jesus—"The white guy with brown hair and blue eyes. You know, kind of looks and acts like we do."

Missiology—"Getting people who are different to look and act like Jesus (or rather: us)."

Ecclesiology—Assimilating people into our way of thinking and behaving.

The Feel-Good Church

Hell—"To be uncomfortable."

Jesus—"God who wants me to be happy."

Missiology— "Helping people feel better."

Ecclesiology—"Satisfying people's needs."

The Club Church

Hell—"Unsure."

Jesus—"That little baby in the manger. The reason for the season."

Missiology—"Don't know. Don't care."

Ecclesiology—"Our church makes pierogies. The town loves it, and we make lots of money."

The Good-Example Church

Hell—"There's no such thing."

Jesus—"A good teacher. A good example of how we should behave."

Missiology—"Be a good example. Don't cuss, don't fuss, don't stink."

Ecclesiology—"Be good. Keep up appearances."

What if our definition of hell were more thought out and realistic and our understanding of Jesus more dynamic? More dangerous?

The Church Practicing Koinonia

Hell—"Selfishness, alienation, isolation from God and others. To be all alone, without meaning, without identity, without love."

Jesus—"Lord and Savior who endured separation from God on the cross, was dead, and was raised to life. Who is alive right now and comes to us bringing grace, forgiveness, reconciliation, redemption, and new life."

Missiology—"To be Christ's Body. To live Christ's life. Living a life of humility, love, and koinonia so that the Kingdom of God is near."

Ecclesiology—"Koinonia with God, others, the poor, the suffering, the Word, and God's mission" (Acts 2:42).

How can it be that John and I think differently, but we both experience salvation in Jesus Christ? Simple. Salvation is not about being right because hell isn't about being wrong. Salvation isn't only about what we believe because hell isn't just about doubt. Salvation is about koinonia; it's about connection with God and with others. Is it possible to connect with God and at the same time not have the exact, right belief? I sure hope so. Because no matter who you are, you do not have complete understanding of who God is and what God is about. On the other hand, koinonia with God is impossible when we deny our own brokenness. Koinonia goes hand in hand with denying one's self. Can John experience salvation by experiencing the kingdom of God? I believe so. Did he experience salvation through the poker game? I'm not sure. All I know is that I'm to live Christ's life and bear witness to his kingdom. If that is the case, then I believe I witnessed the kingdom of God at John's house that night—heaven where I did not expect it. Is

Heaven a place where wild poker games take place? I sure hope so. John has since passed away, but I anticipate laughing with him again over a wild game of Texas hold 'em in the kingdom of heaven.

Look at the parable of the good Samaritan in Luke 10:26-34. A teacher of the law challenges Jesus. He asks him what he has to do to inherit eternal life. (I think we forget as we're reading the rest of the story that this conversation is about eternal life, not just when we die, but right now.) Jesus answers the man with a question, asking the teacher what is written in the law. The teacher replies, "Love the Lord your God with all of your heart, and all of your mind, and all of your strength; and love your neighbor as yourself." Jesus affirms the teacher's answer by stating, "Do this and you will live." In other words, love God and love others and eternal life is yours, in the next life, but, just as importantly, right now.

Of course, this isn't enough for the teacher, and he presses Jesus further saying, 'But who is my neighbor?" Then, Jesus tells his famous story of the good Samaritan in which a man is beaten up, a priest passes by, a Levite passes by, and a Samaritan not only helps the man, but sacrifices his money, his schedule, and his time for the beaten-up man. When the teacher answers, "The one who showed mercy," Jesus responds by charging the teacher, and all of us, to "go and do likewise."

What is so offensive about this story is that the conversation is not about helping people. The conversation is about eternal life. The teacher essentially asked Jesus, "How is one saved?" Then Jesus tells a story to the teacher of the law (who certainly believes that he will receive eternal life) about a Pharisee, who is without question part of the family of God, and a Levite, who is a holy man and should receive what's coming to him. But neither of these help the man. A Samaritan does, and we are instructed to do as the Samaritan did. But Samaritans, at the time, did not believe the same things as a teacher of the law believed. In fact, the Samaritan, in the teacher's view, would have been so off the mark theologically that he would not have been included in the family of God. The Samaritans had a sightly different set of beliefs than that of the Jews. As a result, the two groups hated each other. They certainly would not have been invited to worship and they certainly were not considered worthy to receive eternal life. In other words, in the teacher's mind, Samaritans, based on their beliefs, were not going to get in.

Jesus blows the teacher's mind. And he blows our minds by suggesting that a theologically deficient mutt inherits eternal life, not based on his beliefs, but based on his practice, and more specifically, based on his love for others, which in turn reflects a love for God. Am I saying that you simply have to be nice to get into heaven or have heaven be in your midst? Absolutely not. What I'm saying is that inheriting eternal life, according to Jesus' story in Luke 10, is not based entirely on what we believe. It is the act of loving others, which in turn *is* the act of loving God, which brings salvation.

So, if a no good Samaritan can find eternal life by "loving thy neighbor," then why can't my friend John, who doesn't agree with my theology, find salvation as well?

What am I saying? Am I saying that everyone is saved? That everyone gets into heaven? No. Am I saying it doesn't really matter what we believe? Can I believe that a head of lettuce is God and still experience the kingdom of God? No. One thing we can and should hold in common as followers of Christ is this: Jesus Christ is Lord and Savior.

As followers of Christ, although we might have differing beliefs, we almost all agree that Jesus is Lord and Savior. But what does "Jesus is Lord and Savior" mean? I think sometimes we give lip service to the "Jesus is Lord" thing. I mean, if Jesus is really Lord, don't you think it should have a bigger effect on us than simply changing our language and making us very judgmental? Shouldn't "Jesus is Lord" somehow rearrange our lives? I contend that "Jesus is Lord" means that he is the Great I AM. He is the way, the truth and the life. These are the ways that we are saved. Jesus is the Great I Am. He is Existence. For us to exist as well, we need to connect with the Existence. He is the way, the truth, and the life. For us to be part of the way, the truth, and the life, we have to connect with it. How do we do this? The way is marked out for us in all four Gospels. To narrow the way to salvation down to one or two memory verses is to close doors to heaven that God, I believe, intends to keep open.

To be saved from the hells of alienation, isolation from God, from fear and rejection, one must share in koinonia with Jesus Christ.

You might be wondering if I mean that salvation is heaven when you die, or if salvation is here and now. I mean both, just as Jesus did. Jesus was all about getting to heaven for eternity. He was even more

Who is Jesus Christ? "He is the way, the truth, and the life" (John 14).

But what was his way, what was/is the truth, and how did he live?

His *way* was to suffer. Share in koinonia with suffering and you will be saved.

His *truth* was to love, the greatest commandment. Share in koinonia with love and you will be saved.

His *life* was one of humility—share in koinonia with humility and you will be saved.

His *way* was to be last—share in koinonia with the last and you will be saved.

His *truth* was the Word—share in koinonia with the Word and you will be saved.

He lived *life* as a poor man—share in koinonia with the poor and you will be saved.

His *way* was to make himself nothing—share in koinonia with those who are "nothing" and you will be saved.

His *truth* was to be broken bread—share in koinonia with the broken, with brokenness and you will be saved.

His *life* was poured out like wine—pour out yourself. Share in koinonia with those who are empty and you will be saved.

about bringing heaven to us here on earth. Share in koinonia, and you experience the kingdom of God—heaven here on earth. At the same time, you prepare yourself for what is to come. Those who have practiced koinonia here on earth are not aliens when they get to heaven. But those who have spent their whole lives living for themselves find themselves as foreigners when they finally get before God, no matter how righteous they were here on earth.

"Not everyone who says to me, 'Lord, Lord,' will enter the kingdom of heaven, but only the one who does the will of my Father in heaven. On that day many will say to me, 'Lord, Lord, did we not prophesy in your name, and cast out demons in your name, and do many deeds of power in your name?' Then I will declare to them, 'I never knew you; *go away from me, you evildoers*" (Matthew 7:21-23).

Hopefully, somehow, some way, we can become a bridge for John. Through loving Jesus and through the power of the Holy Spirit, John

Salvation at the Poker Table?

Hell—Rejection, brokenness, alienation from God and from family and "friends" and society.

Jesus—The one who brings new life, reconciliation, redemption, and communion.

Mission—Be Jesus for John. Love him as Jesus would love him.

Ecclesiology—Go to his home, play poker, drink beer and share in community.

can connect with God. Maybe in some small way all of us at the poker table saw our human condition in the light of Jesus, not just John. This very act leads to repentance, which leads to a denial of the self and to a deeper walk with Christ. This will definitely lead to less alienation and isolation brought on by our self-centeredness. If alienation is hell, then has salvation come?

In Luke 19 we find the story of Zaccheus the tax collector:

He entered Jericho and was passing through it. A man was there named Zacchaeus; he was chief tax collector and was rich. He was trying to see who Jesus was, but on account of the crowd he could not, because he was short in stature. So he ran ahead and climbed a sycamore tree to see him, because he was going to pass that way. When Jesus came to the place, he looked up and said to him, "Zacchaeus, hurry and come down; for I must stay at your house today." So he hurried down and was happy to welcome him. All who saw it began to grumble and said, "He has gone to be the guest of one who is a sinner." Zacchaeus stood there and said to the Lord, "Look, half of my possessions, Lord, I will give to the poor; and if I have defrauded anyone of anything, I will pay back four times as much." Then Jesus said to him, "Today salvation has come to this house, because he too is a son of Abraham" (Luke 19:1-10).

When was Zacchaeus saved? I didn't see him come down the aisle during the altar call. When did he say the special salvation prayer? Was he saved when he climbed the tree? Was he saved when he stood up and declared that he would give away his money? Or, did his salvation have nothing to do with his actions at all? Was Zacchaeus saved when Jesus and his whole entourage (which was probably pretty big a week before the triumphant entry) sat down and ate with Zacchaeus? Was Zacchaeus, the lonely tax-collector who ate every meal alone because he had been excluded by all of his family and friends from the table of God, saved when God's son showed up at his house for dinner? If the saving moment for Zacchaeus is koinonia with Jesus Christ, why can't John have the same kind of saving moment over a game of Texas hold 'em?

Whether John did or not, I know I have experienced salvation in the past five years again and again, and not in the way I would have ever expected. Through poker games, a tattoo shop, punk-rock shows, stage diving, hanging out in the lowliest of places with the lowliest of people, I have experienced salvation in all the ways a person can be saved. Somehow, some way, God heard my cries, rescued me from the cesspool of the bastardized, Americanized version of self-centered Christianity and introduced me to something completely different: the kingdom of God. Saved. I was saved. And not by religion. And really, not by faith, either. However, faith is part of it. I think I was saved by something a little more . . . dirty. Saved by koinonia alone. Saved over a game of Texas hold 'em.

"Jesus Saves" Is More Than Just a Bumper Sticker

Jesus Saves. We've all seen that bumper sticker before. But what do we mean when we say, "Jesus Saves"? Do we understand Jesus and salvation in real spiritual terms, or have we made Jesus into another commodity to market? Is "Jesus Saves" just our marketing slogan? Do we really want people to experience the kingdom of God, or are we more interested in people buying into our product so that we can fill seats and fill offering plates?

Salvation is not related at all to our brand of belief. We associate belief with having the right doctrine or having the right set of ideological values and dogma. This might sound like heresy, but following Jesus, following the suffering servant, is about a lot more than having the right doctrine. The Pharisees thought they had the right doctrine! For Jesus, salvation came from experience, from being in connection with God and God's kingdom. Therefore, being in connection has little to do with right doctrine and has more to do with trust, abiding, belonging, and loving. If having the right doctrine leads to trust in God, great. If holding a certain dogma helps you to love, super. But a person can certainly trust in God, abide in God, belong in the kingdom, and participate in love without holding exactly the right doctrine. This is what Jesus was getting at, and this is why he did not get along with the Pharisees.

Yes, I know what you're thinking—Jesus calls us to believe in John 3:14-18:

> "And just as Moses lifted up the serpent in the wilderness, so must the Son of Man be lifted up, that whoever believes in him may have eternal life. For God so loved the world that he gave his only Son, so that everyone who believes in him may not perish but may have eternal life. Indeed, God did not send the Son into the world to condemn the world, but in order that the world might be saved through him. Those who believe in him are not condemned; but those who do not believe are condemned already, because they have not believed in the name of the only Son of God" (John 3:14-18).

Jesus' message here is not, "Say a special prayer, believe in Jesus, sign the card, get your ticket, and get into heaven when you die." His message is the same as it is in Luke: "The kingdom of God is near. Repent and believe the good news." In other words, you are lost in yourself. Step out, grab hold of God through Christ, and you will be saved. Take your eyes off yourself and give your attention to the cross. Trust in God. Put your life into God's hands rather than your own. Share in koinonia with God through the cross of Christ, and you will be saved from the hell of alienation and isolation that comes from self-ishness. Salvation does not come from a set of right beliefs; it comes from koinonia with Christ. Certainly, there is absolute truth, and that truth is centered on Christ. Being in koinonia with that truth is where we find salvation.

When we first began work on launching Hot Metal, we had no building. We had no place to hide. All we had was on the streets. We found places to meet in coffee shops, tattoo shops, and restaurants. There is one coffee shop on the South Side that stays open quite late called The Beehive, and so it attracts many night owls. Naturally, we quickly made friends with those night owls. One of those night owls that we met went by the name of "Fetus." Fetus is a fascinating person who has lived on the streets as a squatter and has traveled the country in railroad boxcars. When we first met him, he told us that he was Rastafarian. If you don't know what that is, the Rastafari movement is a religion that accepts Haile Selassie I, the former emperor of Ethiopia, as God incarnate, whom they call Jah. Fetus would always greet us with a handshake and a "Jah Love, Bro."

One evening as I was leaving The Beehive, I noticed Fetus sitting alone at one of the tables in the back. He was looking a little blue, so I decided to sit down with him and strike up a conversation. I asked him how he was doing and then simply sat there and listened as he gave me the story of his life. It was such an honest moment. I will never forget it. Fetus wasn't trying to fake me out, like so many people do when they find out I'm a pastor. Fetus was being Fetus—cussing, smoking, and speaking his heart. I experienced the great blessing of listening.

When Fetus finished sharing, I had nothing to say. I didn't give him advice and didn't pray with him. I just thanked him for sharing a piece of his life with me. I left The Beehive that night thinking I had let God down somehow. Somehow, I should have brought Fetus to a "saving knowledge of Jesus Christ." I thought, "How will this church ever grow if I'm not willing to share the gospel with people like Fetus?"

But since then, I have learned a great lesson that has change my life and has changed my approach to ministry: *I can't change people!* I can't. And you can't either. There is not one thing we can do that is going to change someone else. The more we try to change others, the more we get in the way of what God is doing. That's who does the changing: God. The Holy Spirit moves in people, moves in me, and brings about change. And I mean real change. The Holy Spirit changes people, not me. My job, as a follower of Jesus, is to bear witness to Christ. All I can really do is point out to others where Jesus is working and where his kingdom is growing. Many times, that job can and should be done without words.

That's exactly what happened in that coffee shop that night. That wasn't the last I saw of Fetus. He began to connect with our community. I would see him in the tattoo shop. I would see him even at worship. Then one Sunday morning, after we had baptized eight people or so, we asked the congregation if there were any others who had never been baptized and if they would like to come forward and do so. Four more people got up and approached the altar. Fetus was one of them. I thought about our conversation in the coffee shop as I read from the book of worship:

> . . . Do you confess Jesus Christ as your Savior, put your whole trust in his grace . . .

I thought about all of the ways we had connected since then as I poured the water over his head and said, "I baptize you in the name of the Father, and of the Son, and of the Holy Spirit." I wondered what it was that had brought Fetus to this place.

The next week I saw Fetus in church again. I reached out my hand and said, "Jah love, Fetus." He didn't shake my hand. He said, "Please don't call me that. From now on, my name is 'Feed Us.'" The man had been changed. God had moved in his life to a point of changing his identity. I thought of Saul and his transformation to Paul. I'm still unsure exactly what "Feed Us" means, but what I do know is that Fetus was changed to Feed Us and he wasn't changed by me. It wasn't the conversation in the coffee shop. It wasn't the words from the book of worship. It wasn't water that was poured over his head. It was God. God did it. Fetus entered into koinonia with God, and he was changed.

I believe that this story of Feed Us is John 3:14-16 played out in the real world. Feed Us found salvation in trusting in the truth of Jesus Christ. This happens every day in a million different places in a million different ways. People welcome koinonia with God, God moves in their lives, and they are changed. Every once in a while it actually happens in a building we call the church, but more often than not, koinonia happens in the coffee shops, the bars, and all of the little places where people gather in this world. "The light shines in the darkness, and the darkness did not overcome it" (John 1:5).

The Kingdom of God Is Near . . . in a Strip Club?

For a long time, it seems that we have been the church centered on John 3:16. "For God so loved the world . . ." has got to be the most well know, most often memorized verse in the Bible. It has been the cornerstone of our modern theological approach to ministry. However, John 3 isn't the only place in the Gospels where Jesus lays down the meaning of salvation and what it takes to be saved. Peter and Andrew were saved when they dropped their nets. The demoniac was saved when Jesus called out the legion of demons. The woman at the well was saved when Jesus knew everything about her. The prodigal son was saved when he ran into his father's arms. The widow was saved when she dropped her two coins into the offering. Lazarus was saved when Jesus called him out of death. And the thief on the cross was saved when Jesus assured him, "Today, you will be with me in paradise." And on and on and on . . . .

In places where Jesus does make a clear call to salvation, he doesn't always call us to the same response. Sure, in John 3, Jesus calls us to believe or to trust in him. But in John 15, Jesus calls us to abide. In my mind, trust and abide are slightly different. Look:

"I am the true vine, and my Father is the vinegrower. He removes every branch in me that bears no fruit. Every branch that bears fruit he prunes to make it bear more fruit. You have already been cleansed by the word that I have spoken to you. Abide in me as I abide in you. Just as the branch cannot bear fruit by itself unless it abides in the vine, neither can you unless you abide in me. I am the vine, you are the branches. Those who abide in me and I in them bear much fruit, because apart from me you can do nothing" (John 15:1-5).

Where John 3 is a call to share in koinonia with the truth of the gospel, John 15 is more of a call to share in communion with God through Christ.

One evening during our first year, while trying to get to know people in the South Side community, we sat down and had dinner with a bright young lady named Melisa. Melisa was surprisingly well spoken with a lot of initiative. With black spiky hair and a seemingly endless supply of tattoos, she dreamed of a tattoo shop that would also double as an outpost for ministry. As she told us her vision, our mouths hanging open, we quickly realized that we needed to team up with this young lady and her freaky band of friends. Within a few months, Melisa and her group, The End Ministries, pulled together what little money they had and established the In the Blood Tattoo Shop. Soon, the shop became a kind of gathering place for young punk-rockers and young people simply yearning for a place to belong. The tattoo parlor came alive on Monday nights when they gathered for Bible study. In the Blood has become a key partner in ministry with us as the young people who run the ministry have found a way to connect with "the lost" like no other ministry that I've experienced.

One Sunday morning we had the great honor of hearing Melisa's testimony for the first time in worship. She stood up and showed us the tattoos on her right arm. What had been drawn on her arm in ink actually looked like cuts from a knife. She shared her brokenness, how throughout her teenage years she struggled with self-hate and depression. She hated herself so much she cut herself. Then she showed us her left arm where, tattooed into her skin with ink, were similar cuts. However, these cuts on her left arm were stitched up with stitches that looked like small crosses. She shared how she had been saved. She shared how she had found refuge in abiding in the unconditional love and grace of God through Jesus and how she had been healed. Now she wears her heart on her sleeve, literally. Her tattoos are her testimony, which she shares with young women on a regular basis.

Melisa's husband, Chippy, is the drummer for a punk-rock band called The Last Hope, which was somewhat birthed out of the tattoo-shop ministry. These six guys, Chippy, Justin, Skull, Dylan, Denman, and Jake, are a whirling dervish of energy, heat, noise, and spirit as they play their music—music that points to Jesus Christ, the Revolutionary One. The guys in The Last Hope see themselves as missionaries sent by Christ to bear witness to the kingdom of God to those young people who would never darken the doorway of a church building. During one very memorable tour, the band was scheduled to play at a bar out in the middle of nowhere. When they got to the bar, they discovered that it was actually a strip club, with mostly naked women dancing on stage. When the guys turned to leave, Melisa, who was on tour with them, stopped them and insisted that they play. While the boys played, trying their best to be light in the darkness, Melisa befriended some of the strippers. In telling the story, Melisa said that she didn't preach; she didn't even share the gospel. She didn't have to; she was the gospel. Melisa had found salvation in the unconditional love of God in her life, and now she was saved again as she simply shared that same unconditional love with those who probably see more lust and lies than actual love.

When we dwell in God's unconditional love, we can't help loving others with the same blindness to flaws. Is it possible for the kingdom of God to come near a tattoo shop? Is it possible for the kingdom of God to come near when The Last Hope plays? Is it possible for the kingdom of God to come near a strip club? I believe it is.

Charley's Prayer Request

The kingdom of God is near in the Goodwill every Wednesday at noon. I work there as the chaplain, and I lead a weekly worship service every Wednesday at noon for the employees, or, as they call them, the clients of Goodwill Industries. As you might know, Goodwill employs people with handicaps and developmental disorders such as mental retardation and autism. Every Wednesday at noon, we gather in a tiny chapel. Every week at that same time, I experience the kingdom of God at its most palpable. Share a conversation with Jack, who uses a walker to get around but proudly wears the medals he won at the Special Olympics, and you can't help seeing the face of Jesus. Every week the service is almost exactly the same. It's the same twelve people, and we do the exact same things every time. We gather and sing songs from a vacation bible school CD—"Jesus Loves Me," "This Little Light of Mine," and "Rise and Shine." I don't feel more ridiculous and more blessed than when I'm jumping up and down singing, "If you're happy and you know it clap your hands!" Then we gather everyone's prayer requests, and we pray together. Each week the prayer requests are exactly the same: Jack prays for everyone in Goodwill; Joe prays for the weather; Jeffrey prays that he'll get a gun for Christmas (this is the last person on earth who needs a gun). Every week the candles are snuffed out and they all go back to work somewhere in the building, moving along slowly, by walker or by wheelchair.

One week not so long ago, something new happened. We had some-one join us who had never joined us before. His name was Charley, and he had just begun working in the kitchen. As we went around the room and gathered prayer requests, we finally came to Charley. I was a little unsure if I should ask a newcomer if he had a prayer request, but I gave it a shot.

"We want to welcome you, Charley, to our service," I said. "Is there anything going on in your life that you need prayer for?"

Charley paused for a long time, thinking. Then he quietly, with sad eyes, looked at me and said, "Would you pray that I would get some friends? I have been very lonely all of my life, and I need a friend or a brother or someone to talk to."

As you can imagine, my heart broke in half. And I prayed that Charley would find a friend.

The following week, Charley attended the worship service again, and again Charley had the same prayer request. Again, I prayed that Charley would find a friend. This happened week after week after week, until one week, before the service, Charley approached me with tears in his eyes.

"Pastor, can I talk to you?"
"Sure, Charley, what's wrong?"
"I just don't know," he said. "I just don't know."

DIRTY WORD

"You just don't know what, Charley?"

"I just don't know what's wrong with me. I try so hard, but no one wants to be my friend. And I have been so lonely. All of my life I have been so lonely. Would you pray that I would get a friend? Lots of friends."

As I listened to Charley's heart-breaking words, I suddenly felt like a complete idiot. Why was I praying for Charley to have a friend instead actually being Charley's friend? Is it because praying for a friend is easier than being the answer to that prayer?

"I'll tell you what, Charley. Instead of praying for you, what if you gave me your number and I'll call you. We'll get together and do something. Maybe you would like to come to our Sunday worship service sometime?"

Charley nodded. I took down Charley's phone number and called him as soon as I had the chance. That Sunday morning, Charley was at Hot Metal Bridge worship service. He sat in the front row and appeared to love every minute of it. During the prayer time, as we gathered people's prayer requests, Charley raised his hand.

"Charley, how can we pray for you?"

Charley began to share the same prayer request that he had given every Wednesday. "Would you pray that I would get some friends? I have been very lonely all of my life and I need a friend or a brother or someone to talk to." But Charley didn't get all the way through the request before two or three hands fell upon his shoulders and his back. The people around him quickly embraced him. As they did, I watched as his body became thirty pounds lighter. It was almost as if all of that sadness just evaporated as a small grin came across his face.

I thought of Jesus' words with Zacchaeus, "Today salvation has come to this house, because he too is a son of Abraham."

It's funny for me to think about Charley finding salvation in the good news of the kingdom of God because he wasn't saved by a prayer. In fact, he finally connected to the kingdom when I decided *not* to pray and actually did something.

At the end of the service that Sunday, I asked if there were eight volunteers who would like to help serve communion. Charley, even though it was his first week at our church, jumped up and grabbed one of the baskets of bread. As Charley stood with the basket in hand, watching person after person go by, taking bread and dipping it into the cup, I thought about what Jesus said when the children came to see Jesus, but his disciples turned them away. "Let the little children come to me, and do not stop them; for it is to such as these the kingdom of heaven belongs" (Matthew 19:14).

Charley found salvation in sharing koinonia in the kingdom of God that day. Charley found belonging. With the same simple faith as one of the children that jumped into Jesus' lap, Charley came with the same longing to be part of the family of God.

Where Fetus connected with the truth, and Melisa connected with the unconditional love, Charley connected with the belonging.

All three were saved by koinonia with Christ.

Love Saves the Day

In short, we're saved when we love others. If we are followers of Jesus, then we are followers with the one who loves, the one who is love. The act of loving others brings salvation. We cannot build all of our theology of salvation around John 3:16 and turn a blind eye to Jesus' call to service expressed in his parable of the sheep and the goats in Matthew 25. Furthermore, this is not a call to works-righteousness or any attempt to save ourselves. No, to be in communion with God one must love God, and to love God means to love others—especially those who are unlovable.

A group of young people meets at the tattoo shop every Saturday afternoon to take lunches to the homeless. Their goal is not just to hand out food, but also to love people who are on society's fringes. The group spends most of its Saturday afternoon just hanging out with the homeless, talking, listening, and getting to know them. The experience, for the group, is much like going to visit Jesus. One day, a forty-something named Doug joined the group on its mission to feed the homeless, and his life was changed. Doug had been living in a rural town in western Pennsylvania, living in a bubble, "in the comfort zone," as he puts it. Doug had been through two marriages and was trying to recover from his second divorce when he decided to move to the city. As Doug tells the story, he was on a mission to find himself. I would put it this way: even though he was already a Christian, he was searching for salvation.

The day Doug spent his afternoon getting to know the hungry, the thirsty, and the homeless, his life was changed. He met a woman named Claudell who was actually a man. Claudell is a transsexual and certainly one of those lepers in our society that no one wants to touch. When Doug met her, he didn't want to touch her either. For Doug, who grew up as an evangelical Christian, Claudell didn't fit into his matrix. But as he got to know her, her hurts, her brokenness, he suddenly found himself looking into the face of Jesus. He found himself saved—saved through compassion. The word *compassion* literally means "to suffer with" or to share in koinonia with suffering, which is all Paul wants to know in Philippians 3. When we connect to suffering, we connect to the sufferer, who is Jesus. To share in koinonia with suffering is to share in koinonia with Christ.

I have encouraged people in the past to change their thinking about who Jesus is and what Christianity is by referring to Jesus as the sufferer. Try it yourself. When you pray or read the scriptures, replace the word *Jesus* with the words *the Sufferer* and see if that doesn't change your faith life.

> As *the Sufferer* passed along the Sea of Galilee, he saw Simon and his brother Andrew casting a net into the sea—for they were fishermen. And *the Sufferer* said to them, "Follow me and I will make you fish for people." And immediately they left their nets and followed him" (Mark 1:16-18).
>
> Now the eleven disciples went to Galilee, to the mountain to which *the Sufferer* had directed them. When they saw *the Sufferer*, they worshiped him; but some doubted. *And the Sufferer* came and said to them, "All authority in heaven and on earth has been given to me. Go therefore and make disciples of all nations, baptizing them in the name of the Father, and of *the Sufferer* and of the Holy Spirit, and trenching them to obey everything *the Sufferer* has commanded you. And remember, *the Sufferer* is with you always, to the end of the age" (Matthew 28:16-20).

WHAT THE HELL?

77

I'm sure you could do the same thing with *the Forgiver, the Broken One, the Suffering Servant, the Risen One,* or anything like that. Sometimes the words we use actually get overused and they lose their meaning. *Church* and *Jesus* are two of those words. Connecting Christianity with who Jesus really is is so crucial to being an authentic follower of Christ.

Has Jesus become another commodity to be bought, sold, and marketed? Is Jesus real? Or is Jesus just the American way? Is Jesus only for those who have it all together, who have gotten cleaned up, at least on the outside? Or is Jesus really found in the face of people like Claudell? Is Jesus present in the broken, dirty faces of this world? Is being a Christian all about knowing John 3:16 or can we also include 1 John 3:16, "This is how we know what love is: Jesus Christ laid down his life for us. And we ought to lay down our lives for our brothers and sisters" (NIV)? Is Christianity the American way, part of our consumeristic society that we all have to conform to? Or is koinonia with Jesus Christ, the sufferer, the dirtiest, the most offensive, the most counter-cultural of activities?

The bottom line: we're saved when we love God. We love God by loving others. We love others by having compassion. Compassion is sharing in koinonia with suffering.

Putting It All Together

Salvation isn't only about believing a certain dogma. It is about more. Salvation isn't just about not going to hell when we die. It's about being saved from the hells we find ourselves in every day.

If our deep need is *assurance,* but we find ourselves living in the hell of *fear,* fueled by our selfishness, then abiding in Christ through *communion* would bring salvation.

If our deep need is *belonging,* but we find ourselves living in the hell of *rejection,* fueled by our selfishness, then finding belonging in the kingdom of God by experiencing *community* would bring salvation.

If our deep need is *meaning,* but we find ourselves living in the hell of *luxury,* fueled by our selfishness, then finding true eternal meaning by loving others and having *compassion* (suffering with) would bring salvation.

If these are our	Then these are	This is the cure:	To finding
Deep Needs	**Four Curses**	**Koinonia**	**Salvation through**
Assurance	Fear	Communion	Abiding (John 15)
Belonging	Rejection	Community	Belonging (Luke 19)
Meaning	Luxury	Compassion	Loving (Matthew 25)
Identity	Superficiality	The Word	Truth (John 3:16)

If our deep need is *identity*, but we find ourselves living in the hell of *superficiality* and masks, fueled by our selfishness, then finding reality in the truth by sharing in and participating in the Word(which is the *truth*) would bring salvation.

Now don't get me wrong here. I'm not trying to compartmentalize salvation. Actually, I'm trying to say just the opposite. Salvation is more holistic than we make it. Salvation is about eternity, which is here but not yet. Heaven is here and now, but not yet, and hell is also here and now, but not yet. Jesus wants us to abide in him, belong in God's kingdom, know God's love, and connect to God's Word all at once. Watch what happens when we reduce salvation to just one piece:

- emphasize belief and you get a fundamentalism that demands you believe before you can belong;
- emphasize abiding and you get a faith that's all about the emotions and little to do with the mind;
- emphasize belonging while reducing belief and you get a social club;
- emphasize love and action, while reducing belonging, abiding, and believing, and you get a faith that's focused on social activism. There is nothing wrong with social activism, but the gospel is dirtier.

The gospel is a call from God to connect with God in all the ways we need to connect to overcome the hells of fear, rejection, luxury, and superficiality.

Connecting Our Brokenness to the Cross

You might ask, "What does this mean for me, as a follower of Christ? How am I to share koinonia with others and help others participate in koinonia?" I believe we connect best with God and with others through our brokenness. We like to think of Jesus being in the faces of the hungry and the thirsty. We like to think "that which we do for the least of these we do to Jesus." We like to think that the kingdom of God is for the last, the least, and the lost. We forget that that's *me*. The last, the least, and the lost—that's *you*. We're all broken and lost people, searching for the light. We forget that we are all Fetus, Melisa, and Charley. We are all searching and longing. We are all broken. But it is through brokenness that we encounter God's overwhelming grace and love. Then the kingdom of God is near. If you've ever been to an AA meeting, you know what I'm talking about. It is when we really cut to the core of who we are that we are ready to surrender ourselves to God. Is it that moment of surrendering ourselves to God that we're really searching for? We can't forget that Jesus broke the bread in half and said, "This is my body, broken for you. Take in remembrance of me." Salvation is also found in sharing in koinonia through our brokenness. Connecting with brokenness connects us to the cross.

I was born on March 9, 1969, but I was reborn, in a sense, on October 27, 1975. That's not the day I became a Christian; that was the day I was adopted by my father. My parents were divorced when I was just three years old. That event has been a large gaping wound across my heart all of my life. Yes, I have found healing in being adopted by my dad, and also being adopted by God, yet the wound is still there. In some ways, it determined who I am as a father, a husband, and a pastor. When my dad adopted me at the age of five, he gave me more than one gift. Adopting me meant that I took his name. It also meant that I could eat at his table every day of my childhood. And it was a covenant between him and me—a covenant to love and to care for me. When God adopted me, God did the same thing. Being adopted by God changed my identity. I became God's son. I took God's name, in a sense. Being a child of God means that I can eat at God's table every day of my life, into eternity. And being adopted is also a covenant, like the broken bread, that God will love and care for me.

Being adopted by my dad and by God have both been healing events for me. Yet, the brokenness is still there. Am I still a broken person? I guess so. But the good news is that being broken is not a bad thing. Being broken means that you're in a place where God can use you. This sounds like blasphemy. We've been sold the line that Jesus makes everything better. Remember, Emmanuel means "God with us." Jesus doesn't rescue us from the suffering; he walks through the suffering with us. Our brokenness can connect us with others and ultimately connect us to Christ, the Sufferer. The Broken One.

Jesus Heals a Paralytic

In Luke 5:17-26, Jesus takes on the Pharisees and the scribes for the first time. Jesus has been popular in Galilee and Judea. Word about him has spread, and he has become quite popular. However, as the story unfolds in Luke 4, he gets kicked out of his hometown for preaching a gospel that the people don't like. It is an offensive gospel of inclusion. In Luke 5, Jesus has gathered with the Pharisees, and they're going to set him straight. They want him to make sure he knows who is in and who is out. At that time, it was up to the priests and the teachers of the law to decide who was in and who was out. When a priest declared someone unclean, he or she was considered out.

In Luke 5, as Jesus is talking with the Pharisees and the teachers of the law, some men came carrying a paralyzed man on a mat. The scriptures say that when the men got to the house where Jesus was teaching, it was so crowded that they couldn't get anywhere close to Christ. Cunningly, the men cut a hole in the roof and lowered the man down to Jesus on the mat. Here's where it gets a little interesting. "When he saw their faith, he said, 'Friend, your sins are forgiven you'" (Luke 5:20). Everyone is either stunned or completely offended by this statement. They say to themselves "Who can forgive sins but God alone" (v. 22)? Then Jesus chastises the Pharisees and heals the man. The scriptures say that everyone was amazed and said, "We have seen strange things today" (v. 26).

Two things are going on here. First, the writer is emphasizing Jesus' divinity. Jesus has the power. Jesus is God. Secondly, Jesus is making a big statement here as to who is in and who is out. See, the paralyzed man would have been considered unclean. The people of the time did not have modern medicine to know what was wrong with the man, so they chalked it up to sin. Obviously, in their minds, the man had sinned somehow and now he was paralyzed. Therefore, since he was a sinner, this man was considered unclean or out. This meant that he was an outcast, a throwaway. He would not have been invited into community. He would not have been invited to worship. The Pharisees, in a sense, had already sent this paralyzed guy to hell. By saying, "Friend, your sins are forgiven you," Jesus was declaring the man clean, delivering him from hell, and welcoming him into the kingdom of God. The man was saved in many ways. Jesus healed his body as well, so that those who were witnessing this would enter into the kingdom, too.

This verse is a great example of how our view of God affects our worldview. If we view God as an authoritarian, then we read "your sins are forgiven" as the ticket into heaven after death, and we make sure we have our ticket. If we view God as benevolent, then we read the verse as Jesus giving a gift to the man, and we wonder how we can get God to give us that kind of gift as well. If we view God as critical, we might agree with the Pharisees and wonder why the man needed forgiveness. What sin did he commit to deserve his disease? And if we view God as distant, we might doubt the whole story altogether. However, if we understand God as communion, then we have to interpret this interaction differently and see that Jesus is opening the door into the kingdom of God for everyone in the room. The man chooses to enter. Others in the room choose to enter. But the Pharisees are the ones who choose not to enter. Strangely enough, they find themselves thinking that they're at the center of God's kingdom, when in actuality they have declared themselves unclean. They are out, and they don't even realize it.

Who in our society have we already sent to hell? Who in our culture is considered unclean? Who do we know who is like the paralyzed man? I'm sure we can give a cute, political answer like the homosexuals, the transvestites, and the pornographers. Those folks are certainly among our unclean. But I wonder, with all due respect, if the paralyzed man is actually *you*? I wonder if the paralyzed man is *me*. I wonder if we have become unclean, and we have alienated ourselves from God and community. I wonder if we have become so broken and so wounded we can't even move. I think about what it must have been like for the paralyzed man to descend into that crowded room on his mat. Everybody was staring at his frozen body. So hurt. So wounded. So broken. So vulnerable. Then I wonder if that's exactly where we need to be? Are we meant to descend into Jesus' presence, completely vulnerable, completely surrendered? It seems to me that we have become very good at covering over our broken places and pretending everything is fine when we are completely paralyzed by our wounds. Are the walls we create, the masks, more harmful to our Spirit than the actual wounds they cover? In other words, maybe it's the masks that are the things that send us to hell, not the brokenness itself.

Scary Jerry

When we first met Jerry (who told us he was "Scary" Jerry), he had no place to live so he was living in the graveyard. He was dressed in all black, from the black hat on his head to the black boots on his feet. Satanic tattoos covered his body, and he wore black eyeliner, shaved his highbrows, and wore a "Misfits" t-shirt—the one that depicts an angry-looking skull. Our first interactions with him knocked us off guard. He would sit in the back of the sanctuary and shout obscenities. During one worship service, when we were preaching on the cross of Christ, Jerry jumped up and bolted for the door, all the while muttering the f-word under his breath. Jerry was angry and lonely—one very lost man.

One Sunday, as we were gathering prayer requests, Jerry shared a little bit of his life. In between the curse words, Jerry talked about how he was alone, isolated from everybody and everything. His own family didn't want him. Jerry had nothing, only the clothes on his back. His honesty and transparency moved everyone in the room, even if he was using such inappropriate language. We were so moved that we thought that we should do something. At the end of the service, as we were about to give the benediction, we placed a paper cup on the communion table. We asked that if anyone would like to give to the Jerry Fund, we would take him out shopping for new clothes. As we made the plea,

Jerry, who was standing in the back, gave a shout of surprise and doubled over in tears. A few hands fell upon his back, as we recited Hebrews 12:1-4 as our benediction:

> Therefore, since we are surrounded by so great a cloud of witnesses, let us also lay aside every weight and the sin that clings so closely, and let us run with perseverance the race that is set before us, looking to Jesus the pioneer and perfecter of our faith, who for the sake of the joy that was set before him endured the cross, disregarding its shame, and has taken his seat at the right hand of the throne of God. Consider him who endured such hostility against himself from sinners, so that you may not grow weary or lose heart (Hebrews 12:1-3).

Those words have never been truer for me or had more meaning than that morning. After we had said them, a throng of people, a "great cloud of witnesses," approached the communion table, dollar bills in hand. By the end of the afternoon, the "Jerry Fund" had swelled to over nine hundred dollars. A group of guys took Jerry to the Army Navy Store (his favorite clothing outlet) and helped him get some new clothes. He told the guys as they were shopping that no one had ever done anything like this for him before in his life.

Soon after that, Jerry was making more and more visits to the tattoo shop, not to get more tattoos, but to cover over the satanic tattoos with ink that proclaimed God's grace. Jerry ended up being baptized not long after that. It was a moment I will never forget as long as I live. When we asked Jerry his name, he said, "My old name is Jerry. My new name is Justice." Jeff and I weren't too sure what he meant by that. We just looked at each other and then began pouring water over his head. Somehow, some way, Jerry found the King by first experiencing the love and grace of the kingdom of God. Now, don't be misled. Jerry is still Jerry. He wasn't transformed into a quiet, happy-go-lucky Sunday school teacher. He still shouts things out, but the language is a little cleaner. He still wears black eyeliner, but he's seeking communion with God and community with others. He still dresses in black, but he doesn't live in the graveyard anymore.

He's been saved, saved by koinonia with Jesus through the kingdom of God.

PART 3: PUT YOUR BOOTS ON. IT'S GOING TO GET DEEP.

Help Wanted: Feet Washers

Not long ago I read a newspaper article about a woman who had a rather elaborate garden in her backyard. The article was in Saturday's "Home and Garden" section. The lady gave the paper the grand tour of her big garden. There were pictures of big bushes in the shape of animals, fancy stonework, and even a waterfall. As she talked about her garden, she bragged about the expense of each element. There wasn't a word about digging, planting, watering, or pruning. As I read the article, a little confused, the reason for this soon became clear. This lady wasn't a gardener. In fact, she hadn't done any of the gardening at all. She hadn't even gotten her hands dirty. She had picked up the phone, called a landscaper, and started throwing money at her backyard. Now, a few thousand dollars later, she's in the newspaper for having the nicest garden in town. But despite the fact that her backyard was absolutely beautiful, for some reason I felt sorry for her. I think she missed the best part of having a garden—actually *doing* the gardening. You know, digging, planting, watering, and just plain old getting covered in dirt. Truth be told, the newspaper shouldn't display her garden. I mean, come on, she really isn't a gardener, is she?

This is the same reason I feel sorry for so many churches and so many so-called Christians today. Some of our churches have become so fat with wealth that there is no need to do our own gardening. We can throw money at the garden, and we end up like the lady with beautiful landscaping and clean hands. Unfortunately, we have robbed ourselves and the people of our churches and communities of the best part of being the church, and that is participating in the kingdom of God. Just like gardening, in order to experience the kingdom of God, we need to get down on our hands and knees and get dirty. If you want to get dirty, you have to get down into the dirt.

Working as a youth worker, I came to realize a key truth about koinonia: it is an action. Remember, koinonia means "to participate with or in." How often does the church help people participate in the kingdom of God? Do we, more often than not, let one or two people do all the participating as everyone else watches? Every year of youth ministry looked the same for me. We spent all year trying to get kids to grow in the faith, come to activities, and stuff. It was always a nice try, but quite ineffective. However, when the summer rolled around and we dragged the young people down to West Virginia on a mission trip, something would happen. Suddenly, we weren't just talking about our faith anymore; we were living it out. The active cause of the mission trip, no matter where we actually went, was enough for us to experience the bonding power of koinonia. Then we would return home, get cleaned up, and get back to life as usual. My question back then, and my question today, is why can't church be what it's meant to be: a 24/7 mission trip? Why do we ever have to get cleaned up?

The church is quick to claim Matthew 28 as its mission statement. We get all lathered up on "making disciples of all nations," but we seem quickly to forget *how* Jesus told us we were to do it. To find those directions, we need look no further than John 13:

> [Jesus] got up from the table, took off his outer robe, and tied a towel around himself. Then he poured water into a basin and began to wash the disciples' feet and to wipe them

with the towel that was tied around him. He came to Simon Peter, who said to him, "Lord, are you going to wash my feet?" Jesus answered, "You do not know now what I am doing, but later you will understand." Peter said to him, "You will never wash my feet." Jesus answered, "Unless I wash you, you have no share with me." Simon Peter said to him, "Lord, not my feet only but also my hands and my head!" (John 13:4-9).

Being the church, making disciples, isn't about conquering people. It is actually a lot like gardening. It's a lot like washing feet. You're down on your hands and knees touching filth, grime, and all kinds of disgusting muck and mire. It's not clean work. In order to avoid it, the church, for the past so many years, has been hiring others to do its dirty work. Pastors, ministers, youth ministers, and church administrators are expected to do the feet washing. The church has been a lot like the lady with the fancy garden. Instead of actually doing the washing, the church in America has simply hired someone else to do it. To top it off, they've hired them to wash their own feet! Pastors are hired, not to care for the lost, but to care for the found!

We need to remember that Jesus is our Master. He is our Lord. As such, he is the model of who we should be. We are to be imitators of Christ. What does it mean to be an imitator of Christ? In Philippians 2, Paul lays down exactly what that means. It means doing nothing from selfish ambition or conceit, but in humility regarding others as better than yourself. It means letting the same mind be in you that was in Jesus. It means acknowledging that he is Lord of all.

Why is Jesus Lord of all? Because he made himself nothing. He became a servant to death. Being a follower of Christ means living Christ's life. Proclaiming "Jesus is Lord" isn't a political statement you say with your mouth or you put on your t-shirt—you live it out. We are to live out "Jesus is Lord" by making ourselves nothing and considering others better than ourselves. How can we consider ourselves better than others, as us church people often do, and claim "Jesus is Lord" at the same time? It is completely impossible. This is how we are to live in an ever-shrinking, pluralistic world—we are to proclaim to the Hindu, to the Muslim, to the Buddhist, to everyone we meet that Jesus is Lord—not with our big, arrogant mouths, but with our lives. We humble ourselves, considering others better than ourselves. Our job is to wash feet. We wash feet, not as a through-the-backdoor evangelistic ploy or because it might bring more people into our church, but because that's how we are to live as followers of the Humbled One. We proclaim "Jesus is Lord" when we consider the homeless, the fatherless, the foreigner, the widow, even the prisoner and the prostitute better than ourselves.

I sometimes wonder, since we're such a Christian nation, why we don't engage the world as Christ would engage it? Does "make disciples of all nations" mean go out and conquer and control or does it mean go out and wash some feet? If being a Christian means washing feet, and we supposedly live in a Christian nation with a church on every block, then why is it so rare to see it actually happen?

Getting Down and Dirty

How can the church become a movement rather than a place? How can we become the means by which people share in koinonia with God and others so that they may experience the kingdom of God? It begins by rearranging the way we think about church altogether. Perhaps one of the reasons that we've turned Jesus into another commodity to be marketed and to be profited from is because we think of church in consumer terms. In the modern church, everything looks more like a store, or a business than a people movement, an expression of the kingdom of God. Churches rely on flyers, signs, and even commercials to get people into the pews. Therefore, people come to church thinking like consumers, looking to get their spiritual goods and services. When a certain church doesn't give them what they're looking for, they move on to the next church, the bigger, cooler church down the street. This breeds a bizarre environment of competition.

I heard a church expert tell a group of pastors the three most important things a church has to have in the twenty-first century in order to grow. The three things were multi-media capability, communicative signage, and an excellent website. As I was listening, I thought, "What does this have to do with the kingdom of God?" Why should the growth of the kingdom of God depend upon web sites and signs? Why should it depend upon anything other than Jesus? Why should money or budgets or salaries or retirement plans or building campaigns or passionless, jaded leaders who never take any risks determine the growth of the kingdom? We stake everything on all of the above because we think of the church in terms of a store. We all do. People who work in the church, people who go to church, and people who have never even looked at a church think the church is a place to find goods and services. The church is just another store. Some look like the old hardware store on Main Street, some look like the area convenience store and some look like Wal-Mart. No matter what form it takes, we still consider church a store where the pastors are the employees and the parishioners are the customers. And, as we've been taught, the customer is always right.

The Difference Between a Store and a Bridge

- A store has doors and walls, most of the time locked; a bridge is open 24/7.

- A store is in one location; a bridge connects multiple places.

- A store has signs and advertisement; a bridge gets used because people need it.

- A store is nice and fancy because it needs customers to survive; a bridge is dirty because it gets walked on, traveled on, and worn down.

- A store is a safe place; a bridge can be, at times, risky, and dangerous.

- A store gets new products, carries brand names; a bridge is a bridge.

- A store has employees; a bridge is made of cement towers and steel beams and little rivets, each one just as important as the other.

- Customers determine a store's worth by how much it has; travelers determine the worth of a bridge by what it connects.

The church of the future is not a store. The church that the people of our world need doesn't resemble a store in any way at all. In fact, the church of the future needs to have the opposite characteristics of a store. The future church looks more like a bridge than a store. The buildings, the money, and the leadership are all still part of it, but they are peripheral. Church isn't a destination; it's a movement, a pathway, a bridge. Think about the difference between a store and a bridge for a moment.

The church's job is to help connect people with God by living Christ's life. This would make the church the most valuable bridge in the world. Yet, we don't think of it as a bridge but as place of business. The church is meant to be walked on by people so that they can connect to Jesus Christ.

What does this mean for today's church? Does this mean that our church buildings will be converted into restaurants and bars, while the body of Christ meets in homes and tattoo-shop basements? Wake up—it's already happening. This might scare you, but it excites me. My passion is to be part of the bridge, even if my role is as small as being a rivet. I'd much rather be a rivet in the smallest bridge than the CEO of the biggest store. The church is mission, and that mission is dirty, raw, dangerous, and makes life worth living. This is actually how Jesus did ministry—real, dirty, and out on the edge. This is how he encouraged his followers to do ministry as well. In Luke 10, Jesus sends his disciples on a mission trip:

> After this the Lord appointed seventy others and sent them on ahead of him in pairs to every town and place where he himself intended to go. He said to them, "The harvest is plentiful, but the laborers are few; therefore ask the Lord of the harvest to send out laborers into this harvest. Go on your way. See I am sending you out like lambs into the midst of wolves. Carry no purse, no bag, no sandals; and greet no one on the road. Whatever house you enter, first say, 'Peace to this house!' and if anyone is there who shares in peace, your peace will rest on that person; but if not, it will return to you. Remain in the same house, eating and drinking whatever they provide, for the laborer deserves to be paid. Do not move about from house to house. Whenever you enter a

town and its people welcome you, eat what is set before you; cure the sick who are there, and say to them, "The kingdom of God has come near to you" (Luke 10:1-9).

I had always read this passage thinking that somehow the lambs had a chance. I believed that the lambs, powered by God's strength, could overcome those vicious wolves. I always thought that Jesus meant that those lambs were going to beat those wolves with super-lamb-meekness. The old kill-'em-with-kindness strategy. Now I don't think that's what Jesus means. He's talking to people who know about shepherding, and they know this truth: lambs vs. wolves, wolves always win. Always. In fact, lambs usually, if not always, get ripped to shreds and eaten. The lambs' only hope is the shepherd. Their hope is that when it comes to shepherd vs. wolves, shepherd always wins.

For the church to become a bridge and really help people find salvation in God through Christ, then the people of the church are going to have to be willing to become sheep. We will have to be willing to get dirty, to let others walk on us, even to die to ourselves so people might go where they need to go—the kingdom of God.

I find it interesting that we pray, "your kingdom come, your will be done" in the Lord's Prayer, but we still insist that heaven is after you die, and that the church is a building. When we pray that prayer, we are asking God to bring heaven to us, to make the kingdom of God, heaven, manifest itself around us. What is in heaven? We won't know entirely until we get there. But we know one thing that won't be there. Read Revelation 21:22: "I saw no temple in the city, for its temple is the Lord God the Almighty and the Lamb." See? You know what's *not* in heaven? A church building. What do we pray in the Lord's Prayer? Come and bring your heaven to us. The kingdom of God has nothing to do with bricks and mortar. The kingdom of God looks nothing like a store at all.

What do we do? How do we go from being a store to being a bridge? Is there a way for the church to make the needed transformation? I would say *yes* and *no*. The church can transform, but in the same way that a field transforms. ". . .unless a grain of wheat falls into the earth and dies, it remains just a single grain; but if it dies, it bears much fruit" (John 12:24). The wheat needs to plant new seeds.

A few years ago, a new company came out with a great idea. Netflix was advertised as a web site where you could order movies; they would be mailed to you, and then you mailed them back with no late fees, no penalties. Netflix began to emerge as an attractive alternative to Blockbuster, the dominant video company. Eventually Blockbuster decided to do them one better. Now Blockbuster, trying to keep up, offers the same deal as Netflix. You can order your movies online, or you can go to the store, drop off the movies you got in the mail, and get new movies in the store. To counter this, Netflix has taken the fight to the next level, offering movies that users can simply download from their site instantly!

Will the church of tomorrow look like a Blockbuster or Netflix? Will the church look like Blockbuster, and have store-style churches and bridge-style churches working together to help people connect with God? Or will the church look like Netflix, with no buildings and instant access? Can the church have store access and bridge access at the same time? Or will the stores be completely dismantled so that new bridges can be built?

The Kingdom of God Is like a Demolition Derby

What does this all mean for how we do church? If hell is the place of alienation and fear and Christ is the bridge that brings assurance, love, and belonging in the kingdom of God, what is the church's role? How can the church become a bridge to God by helping people participate in the kingdom of God?

One potential guide is Dale's Cone of Learning. Edgar Dale developed the cone in the 1960s following some research he did about how we learn things and how we retain information.

Dale's Cone of Learning*

According to Dale, information that comes to us verbally or in written form, we tend to retain the least. After two weeks, we almost completely forget that information. If the information links with a visual example, we are more likely to remember. Therefore, watching a movie or seeing an exhibit can help us retain information. However, as seeing

*See Edgar Dale's *Audio-visual Methods in Teaching.* Third Edition. (Holt, Rinehart, and Winston, 1969).

Dale's Cone of Learning

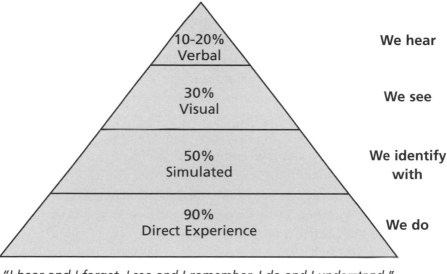

"*I hear and I forget, I see and I remember, I do and I understand.*"
Ancient Chinese Proverb

turns into actually doing, we are the most likely to remember the information. Dale proposes that the best ways in which we learn, and therefore also teach, are through:

1. Participating in a discussion;
2. Giving a talk or teaching the information ourselves;
3. Doing a dramatic presentation;
4. Simulating the real thing;
5. Doing the real thing.

What do we use in church to help people connect with God? Do we invite people to participate in discussions, or are we more likely to preach a sermon and have people read the words on a bulletin? Do we get people involved in the service, let them participate in the learning, or is it a one-person show? When it comes to helping people know God's grace and love, do we help people experience the real thing, or are we more likely to make people sit and listen?

When I was working as a youth pastor in a small-town church in western Pennsylvania, I was helping to clean out a closet with Earl, the church janitor. We stumbled across a box filled with old church brochures. We rummaged through the box like a couple of raccoons. We were amazed at what we found: brochures and flyers going all the way back to the turn of the century. What interested me most were the oldest flyers that advertised weeklong church gatherings. The brochure boasted 7 am to 11 pm church gatherings, with speakers talking for hours on end. "The world sure has changed," I said to Earl. "No one would ever sit through all of this these days."

Times have changed. We live in a digital world, with the whole world at our fingertips, but somehow we're still convinced that people will sit for hours on end. We have to get it into our heads that church isn't about sitting at all. There's no sitting and watching when you're a bridge. There's no coming or going when you're a bridge. When you're a bridge, you're part of the bridge. You're a piece of it. You're participating in the bridge.

Remember what koinonia means: participating in. When we help people participate in the bridge rather than come to the store, we help people connect with God in the way we were designed to connect. Think of Dale's Cone again. When we go to a store-style church and we sit and listen, how likely are we to retain any of it? How likely are we to connect? But what if we didn't go and sit, but we were instead a part of the church? What if we participated actively and actually shared in koinonia? How much more would we learn? How much more likely would we connect and be connected with? We need to stop talking about sharing in communion, community, compassion, and the Word with God and actually practice koinonia. Koinonia isn't something we talk about, read about, or sit and watch. Koinonia is action; it's what we do.

When I was learning to drive, I was told and I was shown. I even got to use one of those driving-simulation machines in high school. But it wasn't until I actually got behind the wheel and hit the gas that I learned how to drive. Does the church teach people to drive by putting them behind the wheel? Do we help people experience the kingdom of God? Or is church a big tour bus where everyone piles in, and there is one driver who points out the window at the kingdom of God, but no one actually gets to get out and experience it?

The kingdom of God is more like driving school, where everyone learns how to drive. Scratch that . . . start over—the kingdom of God is more like a demolition derby, where everyone gets to jump in and hit the gas and go. In a demolition derby, cars fly everywhere, it's chaotic, cars slam into each other, metal crushes, and mud covers everyone. It's fun. I mean, come on—which would you rather be in, the window seat of a nice safe luxury tour bus, or behind the wheel of a junked-up 1978 LTD? Too many church people pick the tour bus and miss the real adventure of following Christ. The kingdom of God is meant to be lived in, not simply talked about or put on exhibit for people to see. Dale is right. If we want people to experience the kingdom of God, we need to stop reading Philippians 2 and preaching Philippians 2, and we need to step out and find ways to live, experience, and participate in Philippians 2. I wonder if reading and preaching scripture from behind a pulpit, with people just sitting and listening, will have any real impact on people at all in the church that is to come. The young people I work with would much rather be in the fray, part of the demolition derby, than sitting in the tour bus. The times are changing. In the Industrial Age, the apologetic was found in reasonable explanations and proofs. In the Information Age, the apologetic is found in experiencing koinonia.

Late one Friday night in some God-forsaken bar, I stood against the back wall listening . . . er . . . I mean taking in The Last Hope. One doesn't just listen to The Last Hope. The punk-rock band has to be experienced with all of the senses in order to get the full impact. The six musicians completely took over the stage and the whole room, slamming into each other and whatever was in their way. I stood in the back, near an exit. I was the exception. Everyone else in the audience stood as close as they could to the speaker stacks, the screaming guitars, and the band's growling, menacing lead singer Justin. Some of the kids practically stood inside of Justin's shoes. The entire room was rocking; kids were jumping up and down, yelling, and their fists were pumping in the air. As I stood there near the exit, wondering what this was doing to my hearing, Derek approached me and said something. I'm still not sure what it was. But Derek, a faithful member of Hot Metal, uttered something mysterious, turned toward the band and the crowd of young people dancing near the stages, and launched himself into the fray. As Derek ran, with all the power he could muster (and Derek's not a wimpy guy), I thought to myself, "It looks like we'll be making a trip to the hospital." If Derek had run into a crowd of forty-something golfers like he ran into this crowd at the bar, he would have left a trail of dead bodies in his wake. But to my surprise, Derek's outside-linebacker blitz into the crowd left not a trace of blood. As matter of fact, the effect was just the opposite. The crowd welcomed, if not expected Derek's violent blow with a shout of joy and an intensified energy and heat. Derek's run at the crowd was simply gas on the fire. The whole room erupted and spun into complete chaos. Young people, covered with black clothing, tattoos, and piercings of all types, went flying in all directions, not out of fear or anger, but out of sheer joy. The music blared, and everyone ran, jumped, and slammed into one another. Two twenty-something girls, who should have been trampled to death, were arm in arm as if it were a game of skip-to-my-loo. They were laughing, shouting, dancing, and running as if they were both kids again. So, on this particular Friday night, as I watched the feverish, Red Bull-induced frenzy happening before me, I couldn't help but cup my hands around my wife's ears and shout, "The kingdom of God is like a mosh pit!"

And it is. The kingdom of God is wild, chaotic, and uncontrollable. It is like a demolition derby or a mosh pit at a punk-rock show. It involves everyone. Everyone has a role. Everyone gets to play. In Matthew 22:1 Jesus compares the kingdom of heaven to a wedding banquet. And what happens at a wedding banquet? Singing, dancing, laughing, running, jumping, eating, drinking, and a whole bunch of carrying on. It involves everyone, everyone has fun, and everyone connects. Persons don't easily forget the time they share at a wedding banquet. In contrast, nowhere in the Gospels does Jesus compare the kingdom of heaven to standing in line at the bank. The line at the bank bores everyone stiff, people can't wait to go home, and no one connects. Everyone is in line at the bank for one reason, and that one reason is "me." At a wedding banquet, there is an abundance of koinonia. In line at the bank, there is none. Let's step out of that line and into the mosh pit.

A few months later I found myself at another punk-rock concert.

This time, instead of lurking near the safety of the exit, I tossed myself into the fray. Let me assure you, there is no more invigorating feeling than leaping off a stage into the waiting, supporting hands of a crowd of spiky-haired freaks. As I ran to the edge of the stage and tossed my body into the crowd, I thought, "Now this is church."

Missional Koinonia: Creating Doorways into the Kingdom of God

For the church to move from a store-model of ministry to a bridge-model of ministry, we need to embrace the spontaneous, uncontrollable movement of the Holy Spirit through practicing koinonia. "Now, wait a minute," you might reply. "We practice koinonia in our church all the time. On Sunday morning we gather, and on Tuesday we have a potluck supper, and Friday night is family night at the church, and . . . ." No, I don't mean that we should hunker down in our church building and practice koinonia between the pews. We need to practice koinonia everywhere *but* the church building. We need to flee, run screaming out of our safe and comfortable churchy surroundings, and slam as hard as we can into the mosh pits of this dark and lonely world. We not only have to practice koinonia actively and help others experience the kingdom of God through koinonia; we also have to get out of our pews and onto the streets, into the coffee shops, and into every nook and cranny of this world. This is practicing *missional koinonia*. This is not handing someone a tract; this is listening to someone. This is not walking around wearing a clever t-shirt; this is loving and caring for people, not in the church, but out there in the real world.

Simply put, we need to look like the church in Acts 2:42. According to that verse, the early church centered all of its energy on four activities: the apostles' teachings, fellowship (koinonia), the breaking of bread, and prayer. As a result of practicing these four things, its members were motivated to meet every day and to share all they had with one another. As a result, the church grew in number every day. What if this is all that we did, actively but simply? After all, what is prayer but sharing in communion with God, dancing with God? What is breaking bread but sharing in community over a meal? What is fellowship—real, authentic, intimate fellowship—but sharing in compassion by simply listening? What is sharing in the apostles' teaching but sharing in the stories of our faith, the stories from scripture, and the stories of our own lives? What if this is all that a group of followers had to do for the kingdom of God to be near: dance with God, eat with friends, listen, care, and tell stories of our faith? Does that sound like standing in line at the bank? Or does it sound more like heaven?

Practicing Missional Koinonia

Communion—dancing

Community—eating

Compassion—listening

The Word—storytelling

These verses in Acts have always made me a bit curious. I wish I could go back in time and see exactly what this looked like. I mean, obviously they didn't have any church building, so they met in all kinds of places. The scriptures say that they met in the temple courts and broke bread in their homes. So, the gathering that we call the church was a public gathering. Who was there? Only people who believed? Or were there people of all different kinds of backgrounds and interests? Were Peter and Andrew there, who had been with Jesus from the beginning? Were there people there who had just heard about the Risen One earlier that morning and were still trying to piece it all together? What did it mean for this group of people to share in koinonia? What did it look like?

What did it mean for the early church to share in the apostles' teachings? They didn't have the New Testament or any formalized, systematic theologies. What did they do when they gathered? I wonder if the gathering felt like a gathering in someone's living room with many different people sharing their memories of Jesus and reflecting on how those events affected their lives, not just individually, but, moreover, communally. What did prayer look like? Did it resemble what we do in our churches today? Or with daily gatherings, with no apparent beginning time or ending time, was prayer much lengthier, more interactive, and spontaneous? How about the breaking of bread? Were there big silver goblets, special liturgies, pomp and circumstance? Or did the Lord's Supper, as we call it, have the feel of a great banquet or maybe a picnic or tailgating at the Steelers game? How did the early church practice koinonia? What can we learn from them? What if all we did was dance, eat, listen, and tell stories of our faith? Would what happened to the early church happen to us?

While I believe that learning about the early church's ecclesiology is important, to try and recreate its practices would be a mistake. That was two thousand years ago. The world that the early Christians lived in was completely different from the one we live in now. They lived with a different mindset altogether. Their main source of proof of God was the Logos or the Word or the Reason. This is why the Greek philosophers loved to gather and argue. That was their entertainment. Our world is completely different. We live in a new age: the Information Age. Well, some of us do—some of us are still living in the Industrial Age (and some are still living in the Medieval Age). However, for those who have gotten rid of their "land line" and who carry the Internet in their pockets, the world is much different. For the person living in the Information Age, the main source of proof of God is not reasonable arguments or scientific explanations. (How do you argue with a person who has Wikipedia in his or her pocket?) No, actually the person living in post-modernity looks to art to explain God, or more specifically, the art of story. And what is a story? It is a connection of relationships and experiences with our lives. Story is koinonia: sharing in communion

Era	The Main Source of Proof of God
Ancient Age –	Oracles, Prophets, Kings
Classical Age –	The Logos, the Word, or the Reason, Philosophers
Medieval Age –	The Church, Religion
Enlightenment Age –	The Reason, Logical Explanations
Industrial Age –	Science, Mechanical, Analytical Thinking, Methods
Information Age –	Art, Relationships, Experiences, Stories

with the people and the conflicts and the problems and the resolutions of the story.

Not long ago, we took a group down to Chiapas, Mexico, on a week-long mission trip. We helped build a medical center, saw the backwoods of Chiapas, and met some radical missionaries. One evening, when we thought the day was done, they led us down a back alley to the home of one of the pastors. There in the back courtyard was a party, already in progress. Music was playing, people were dancing, there was food, laughing, and kids were swinging a stick at a piñata. We had a blast. I can remember thinking that I had never been to party like this one before in my life. There was so much energy, love, and fun. Standing in the middle of that courtyard, looking around at all of the smiling, joy-filled faces, most of them much different from my face, I connected in a very tangible way with God. You could have sat me down and tried to explain God with charts, graphs, and all kind of proofs based on mechanical, methodical thinking. I didn't need that. I believed in God at that moment and connected with God at that moment because God was real in the faces and in the community that gathered in that place.

In Matthew 18:20, Jesus says, "For where two or three come together in my name, I am there among them." I always hear that verse in relation to poor worship attendance. When eight people show up but two hundred were expected, someone will say, "Whelp, where two or more are gathered, right?" Maybe Jesus meant that in another way. Maybe Jesus meant that if you want proof of God, if you want to see me, if you are searching for me, then look no further than that party in the courtyard.

One of the reasons that it will be difficult for the store-style church to be become a bridge-style church is control. The store-style church does not welcome the randomness and the unstructured chaos of the bridge-style church. This is because the store needs to be in control of the product. The store is convinced that it needs to provide consumers with what they perceive is the "right stuff." In aisle twelve, you'll find your core values; in aisle fourteen, you'll find your spiritual disciplines; in aisle five, you'll find your vision statement; in aisle eight, you'll pick up your programmed ministries. What if we've got it all wrong? What if these things weren't the church's products that we sell through our sermons, our studies, and our marketing, but rather these things were the by-product of practicing koinonia?

In the modern church, everyone comes to the building to pick up his or her Christianity. It comes in the form in which the leadership of that particular church has packaged it. This is why people jump from church to church, building to building, searching for the right product in the right packaging that will make everything better.

What if we're wrong? What if our approach is completely backwards? What if, in our attempt to conquer and control others out of fear, we're actually sabotaging the Holy Spirit's work in people's lives? What if core values actually form, not when they are force-fed to us, but when we actively practice koinonia with the Word? We develop our core values on our own when we don't listen to the gospel, but when we become the gospel, when we live the gospel. What if spiritual disciplines develop naturally within us when we practice communion with God? What if vision isn't supposed to be handed down to us from on high (from the pastor's study or the program team); rather a vision of God's kingdom reveals itself when we actively sit down and share in koinonia with someone over a meal? In sharing a meal with someone, the Holy Spirit opens our

By-Products of Koinonia

Koinonia with the Word	leads to	core values developing naturally
Koinonia with God	leads to	spiritual disciplines, giving
Koinonia with others	leads to	vision
Koinonia with suffering	leads to	ministry (foot washing)

eyes to the needs of the world. Sharing in koinonia with others produces a vision. What if pastors, associate pastors, program directors, or even ministry teams aren't supposed to create ministries? What if ministry, or service (foot washing), is a by-product of listening to someone? Wouldn't that make sense? Wouldn't taking time to listen to someone, I mean really listen, become a catalyst for service?

This is how Jesus lived the Way, the Truth and the Life. This is how I believe the early church behaved, and it is why it grew so fast. They simply lived the Way and the Truth and the Life as well. People didn't go to church to pick up spiritual goods and services. There was no marketing or slick advertising. They formed core values when they actively shared the apostles' teachings and when they experienced those same stories, or similar events, firsthand. Spiritual disciplines developed in the church as disciples came together and prayed. Giving, for example, didn't just magically happen. Giving was a by-product of sharing in koinonia. Vision wasn't part of the church's marketing campaign; it actually came from sitting down and sharing a meal together. The early church didn't have a fancy brochure boasting a long list of ministries and programs. Ministry, or foot washing, happened when people listened, saw a need, and then filled that need. This is the church's job: to live Christ's life; to share in koinonia. When we do, the things that we've been trying to force down people's throats will grow naturally within each and every follower.

If the church's job is to live Christ's life by practicing koinonia, what does it mean for the professional minister or pastor? Is she or he out of a job? By no means; it just means we need to change the job description. Instead of commanding the church from the director's chair, perhaps the job of the pastor is to be a catalyst for koinonia or maybe a farmer who creates fertile ground for authentic, intimate community to take place. Instead of trying to indoctrinate people with our core values, force people to do spiritual disciplines, annoy people with our vision statements, or establish ministries that no one will ever come to, what if the pastor's job were to create a koinonia playing field? What if the job of the pastor were to create doorways into the kingdom of God by helping people to practice missional koinonia?

Finally, I'd like to propose that dancing, eating, listening, and sharing don't just help us develop core values, spiritual disciplines, visions, and ministries, but they also become doorways into the kingdom of God. What am I saying? I am saying that people like Reagan don't necessarily need to "believe" to experience the kingdom of God. Sharing in koinonia can become a touchstone for those who are not yet followers. Faith is like swimming in the ocean: you don't always get completely wet right away. For some, they get their toes wet first; then they wade out a

Doorways into the Kingdom of God

Communion—prayer, the sacraments

Community—a meal, a conversation

Compassion—listening, caring

The Word—experiencing the stories of faith

bit and get hit with a wave. They may wander back to shore, and then they get up enough courage to run with all their might into the water. Before they know it, they can't touch the bottom. Should we deny those who are wading a place at the table? Absolutely not. For those who are just wading into faith for the first time, practicing koinonia can help them understand what the kingdom of God is all about.

Getting people involved is the key. From the beginning of Hot Metal Bridge, we imagined a church that involved everyone. From creating and doing the drama to leading the music, to serving communion to caring for the kids to making and serving the food, we have tried to get as many people involved as we possibly could. On some Sunday mornings, we've had forty to fifty people directly engaged in leading the service, and on all the Sundays we have encouraged everyone to be involved in the caring and loving of one another. More than once, I have had a visitor approach me and ask me who the pastor is. That, for me, has been the ultimate complement. If you can't figure out who the pastors are, that means we're doing something right.

At Hot Metal, we've tried to make it a priority to get people involved and participating in koinonia so that they may come to know and live Christ's life. This very simple idea determines everything we do. We've asked ourselves, "How can we be a bridge?" How can we help people connect with God, with others, with suffering, and with God's Word in an intimate and authentic way? In some ways, this has been quite easy. In other ways, it's been difficult. Although we are moving into a new ocean, we haven't quite arrived there yet. People of this generation still think of church in terms of a store. Whether they are long-time churchgoers or church hoppers or they haven't gone to church in a long time, they still are looking for their spiritual goods and services. As a result, some folks have come to Hot Metal looking for a store, and when we invite them to be part of the bridge, they don't understand, they get angry, and they move on. As pastors, this has changed our role from salespeople to fellow participants—just a couple more rivets in the bridge. We realize that if we want people to get dirty, we're going to have to get dirty ourselves. This is what we've been all about. Sometimes, when people are expecting a salesperson and they get a rivet, it disappoints them. In the end, however, practicing koinonia works and is especially helpful for young people to connect experientially with God and faith.

If you need proof of this, ask Chris Massa, a young man in our church who was part of our worship drama the first week he attended Hot Metal. If you've been wondering if we train people before we let them get up in front of everyone, the answer is *no*. Many times, we'll recruit people as they walk into the gathering for the first time. On one particular morning, I was recruiting people for the drama as I stood at the door and greeted them. I do this every now and then to remind everyone that we've gathered to participate, not just watch. Chris, who is rather outgoing, agreed to be in a worship drama based on Luke 8. Being part of this piece of scripture was so intriguing to Chris, who found himself reciting pieces of the Bible his first week in our worship service, that when I saw him the next week (sure, he came back, wouldn't you?), he had read the entire book of Luke and was ready to talk theology. Perhaps if Chris had sat and listened to one of my clever sermons, I would never have seen him again. But when Chris participated in the Word, the Holy Spirit did something significant in Chris' life. He connected closely with God.

These kinds of things happen all the time when we abandon the store model and become a bridge to the kingdom. We've had people like Debbie approach us in tears one Sunday, telling us she has never experienced God in such a real way before. She had gotten to hold the basket of bread and watch as person after broken person grabbed a piece. We've had Pete and Joe, two guys who did not know each other, sit down and share lunch together and then spend the rest of the day working on Joe's car. We've had young people like Chris sit down and listen to Dewey and Marie, an older couple, talk about their needs and then get up and go and meet those needs. I never asked Chris if he was a believer. I never asked Pete or Joe or Debbie, either. I guess I don't really care what kind of bumper sticker is on their cars. Are they living Christ's life? Yes! And that's the mark of a follower of Christ. These folks have walked through the doorways of koinonia and have experienced the kingdom of God. And by experiencing God's kingdom, the Holy Spirit has moved and has left a mark on their lives.

Missional koinonia is really the key to moving from a store that provides spiritual goods and services to becoming a bridge to the kingdom of God. The only real obstacle that I see that keeps the Christian church in America from making this move is our selfishness. That, our absolute fear of one another, compounded by our deep-seated resentment toward everyone and everything, coupled with our ever-widening gap of isolation and alienation, caused by our addiction to technology. Hmm. Doesn't sound easy, does it? I wonder: is it really possible for a store to become a bridge? Or do we need to scrap it all and start over from scratch?

Get Dirty and Holiness Happens

One of the toughest questions I've been wrestling with lately is, do I really know what it means to be in communion, or have I just gotten small glimpses, little tastes of it here and there? If you think about it, we can share several levels of intimacy with others. There's me and God, one-on-one. There's me and one other, two. There's me and a small group of people, perhaps my family or group of friends, three to twelve or so. Then there's me and the larger community. My question is this: have I ever really enjoyed intimate communion on any of these levels, or have they all been tainted in some way by fear, rejection, superficiality, or unrealistic expectations? Have I ever really connected with God intimately? If it ever happened, how would I know? Am I connecting intimately with God right now and don't even realize it? I don't know. I wonder if I really do not understand God at all because I don't understand what it means to be in true communion.

Is it rare for us to experience true communion, or does it happen all the time? Could you be living in the same house with others and never share in communion with them? I mean share in real communion, in a relationship that is free from fear, doubt, rejection, superficiality, or conditions? Do we have the first clue what it means to share in unconditional love with someone else? I don't know if we have that capacity, or if we do, it quickly slips away from us. Where, on Dale's cone of learning, would I put myself when it comes to understanding grace? Do I talk and read about grace, see grace all around me, act in dramas about grace, or do I actually participate in grace? In my life, is grace a concept, or is it a reality? Can I safely say that I am up over my head in grace? Or are all of my relationships handicapped by fear, rejection, superficiality, high expectations, and conditions?

We need to put ourselves into situations where we are free of those obstacles. Somehow, we have to find means of training ourselves to experience grace. Our culture, through all of its media, shouts to us from all directions to be afraid of, reject, or value others based on what they look like. To counter this, we should put ourselves in "dirty" situations, interact with dirty people, or people that our culture considers dirty for whatever reasons. When we find ourselves sharing in authentic koinonia with the dirty and broken people of this world (and don't forget, that means you and me as well), then we begin to understand the real meaning of grace. When we encounter unconditional love, we might get a small glimpse of God. Then grace will become a reality that we live rather than a concept that we talk about.

John Wesley started a kind of koinonia-training group when he began meeting with a few other guys, shared the scriptures, prayed, broke bread, and sought ways in which to wash feet. As the group's methodical ways began to get attention, they earned the nickname the Holy Club. I am sure John Wesley wasn't insulted by the name. Wesley was all about holiness. For him, it was more than just obedience or fleeing from sin. Now, make no mistake—Wesley encouraged obedience and fleeing from sin, but he saw holiness in terms of connectivity with God and with others. For Wesley, obedience to God, and therefore holiness, had a lot to do with washing feet and discipleship, as well as piety. In other words, to get holy one has to get dirty. Oddly enough, when we encounter the dirty people of this world, our hearts break, we fall to our knees, and we find ourselves living in obedience to God. Get dirty and holiness happens.

Holied Up by Hurricane Katrina

We've experienced the same phenomenon at Hot Metal. Our church began weekly worship gatherings in the fall of 2004. Until that point, we had met in what you might call smaller "cell groups." For the rest of 2004 and into 2005, our church grew in number and in spirituality in small baby steps. Many of those who began joining our new congregation came because they were lost, depressed, or felt isolated and alone. The worshippers at Hot Metal started to reflect the hard, coarse ways of the streets and alleys of the South Side. For some reason, Hot Metal became a gathering place for those who live as outcasts, as throwaways. Because of this, sometimes worship services would become dark and somber as people shared their brokenness during times of prayer. Then, in the fall of 2005, something happened. At end of August, Hurricane Katrina hit the Gulf Coast, and as we watched the tragedy unfold on television, our small core group couldn't help relating with those who were suffering. A group of thirty "losers" decided to organize a trip to Biloxi to help in any way we could.

We planned the trip for the week of Thanksgiving, which turned out to be a great blessing. On Thanksgiving Day, our rag-tag bunch of outsiders and misfits deep-fat fried almost forty turkeys and helped feed a Thanksgiving meal to close to two thousand hurricane victims. At one point, a small group of us took a short break from cooking turkey, grabbed some food, and went to find a place to sit and eat. As we walked down the row of tables, in what had to be the biggest tent I had ever been in, we spotted a man sitting all alone. We decided to join him. I don't think we ever actually finished our meal, or even started it for that matter. When we sat down and began to listen to the man's story, our hearts broke and our appetites left us. The guy was at the end of his rope, physically and emotionally. He had lost his home, all of his possessions, even his best friend, a dog named Paulie. He was dirty and greasy, as if he hadn't taken a bath for a month. He told us that even three months later, he was still dizzy from the storm. The man was shell-shocked.

For a long time, we sat in silence. We didn't know what to say. Then Derek, who sometimes walks around with a dark cloud over his own head, and sometimes puts his foot in his mouth, began to speak words of hope into the man's life. They were words of hope, but not words you would expect. Derek didn't quote any Bible verses, or give the man some cliché bumper-sticker greeting-card catch phrase. Instead, Derek said, "You know, all this—what you're going through—sucks. It does. It really, really sucks." The rest of us thoughtfully nodded in agreement, "Yeah, it does. It sucks." One of us laid a hand on the man's shoulder, and we sat in silence again. For a moment there was silence, and then the man looked up, smiled a sad smile, and said, "Yeah, it sucks. But this turkey doesn't." He smiled and in less than a moment we went from despair to hope. "Deep-fat fried in peanut oil," Derek replied, holding up a drumstick. "It's the only way I'll eat it." Then Derek began telling one of his elaborate stories that got more than one laugh. We ate some more, and we shared some more and we laughed some more, and then we went back to work. There was no fuzzy moment; we didn't even pray with the guy. But I believe that we shared in koinonia with that guy, and he shared koinonia with us. Through that encounter, somehow, being connected by our suffering and our brokenness, the Holy Spirit moved and there was holiness.

When we returned to Pittsburgh and gathered on Sunday morning for worship, the room was electric. You could tell that people's hearts had been touched, and lives had been changed. There was a sense of "God-seeking" in the room by people who had gone on the trip and people who hadn't. Voices sang loud, hands were raised, faces were on the floor, and there was rejoicing. At one point during the singing, Jeff, who was standing next to me, turned and whispered: 'Do you realize what happened this week? This faith community was finally planted. God planted this church." It was true. After a year of struggling and praying and plodding along, God had moved in the lives of the people of our congregation and brought holiness and sanctification through connecting with the broken. As a result, there was a new sense of hope as people craved the Word of God, seeking holiness and sanctification. There was a new pursuit of obedience and righteousness.

See, sitting and watching television shows where people are judged or rejected is not koinonia-training. As a matter of fact, it is the opposite. Accumulating friends on Myspace is not koinonia-training. Neither is gossiping about others or watching porn or finding ways to put yourself above others. Putting your arms around a guy who's lost everything and sharing in his suffering—that's koinonia-training. And that's what sanctification is really—koinonia training. We think of holiness and sanctification as piety, or an effort to become sinless. But we don't avoid sin just because God said so. We avoid it because it acts as a barrier to koinonia and therefore a barrier to life abundant. Conversely, holiness isn't something we strive to gain for our own pleasure or to make ourselves feel righteous. Holiness is the product of koinonia and is koinonia-training at the same time. We prepare ourselves for kingdom-living, we become sanctified, by actually connecting with the kingdom. That means to become sanctified, to experience holiness, we have to share in communion with the lepers, the outcasts, the losers, the loners, the broken, and the "dirty" people of this world.

Koinonia acts as a bridge to Christ. It is how the church of the future will do what the modern church called outreach and evangelism. It is how the church of the future will do what the modern church called discipleship. It is the means for worship; it is the catalyst for spiritual disciplines such as giving. Koinonia is the mission, the purpose of the church. It is how the kingdom of God manifests itself in our midst. It is being in communion with God, with others, and with the poor and suffering.

Bridges Get Dirty, Churches Stay Clean

This all means that if the church is to be a bridge, connecting people with God, we will have to get dirty. We will have to step into the lives of others and really get to know them, warts and all. The modern church has been slowly fading away for quite some time. In an attempt to find a solution, we have decided that our ecclesiology is broken. In other words, *how* we're doing church is all wrong, and if we fix the *how* we'll fix the problem. The result has been arguments over traditional worship versus contemporary worship and this program versus that program. These days, "emerging worship" is the catchphrase, or "ancient/ future worship" is the new thing. Put away your candles, your incense, and your prayer stations. Practicing koinonia, being in communion with God and others (or quite simply, love), is not a catchphrase or a fad. It doesn't require candles, guitars, prayer stations, drama, or tattoos. It is quite simple and can be done very cheaply. So why don't we want to do it? Why do we prefer the latest catchphrase?

Because, face it: We don't want to get dirty!

For some reason, people in our churches have come to associate Christianity with clean appearances. Nothing could be more ludicrous. The truth is the very opposite. The ways of Christ are the ways of a guy who had one set of clothes and no place to lay his head. The ways of Christ are the ways of a guy who insisted on touching the untouchables of the world. I was a guest speaker at a suburban church not too long ago and when I started my message about Jesus healing the leper with lyrics from a Green Day song, a whole row of people stood up and walked out. Apparently, using a punk-rock song as a sermon intro was heretical. Have we forgotten what Jesus was all about? Have we forgotten that Jesus came for the lost? Have we forgotten whom Jesus encouraged, and whom Jesus rebuked?

The church needs to get clean, holied-up, by getting dirty. The church of the twenty-first century needs to practice koinonia out in the streets, tattoo shops, laundromats, stores, at work, and in homes. Rather than sending out mailings and flyers in an attempt to fill the pews, why not get dirty and help people plug into community? Imagine how different church would be if we were a bridge to Jesus Christ by helping people participate in the kingdom of God? Koinonia should be our mission. Koinonia should put the wind in our sails and propel us across the waters.

Stuck in the Mud

The modern church, which did great things during its healthier years, is not the kind of church we need in this new world. The modern church, which looked a lot like a store, exploded and rode the wave of progress like everything else did in the Industrial Age. From 1800 to 1830, the Second Great Awakening became the catalyst for new churches, and new ministries and social agencies were born. This church was like a great big ship with a massive hull and great big engines with mighty pistons and a strong propeller. This ship sailed the oceans of the Industrial Age with speed, strength, and effectiveness. Think about how many people this ship's work touched. Think of how many people it pulled from the water, pulled from certain death.

Now, this ship has run aground. In an attempt to cross over from one ocean to another, from one age to another, it has been stuck in the shallow water of the strait that connects the two oceans. The crew has tried to get it out of trouble, pushing the engines to their max, only to sink it deeper in the mud. There it sits, stuck in the mud, like a car broken down on the side of the road. Sure, ministry still happens here and there. Every now and then a desperate, drowning soul floats close enough to the ship for the crew to throw out a lifeline. But that's it. Everyone on the deck chairs just looks at one another. Some play the blame game; some give up and lay out on a deck chair. What's going to happen next? Will this ship ever sail again? Will the ship ever get out of the mud?

Meanwhile, some of the crew gathers in the engine room, duct tape in hand. Somehow, they are determined to fix the engines. Others taken some small pieces of the mighty behemoth, pieces of the deck, pieces of the masts, and they build a small raft and head into the new ocean alone. This crew of brave explorers and pioneers go to put their lives on the line for the cause. They hear people crying out to be saved, and, one by one, they're pulling people onto their small, makeshift craft. But there is a third group. They aren't stubborn or unchanging like the folks in the engine room, and they aren't adventurers like the servants on the raft. They are simple, practical folks who have stumbled onto, almost by accident, a very old treasure chest. When they open it up, they cannot believe their eyes: it's the sails. As some try feverishly to get the huge engines restarted, and others paddle out into the new ocean in a capsizable dingy, this third group rushes from the treasure chest to the deck, screaming and yelling, the big white, billowing sails clenched in their fists.

What's going to happen next? Will the crew in the engine room finally concede that the ship is too heavy, drop the engines to the bottom of the sea, and help hoist the sails? Will the adventurers come back to the ship, return with the map and the compass, and take their place in the crow's nest? Will the wind of the Holy Spirit blow through the ship's precious treasure once again, pulling the mighty servant out of the mud?

Perhaps the engine crew will emerge from the engine room once again, insisting, "She's still got some life in her." Or maybe the adventurers will drift deeper out into uncharted territory, never to be seen again. Possibly, the mighty vessel will sink deeper into the mud as the cries of the drowning grow louder and louder.

The church in America is like a ship that has run aground. We're too heavy and we've lost power. And let's be honest, we're taking water pretty fast. Sure, good things are happening. God always moves, even when the ship is stuck in the mud. But to be satisfied with this is to ignore the call. We need to dump the heavy weight of the modern engines, the store-style church, and hoist the sails of missional koinonia so that we can push out into this new ocean of the Information Age and pull people from the water.

The good news is that eventually the massive engines will rust away and the ship will break free. Why wait for that day? Why not begin shedding the weight now? If you are one of the members of the crew—a pastor, lay leader, or even a superintendent or bishop—why not lead the charge? Instead of pouring money into buildings, why not pour money into the poor? Instead of spending thousands on advertising, why not spend it on freeing the oppressed? Instead of honoring and giving out trophies to the best salespeople and CEOs in our denominations, why not honor those who get themselves dirty?

What does it look like to get dirty and practice missional koinonia? How can we help people, living in the Information Age, to share communion genuinely with God? How can we help bring about real community? What does it mean to have compassion? How do we facilitate it? How do we communicate the gospel? How do we help people participate in the sharing of the Word? The next four chapters are about what it looks like to get dirty. They are about what it looks like to hoist the sails.

PART 4: CRAZY OR COMMUNION?

Those Crazy Christians

Years ago when I was thinking about going to seminary, I registered for a single class at a local Bible college. I use the term "Bible college" very loosely. As I think back on it, there wasn't much about this place that looked or acted like a college, and now that I've actually studied the Bible at an actual seminary, there wasn't much of that either. On the first day of class, a middle-aged woman sat down at the desk next to me. She seemed like a joyful person. She wore a big smile on her face, and she acted as if she had just heard a funny joke. It must have been pretty funny, I thought, because she kept giggling. Then, as the professor began to teach the class, this woman wouldn't stop. She kept giggling. And when the teacher didn't address it, she began laughing, I mean belly laughing. At one point, I thought this lady was going to fall out of her chair and roll on the ground, she was laughing so hard. Still, the professor did nothing. In fact, it seemed that he was encouraging the laughing. Thinking back on the moment, I don't think he was waiting for the woman to stop laughing; he was waiting for the rest of us to join her. For this went on for another ten to fifteen minutes, until the teacher finally went to the chalkboard, and underneath the place where it said, "Today's lesson" he wrote, "Laughing in the Spirit." Evidently, this woman was so connected with the Holy Spirit that she was laughing uncontrollably. That was my first and last day at Bible college. As I ducked out of the classroom, ran to my car, and drove away as quickly as I could, all I could think was, "Those people are crazy!"

Am I Crazy?

It's easy to pick out a crazy person, isn't it? But then I think, what about me? Am I just as crazy? Am I much different from the crazy laughing lady? All of my life I have been on this quest to find God, to figure out God, somehow to connect with God, or to simply know if there really is a God at all. And you know, I'm not stupid. In my search, I've stumbled upon some other possibilities that sometimes make my stomach turn and my head ache. For example, I know that it's possible that Sigmund Freud was right when he proposed that we all make God up in our heads to make ourselves feel safe. Freud taught that there is no God, that we construct God out of our own fear. I could easily be called to be exhibit A in the case of "'Fraidie-cat makes up deity to save himself from the black hole of fear and nothingness." I am like a scared little bunny, legs running, heart pounding, eyes bulging out of my head. Why would a guy like me go on a perpetual God quest? Is it a desire for holiness? Maybe, maybe not. Maybe my deep fears of rejection drive me. And those fears are the paint and the paintbrush that help me create this piece of work that I call God, a God that loves me unconditionally and won't reject me no matter what. How convenient? So, there you go. If you've been trying to psycho-analyze me, I'm way ahead of you. I already know I'm crazy. But the important question isn't about my sanity; it's about the existence of God. My being crazy doesn't negate God's existence.

Look at the other side of the coin. Is God formed by my fear, or is fear the result of my self-centeredness? Is fear actually the fruit (if you can call it that) of anti-communion? Perhaps there is a God and that God has created me with a certain wiring toward communion. I'm created for communion. Perhaps I'm created in the image of God. In other words, God is communion. God is, and for me to Be, I need to be connected to that communion. Perhaps what I am experiencing isn't fear at all, but the negative of communion, and that void actually compels me toward the communion.

There is something in me that bends me toward communion, just as it is within us all. If we weren't created that way, wouldn't we all live perfectly happily in isolation? We don't. Look at all archeological records, and you will find people living in tribes, living in communities—people living together. If Freud is right, then every single connection between every person and tribe since the beginning of time has been motivated by fear. All of our social connections, families, tribes, and congregations have been formed by fear. I find this unlikely. There must be something wired inside of our being that propels us toward communion.

As I think about both sides of this argument, and when I think of all of the crazy people who have come before me, it makes sense to me that God would not only exist, but God would exist as a Trinitarian God, a God that is three in one. For God to be communion, God must be one, yet be communing—Father communing with the Son, Son communing with the Holy Spirit, Spirit communing with the Father.

There have been a few moments in my life when I have detected communion with God. I use the word "detected" because I'm unsure what other word to use. I guess I could use the words "see, sense," or "be aware of," but the experiences weren't magical. It wasn't like I saw God's face with my eyes or heard God's voice with my ears. The events were more like moments when I detected God's presence in a way that was very real to me. These moments have been quite meaningful for me; I hold them as precious, if not sacramental. In those moments when I wonder if I'm crazy, I dwell upon these memories as a sort of touchstone. Interestingly enough, none of the moments occurred in a church or anywhere close to a church.

The first occurrence took place in a small lake in Germany when I was only eleven years old. My dad, who had married my mother and adopted me five years earlier, joined the U.S. Army because he couldn't find work. In a matter of weeks, my dad received orders and was stationed in a small arms depot on the German/French border. (The depot was small, but not the arms). We sold the house, put all of our stuff in storage, and moved to Fischbach, Germany. Inconveniently enough, the army base did not accommodate soldiers with families, so we had to live "on the economy" or in a small village outside the base. We moved into a hole of an apartment, over a bowling alley, across from a fish hatchery, and down the dirt road from a sheep farm. I didn't know where I was, why I was there, or what language people were speaking. Talk about being a lost, frightened soul. I slept with the Bible under my pillow.

It wasn't long after we had moved to Germany that I asked my mother if I could be baptized. I'm still unsure what I was thinking. Who does that? What eleven-year-old kid asks his mother if he can be baptized? I should have been building tree houses, throwing rocks at cars, and learning to smoke. Clearly, I was either crazy or longing for communion with God. Through the base chaplain, it was arranged, and a small group of parishioners from the depot's multi-denominational, Protestant chapel gathered on the shores of a lake in the middle of nowhere. I couldn't have been further away from home. I have few very vivid memories from my childhood, but being dunked in the water in that lake is one that will stick with me forever. Although I know I could have only been under the water for a brief moment, it seemed like forever. Yet, I wasn't afraid. When I was pulled back to the surface, I grabbed a breath, opened my eyes and—there is no other way to describe it—I felt that God was near. That's it. God was near. I can't really prove it; I believe that God was very near. I believe that the overwhelming assurance of God's presence I received through that short moment in the lake sustained me through the rest of that troubling time in a foreign land. It has sustained me through all of my life, even to this moment.

What do you think? Was I crazy? Did I create a God in my own mind? Did I conjure up this pacifying event out of fear, or was I compelled towards communion by the one who is Communion? When I dwell upon only my experience, I would say I was and am crazy. Any first-year psychology major could see that I have formed a god based out of my deep-seated fear and resentment. But when I add to my experience all of the things I have read, written by many, many people spanning many centuries, people who seemed to be just as crazy and fearful as I am, I believe the latter. Do you think that the Israelites who put together the scriptures while in exile in Babylon weren't scared? Do you think the early Christians who passed down the stories of Jesus and then eventually wrote down those stories to form our four gospels were without fear? Do you think the Apostle Paul wrote his letters from jail without an ounce of fear? Or how about Dietrich Bonhoeffer or Martin Luther King? To be sure, all of these people had great faith, but I'm sure their hearts pounded just as fast as mine has. Even Jesus was sweating blood in the garden. Fear is a reality of life, and if somehow you think that you walk around without fear, you're a mask-wearing liar. We are all scared little bunny rabbits. The question is, is Freud right? Does God only exist in our minds, acting as a pacifier? Or is God real, and the fear we experience actually the void, the anti-communion, brought on by our self-centeredness that draws us to God? Is fear actually the negation of God's assurance in our lives that prompts us to seek out that assurance?

As I have hunted down the answer to this question, I have found it interesting that throughout the whole of scripture, whenever God or an agent of God interacts with someone, the very first words are almost always, "Do not be afraid." Again and again, God says, "Do not to be afraid." Is it because God is so scary? Or is it because fear is the real enemy? Grab a concordance and look at all the places God says, "Do not be afraid."

Clearly, God does not want us to be afraid. Is this because God is just trying to be polite or nice? Or is it that we have been wired in such a way that the negation of God brings fear, and when we are in communion with God, that fear diminishes and we may live life abundant. The assurance that I have experienced in my life through communion with God has driven away my fears and has kept me alive. It has kept me seeking God every day as well. The moment of my baptism is a moment I point to as proof of God. It was a moment when I detected something that I identify as koinonia. It was a sacramental moment. It was a moment I remember whenever I'm afraid.

I had another moment more recently. I had gone downstairs to change the laundry from the washer to the dryer. As I pulled out a wet pair of pants that belong to my son, who was away at summer camp, I stopped for a moment and thought of Daniel. For a short instance, I thought, "God, keep him safe." Then I continued loading the dryer. That's it. That's the whole God moment. Nothing special. No big lake, no minister, no glistening sun. It might have been short, even insignificant, but I found for an instance that same assurance that comes from

God being near.

I share these two stories, the story of my baptism and my story about changing the laundry, to bring up this question: was God somehow more present, more loving, or more connected to me when I was being baptized than when I was changing the laundry? The answer is *no*. How could that be? God is God. God is everywhere. When the Christ was born, they called him Emmanuel, meaning "God with us. That's who God is. That's God's character—"with us." God is near. God is near when we are being baptized, God is near when we're changing the laundry, and God is near when we don't even realize it. God's love is like an ocean. God's grace is like a river that flows everywhere. God is communion, and that communion is available to us like radio waves; we simply have to tune in to experience it. Communion is always available to us.

> Ho, everyone who thirsts, come to the waters; and you that have no money, come, buy and eat! Come buy wine and milk without money and without price. Why do you spend your money for that which is not bread, and your labor for that which does not satisfy? Listen carefully to me and eat what is good, and delight yourselves in rich food (Isaiah 55:1-2).

There is something we want more than anything else, and it is communion with God. Just as our physical bodies need food and water to survive, our spirits need communion with God to survive.

Communion with God

To be able to share in communion with God, only one thing is required: surrender. Think about the two moments I have shared. What do they have in common? Surrender. Surrender to Christ. When we let go of ourselves and put the focus on God, God's love and grace are instantly available to us. Remember in Matthew, as Jesus dies on the cross, the curtain in the temple tears in two. Some scholars believe that the curtain had art on it depicting the moon and the stars, a celestial scene. This was symbolic of God's majesty, sovereignty, and God's mystery. In other words, God was untouchable and out of reach. With the curtain torn, with the death and resurrection of Christ, God is very touchable.

We can share in communion through Christ. For us to experience communion with God requires surrender of ourselves to Jesus. How can we connect with God when we're wrapped up in ourselves? Selfishness is actually the anti-communion, the negation of communion.

Think about prayer. Isn't prayer just moments of surrender? Moments when we take our thanksgiving, our confessions, our supplications to God aren't moments we spend for God's benefit, but for ours. We pray so we might experience life-giving koinonia. Even moments of complete silence and contemplation are moments when we let go of ourselves and put our attention on God.

There is a story about Mother Teresa and her prayer life. Tom Brokaw was interviewing the humble servant of God when he asked her about prayer. Mother Teresa told Tom that she awoke early every morning, around three or four o'clock, and prayed for several hours. Stunned, Tom asked Teresa what she said to God during all of that time. She responded that she didn't say a thing. Instead, she sat and listened. Even more surprised, Tom wondered what kinds of things God said to her. Mother Teresa quietly answered, "Nothing. God just listens, too." What amazing understanding of God and of prayer! God isn't a celestial vending machine that we can bribe blessings out of. God is good, but God's goodness is born out of God's character, which is communion.

Isn't that what we all really need? However, for some reason, more often than not we choose anti-communion. We choose ourselves, because we love ourselves. Unfortunately, this leads to the hell of fear. Not just in the world to come, but right now. The results of fear compound almost daily. The fear that someone might get to know the real us, figure out we're not worthy to be loved and reject us, causes us to put on masks and pretend to be something we're not. We put on layer after layer, cover after cover, trying to hide from others, hide from God, and sometimes even hide from ourselves. We throw on layers of busyness and hurriedness. If we move fast enough, running from one thing to the next and spending our down time worrying about the running around, we don't give ourselves a chance to be afraid.

We also throw on all of the many layers of sin. Our lusts, our pride, our greed are all efforts on our part to cover over our fear. Popping pills, getting drunk, looking at porn, trying to control things, putting ourselves above others, insisting that we're right and everyone else is wrong are all efforts to cover over our fears.

There are also the many layers of resentment that act like steel prison bars, locking us into dark places and hardening our hearts toward communion. We feel resentment toward our families, who we might believe have wronged us somehow. We feel resentment toward our friends, who we think have ignored us. We feel resentment toward ourselves, since we can't seem to do anything right. We even feel resentment toward God. We love to play the blame game and hold grudges against everyone, even ourselves, because of the hurt and fear that we suffer on a daily basis. When we let fear control us, we cut ourselves off from the life-giving communion that God provides. Fear is the illness. Our masks, our busyness, our sin, our resentment, our isolation, our hell are the results of this illness. They are the symptoms of the deeper problem of fear.

The prescription is surrender. Surrender is really the only thing that we can possibly do to share in communion with God and escape fear. Remember, Jesus said,

> "Come to me, all you that are weary and carrying heavy burdens, and I will give you rest. Take my yoke upon you, and learn from me; for I am gentle and humble in heart, and you will find rest for your souls. For my yoke is easy, and my burden is light" (Matthew 11:28-30).

Out of fear, we have thrown yoke after yoke upon our backs until we are so overloaded that we cannot move. Surrender. Jesus is calling us to surrender our yokes to him. Jesus is calling us to experience "rest for our souls" by sharing in koinonia with him. Jesus wants us to surrender our self-centered busyness and throw on the yoke of peace. He wants us to give up our self-centered masks and superficialities and throw on the yoke of authenticity. He wants us to lay down our self-centered sinfulness, abandon self-gratification, and put on the yoke of holiness. He wants us to let go of our self-centered resentment, even our self-hate, and put on the yoke of grace. It is surrender, abandoning our "self," that leads to communion with Christ and brings grace, love, peace, holiness, and all of the fruits of the Spirit. Communion with God is the cure for the fear that rules our lives, and it is God's gift to us in and through Jesus Christ.

This is the meaning of the cross. Throughout Christian history, the meaning of the cross has been explained using many different metaphors. Early in the Medieval Age, warfare imagery was used. Jesus had gone to hell and defeated the devil, like a knight defeats a dragon. Later, an economic metaphor was introduced. Jesus paid the price that we owed God, which was our very lives. Then there was more of a penal metaphor or a courtroom analogy. We are guilty of sin and we must be punished, but God sent Jesus to take on the punishment so that we can be free. All of these metaphors are right and good, and they point to truth. But these analogies only uncover part of the truth. God has given us an even bigger gift than just freedom from evil, death, or punishment. God has provided a means by which we can share in communion with God and thereby live life eternal, not just when we die, but right now.

I wonder if there is room for another, just as valid, analogy to explain the meaning of the cross, a bridge analogy. Jesus, the Son of God, stretched his body upon the cross to become a bridge that we could walk upon to be in relationship with God. Where's the atonement in this analogy? God somehow experienced fear, isolation, and alienation so that God might become a bridge from fear to communion. Look at what Jesus says on the cross: "My God, my God, why have you forsaken me?" (Matthew 27:46). Perhaps this is more than just a cry of agony. Perhaps the writer is trying to explain the meaning of the cross to us by leading us to read Psalm 22, which begins with this exact phrase. As I read Psalm 22, I can't help thinking that the writer is experiencing what we all experience: fear, isolation, and alienation in their extremes. The poem talks about being mocked, despised, and feeling abandoned by God. Verse 6 of that Psalm says, "But I am a worm and not a human, scorned by others and despised by people" (Psalm 22:6). Is this bridge analogy we've been throwing around really a *worm* analogy? That Jesus, who becomes the bridge to communion on the cross, does so by becoming nothing, by becoming a worm? A worm is probably the most vulnerable, defenseless creature in all creation, isn't it? Snakes bite. Bee's sting. Ants scurry. But what does a worm do? Nothing. All a worm can do is lie on the ground and be vulnerable. All a worm can do is be stepped on and hope for the best. A worm is easily crushed, completely open to attack, defenseless, and utterly surrendered. This is the meaning of the cross. Jesus Christ becomes nothing on the cross, to the point of surrendered wormness, so that we might walk on him, the worm, the bridge, so that we might be in communion with God and live.

If this is the real meaning of the cross, the real meaning of being a follower of Christ, then why do we need church? Can't communion with God happen any time, anywhere, and not just from eleven to noon on Sunday morning? Does one really need to be in a church or a human-made "holy place" to enjoy the benefits of communion? The answer is obviously, "No." This is why the writer of the gospel describes the curtain in the temple being torn in two. There is no need for the temple. God is the temple and, when we are in communion with God, we become the temple as well. It's not the church's job to be a store where you can pick up your Jesus; the church's job is to live Christ's life, to be a bridge, by being vulnerable, surrendered worms so that others might enjoy the communion as well. When we do this, we become the temple, the body of Christ, which has no building, no location. This temple, with its curtain torn in two, is a bridge to God.

Becoming the Temple, a Bridge to God

How can we as a people become the temple, rather than building temples out of brick and mortar, so that people can connect with God intimately and authentically? How do we manifest the body of Christ in our communities so that others may find salvation? I think it begins by creating, or helping to create, through the power of the Holy Spirit, an atmosphere of surrender. To do this, we must become people of surrender ourselves. If there is no sense of surrender, no sense of repentance and worm-likeness, than how can we even begin to be the temple, the body of the Sufferer? When we gather, we need to have the mindset that we are the temple gathering as the people of God, rather than the people of God gathering at the temple. This means gathering to practice koinonia with God by surrendering rather than gathering pointlessly at a certain building.

The problem is that the act of surrender is sometimes, if not all the time, uncomfortable. Many times surrender can be painful. I think that sometimes we confuse quitting with surrender. We mistake one for the other. We think that we're surrendering something when we're really quitting. Quitting and surrender are two completely different things. Here's an easy way to tell the difference: we *quit* the things we don't want, but we know we should keep; we *surrender* the things we want to keep, but we know we should be giving up. Quitting is for me. Quitting is for self. Surrendering is for the Spirit. Surrender is laying our lives before God, completely vulnerable, completely wormlike. The flesh loves to quite, but the spirit hates it. The spirit loves to surrender, but the flesh hates it. We quit having patience. We surrender our will. We quit persevering. We surrender our addictions. We quit a broken relationship. We surrender our pride. We quit "life." We surrender our lives.

As people who are followers of Christ, we follow Peter and Andrew's cue by dropping our nets and following the sufferer. What does that mean? What nets do we hold on to? What things do we carry that we refuse to give up, to surrender? Surrender is an act of sacrifice. It is giving up that which you want to keep for yourself. Usually, these are the things that we prize the most: money, creativity, sexuality, energy, priorities, and time. Time. That's a big one, isn't it? What is more precious, really? Throwing money in a plate, giving up our sexuality, or realigning our priorities all pale in comparison to surrendering our time to God. Time is one of the most, if not the most, precious thing we can surrender. We want to spend our time on ourselves. We want, even need, our "me time." Time surrendered to God doesn't sound very productive. God time doesn't sound like much fun. But that's exactly what it means to surrender. Surrender is sacrifice, and it is within that sacrificial act that we experience koinonia with God, which gives us life. As life gets busier and busier, and we fill our lives with more and more noise, we trim our time with communion shorter and shorter until we have no time to surrender at all.

This is where the body of Christ comes in. This is where the church, the bridge to God, living Christ's life, goes to work and does its job. If the church's job is to help people connect with God and practice koinonia with Christ, then it is the church's job to help people surrender. Ultimately, this is the mission, right? To help people surrender their lives to God. I believe this happens most poignantly by helping people surrender their time. If this sounds counter-cultural to the point of impossible, it is. Our culture has somehow found a way to suck every last bit of time from our lives. We are trained to fill our time with all kinds of pointless busyness, noise, television, distractions, and unimportant worries.

In Mark 10:17, a young man runs up to Jesus and asks him how he can inherit eternal life. Isn't that the same question we're asking in this chapter: how can we be in communion with God so that we can live life abundant, now and in the afterlife? When Jesus responds by telling the young man to follow the commandments, he insists that he has followed all of the commandments since his youth. Then Jesus says, "You lack one thing; go, sell what you own, and give the money to the poor, and you will have treasure in heaven; then come, follow me" (Mark 10:21). In other words, to share in koinonia with God, to experience the treasure of the kingdom of heaven (which *is* the treasure), we need to surrender that which we hold dear, but really has no eternal value. For the rich young man, he needed to surrender his wealth. But the man couldn't do it. When he heard Jesus' words, his face fell, and he went away sad. In response, Jesus declares, "Children, how hard it is to enter the kingdom of God! It is easier for a camel to go through the eye of a needle than for someone who is rich to enter the kingdom of God" (Mark 10:24).

Now, what Jesus is referring to with the camel imagery is not a bizarre, random; comical act of stuffing a large camel through a sewing needle. Rather, Jesus is talking about the process it takes for a camel to enter the gates of a city. The city gates, the entrance into a walled town, were called "the eye of the needle." To get the tall camels through the eye of the needle, the camel had to be completely stripped of all of its baggage. Everything that the camel had been carrying, including all of the traveler's supplies and most treasured possessions, had to be taken off the camel. Then the camel had to be brought to its knees and maneuvered through the gate. What Jesus is saying is that to get into the kingdom of God and enjoy koinonia with God, one needs to surrender all baggage and fall to his or her knees. This makes Jesus' statement true; this is, for many people, especially those who have a lot to surrender, practically impossible. When the people standing there hear Jesus talking about the camel going through the eye of a needle, they declare, "Then who can be saved?" Jesus responds, "For mortals it is impossible, but not for God; for God all things are possible" (Mark

10:27). Jesus proves this very statement by surrendering everything on the cross, not just as an example, but also as the divine power in which we can be saved. It is only through the sacrificial, surrendering act on the cross that we can be in koinonia with God.

This is why it is so hard for us who have so much to surrender. Surrender requires that we give up our wealth. Surrender requires sacrifice, including those things that comfort us—our treasures and our time. For those who have abundant wealth, luxurious comforts, and plenty of leisurely "me time," this is quite difficult to the point of impossible. This is why we prefer church as a store rather than a bridge. A store caters to customers rather than demanding surrender and sacrifice. For those looking for a store to provide for their spiritual needs, the bridge-style church is confusing and unattractive. But for those who have nothing, for those who are hurting and broken, for those who are at the end of their ropes, the bridge becomes the vehicle that facilitates surrender and therefore healing.

The Psalms repeatedly emphasize this theme of God being near and available to those who have bottomed out. "The Lord is near to the brokenhearted, and saves the crushed spirit" (Psalm 34:18). "The sacrifice acceptable to God is a broken spirit; a broken and contrite heart, O God, you will not despise" (Psalm 51:17). Connecting to God means shedding all of our masks, all of our baggage, getting on our knees, and surrendering our lives—including our wealth, our luxury, and our time. For those who have accumulated layer after layer of coverings to hide behind, this is bad news and requires almost impossible sacrifice. But for those who have nothing, who have "a broken spirit," this is good news. God is near because surrender is not quite as difficult when there's nothing left to give up.

There's a guy in our faith community named Doug who experienced this first hand. Doug, a nonconforming, punk-rock tattoo artist, came to Pittsburgh from Altoona a few years ago with almost nothing. He didn't have any money or a place to go, yet he carried a lot of baggage with him. One evening, he and his girlfriend at the time wandered into a local hangout just about at the end of their rope. Doug connected with some of the young punks at the tattoo-shop ministry. Within just a short time of experiencing the kingdom of God with these punk kids, Doug let go and surrendered his life to the King. At that moment, Doug was transformed, and his life was redeemed.

Doug has been involved in our church for a few years now, and I can honestly say there is no one who typifies surrender more than Doug does. Doug now works as a talented tattoo artist at the In The Blood Tattoo Shop on the South Side. He has very few possessions and lives very simply. He is a walking billboard for the counter-culture lifestyle, covered head to toe with tattoos and piercings of all kinds. He even has the outline of the earth tattooed on his head. During many worship gatherings, Doug can be found lying face down on the floor in worship. The faith that he shows through his acts of surrender has inspired others to follow suit.

During the church Christmas pageant last year (yes, we do Christmas pageants), Doug played the biggest bully, Ralph Herdman, in the play, "The Best Christmas Pageant Ever," a story about a family of bad kids who take over the church Christmas play. I still have not stopped laughing from watching Doug wrap his bullet belt around his Joseph robe during the production. And Doug has been involved in our church on all conceivable levels. He was part of our Apprenticeship program, went to Mexico on a mission trip, and created the huge paintings that we use as stained-glass windows during worship. What has amazed me the most about Doug is the intensity with which he has surrendered his life over to God. He has surrendered his priorities, his time, and his very life to the point of hosting a 24/7 prayer chapel in the basement of his house, which he calls "the alpha house." Doug has surrendered and become a beacon of light for our community.

Means of Grace

How do we become a bridge to God by helping people participate in koinonia? How do we become a community of surrendered people? Do we put together a surrendering ministry or program, where we put up a sign, advertise in the church bulletin, and gather at the church every other Tuesday night for forty weeks for our 40 Weeks of Surrender Program? It seems to me that surrender doesn't work like that, on a set schedule, within a set program. Surrender can't be manufactured in a factory. Surrender is a lifestyle, a way of living together. Does this mean we never gather to share in corporate surrender? No. We need to gather. We need to gather and take time—lots of time—to connect with Jesus Christ by surrendering both our lives individually and ourselves corporately. However, we cannot set out a sign and expect people to come to our "surrender event." We need to find ways of taking the gathering to the people.

In our community, we have found many different, sometimes strange kinds of gatherings that have made koinonia with God available to people who might not ever go to a church. Sometimes these gatherings are large-group moments, such as our Sunday morning worship in the Goodwill Industries building. Sometimes they are small-group moments, such as our mentoring connections in coffee shops. The basement of the tattoo shop has been the scene for many 24/7 worship weeks; where we have devoted an entire week to prayer and surrender. And like Doug's "House of Prayer," we have individuals who make room in their homes and in their lives for long periods of prayer and surrender.

In our quest to practice missional koinonia, we've even gathered underneath the local bridge and found a place of solitude in an old abandoned church. In December of 2006, we received notice from the Goodwill Industries that they would begin renovations on the building and we would have to relocate our Sunday morning worship gatherings. They gave us two months to find a new home. It seemed, at the time, to be Godly timing. Our Sunday worship attendance had been maxed out, and we weren't too excited about the idea of creating a second service as so many churches do in that situation. So, as we began looking for a new space, it became very evident that the best space on the South Side was the space we were already in. We looked at building after building, schools and warehouses. Nothing seemed to fit our needs. The one place that seemed to be the best fit for our community was a rather large, state-of-the-art wedding banquet facility at the end of the Hot Metal Bridge. The space was perfect except for the price: eight hundred dollars per week. That might not seem like much for some churches, but for our community, it was outrageous. With only one week to go until we had to move, we made the brave and, now looking back, the very stupid decision to meet underneath the Birmingham Bridge. It was February, mind you. The thought of taking our faith community to the streets was appealing, but the reality of sitting on the gravel in twenty-degree weather didn't sound like fun. However, we were undeterred. We began planning for our move to under the bridge. We refused to pay eight hundred dollars a week.

Shortly after we made that fateful decision, God provided. First, as we were literally sitting down to lay out the first "under the bridge" worship service, (the forecast called for snow), we received a call from one of our parishioners telling us of a rumor that Goodwill had canceled their plans to renovate. When we called the Goodwill, it was true. The plans had been canceled, and we were welcomed back in the building indefinitely. It was a good thing, because that Sunday was deathly cold. I don't know if we would have survived under the bridge. However, the idea of meeting under the bridge for worship excited us so much that we planned to gather there a few times over the summer. Those moments under the bridge, boats chugging along on the river, the trains roaring by, and the traffic overhead, were great moments of surrender, not just individually, but as a community. The act of gathering under the bridge instead of meeting in the luxury of the wedding banquet hall, which would have probably doubled our attendance, not to mention our weekly giving, was an act of corporate surrender that has brought life to our church. At the same time, meeting out in a public place like that became, for us, a model of what it might look like to practice missional koinonia.

The second miracle occurred a few weeks after our call from the Goodwill. We received another call. This one was from a local couple who had purchased an abandoned Catholic church from the local diocese, had built a condo-like home in the balcony, and was looking for tenants to utilize their gutted-out "family room" which at one time had been a glorious sanctuary. When we walked into the place, we knew we had to find time to gather in the space. The sanctuary was a wreck. The pews were gone, the walls had giant holes in them where religious pieces had been ripped out, and the ceiling was a patchwork of rotten wood, plaster, and dark holes. It was perfect. We have gathered in this abandoned church every week for a time of silence, solitude, and contemplation. There is a little singing, we share the scriptures, and we break bread. But the main reason for gathering is to take time to surrender. We don't have a set beginning time or a set ending time. Some folks come late; some leave early. It is a time dedicated to the counter-cultural practice of koinonia with God, which requires surrendering our need to be entertained, our preconceived expectations of worship, and our time.

When you think of all of the ways in which we need to surrender ourselves—our time, our priorities, our very lives—it can seem impossible. In actuality, it is. I think this is what Jesus means when he says to the crowd, "For mortals it is impossible, but not for God; for God all things are possible." In other words, good luck surrendering, laying down your life on your own, because you're not going to be able to do it on your own. Our flesh makes it impossible. Surrender is only possible by God through the cross. This is where grace comes in. Our act of surrender is really an act of God's grace. In the Wesleyan tradition, we use different language to describe the ways in which God's grace moves us toward surrender. Simply put, prevenient grace is the grace that God provides in our lives to reveal our need for surrender. Prevenient grace is God's love for us before we've gained the capacity to acknowledge that love. This love leads to repentance, which leads to another kind of grace we call justifying grace. This is the grace that God provides us that gives us the means to surrender for the first time. Finally, as we live a life of surrender to God, it is not by our means that we surrender, but God's grace moving constantly in our lives, drawing us ever closer to God. This grace we call sanctifying grace.

This might seem basic, and if you've ever been in a Sunday school class, you already know this. But here's why I bring this up: if it is only by God's grace in which we are able to surrender, what does that mean for the church? I guess I'm talking about our *ecclesiology* now. Remember, our *missiology* is the church's job; *ecclesiology* is *how* we do that job. So, if our mission is to help people surrender to God so that they may connect and share koinonia with God, how do we do that job when it is really God who does the job? The answer is *means of grace*. We participate in the different means of grace. In Methodism, the *means of grace* are ways in which God works invisibly in us, quickening, strengthening and confirming faith. We use different means of grace to help us to open our hearts and lives to God's work in us. According to John Wesley, the *means of grace* (or the ways in which we connect with God), are divided into two categories: works of piety and works of mercy. In other words, we connect with God by loving God and loving neighbor.

Wesley's Means of Grace

If it is by God's grace that we encounter surrender in our lives, then practicing the means of grace is the "how" of koinonia with God. And when we practice the means of grace together as a whole community, the kingdom of God is near. That manifestation of the kingdom of God becomes a bridge to God for those who are not yet surrenderers. Wouldn't it make sense then that, if the church is not a building but instead is a mission, the means of grace would be practiced out on the streets of our communities? Wouldn't it stand to reason then, if we are to be taking the kingdom of God to the people rather than insisting that the people come to church, we take the bread and the cup into the places where people gather, offering the grace of God so that people might experience the kingdom of God and surrender? Is communion intended to be a means of grace for those who are being sanctified? Is communion a vehicle of sanctifying grace only, or can the Lord's Supper be a means of justifying grace or even prevenient grace? Can the Lord's Supper actually be, in the missional church, a means of prevenient grace?

Am I suggesting what you think I'm suggesting? Yes, I am. I would like to propose that maybe God can work God's prevenient grace in the heart of what we might call an unbeliever, a not yet Christian, or a non-surrenderer through all of the means of grace, including the sacraments. If the church is mission, why wouldn't this be so? Every time we gather as a body, there should be people in our midst who have never walked on the bridge. If there aren't, the purpose of the bridge would be lost, right? The sacraments, especially baptism and the Lord's Supper, are *not* meant to be activities that we withhold from anyone. In fact, I would contend that communion was originally intended by Jesus and the early church to be a missional tool, if not *the* missional tool. Doesn't the scripture say, "Taste and see that the Lord is good?" Why would we withhold a taste? Why would we insist that people believe the gospel first and then offer them communion with God through the means of grace, through the broken bread and the poured-out cup? Isn't the broken bread intended for broken people? Isn't the poured-out cup intended for empty, poured-out people?

For some people who have grown up in churches where communion was practiced once a month, once a season, and offered to members of the church only, sharing in the Lord's Supper every week and

Works of Piety

Prayer

Meditating on the Scriptures

The Sacraments

Fasting

Koinonia (Community)

Works of Mercy

Doing Good

Visiting the Sick

Visiting the Imprisoned

Feeding & Clothing Those in Need

Earning, Saving, and Giving All One Can

Seeking Justice

inviting everyone to the table is completely offensive. Every now and then we have a visitor or two who will get upset by the way we treat communion, and they'll walk out in a huff. I sometimes wonder if, as they're walking all alone to their cars, they see the irony of their actions as they alienate themselves because of the belief that not everyone is welcome. This is silly. Think of the juxtaposition of an "outsider" walking up to the table to share in the body and blood, while an "insider'" angrily drives away alone in his or her car. Who is really in hell and who is experiencing the kingdom?

Am I suggesting we walk down the street, break bread, and hand it out to whoever we pass on the street? Absolutely not. The Lord's Supper is uniquely a means of grace that points to the body and blood of Jesus Christ. To share in communion is to be in koinonia with the body and blood of *Christ*, not Buddha, Muhammad, or anyone else. The sacraments are distinctively Christian. When people share in communion, they need to understand this. This means that the gospel, the word, the good news of the kingdom of God, must be shared, some-how, some way, so that those who take it have a clear understanding that they are participating in a means of grace. When we share in the bread and the cup, we acknowledge God's work of grace in our lives. We participate in an outward sign of an inward grace.

That's what the elements of the means of grace are: signs. The water for baptism, the bread and the cup for communion, the rings in a wedding, the oil used for anointing—all of these things are outward signs of an inward grace. The signs are not God; they are simply signs. The water isn't a magic potion that makes one clean in baptism; it is the Holy Spirit that cleanses. The bread and the cup do not work like some sort of elixir, making us holy. To give the elements special pow-ers is to say that the elements do the work. This is to say that the ele-ments are God and makes an idol out of the elements. God is God; God does the work, not the water. To say otherwise is idolatry. These are just signs that we use to remind us of what God has been doing, is doing, and will be doing within us, as individuals and as a community.

What makes these signs unique, and the reason we should use them every time we gather, is their depth and dimension in meaning. A stop sign, for example, is a sign that has only one meaning: stop. However, elements that we use in the sacraments have multiple meanings, giving the moment of grace multiple meanings as well. The water used in bap-tism reminds us of God's hand over the waters of creation. It is also a reminder of God's covenant with God's people, the one with Noah in Genesis, and the one made at the parting of the Red Sea in Exodus. The water also points to the womb and speaks of rebirth. When we think of John the Baptist's work at the edge of the Jordan, we think of repentance—turning back to God. Then there is the imagery of being cleansed of our sin, of healing, and the new life we receive in Christ. The waters of baptism are layered with meaning, giving the act of bap-tism layered meaning as well. This means, for all those involved—those who are being baptized, those who are remembering their baptism, and those who are just watching—the sacramental moment takes on these meanings as the Holy Spirit works. In one person, the Spirit works repentance, in another, the Spirit works healing, in another, the Spirit works new life. The Holy Spirit is like the wind and blows where it wants to blow. For us to put limitations and to control the *whos* and the *hows* is for us to throw a wet blanket on a wildfire.

The bread and the cup have multiple layers as well. Preach on the Lord's Prayer, and the phrase "give us this day our daily bread" takes on one meaning if communion follows. Preach on forgiveness and mercy, and the elements take on that meaning. Preach on the cross and the meaning of atonement, and the Lord's Supper becomes that reminder. Preach on the body of Christ, and we gather at the table as the body to share in the body. Preach on how "God is close to the broken" or "blessed are the poor in spirit," and the broken bread becomes a powerful symbol of our koinonia with Christ's brokenness. Preach on missions or the importance of service, and the wine or juice poured into the cup becomes a reminder that Christ's spirit pours into us, motivating and sustaining us. Again and again, we come to the table, and again and again we are reminded of how God's grace is working in us, not just rubber-stamping our foreheads so that we can get into heaven when we die, but marking our hearts in that very moment so that we can experience heaven on earth. The church's job is to live Christ's life and become a bridge so that others may experience the love of God. The church exists to help people find salvation through surrender and through experiencing God through the means of grace. Isn't it also the church's job to help people share in the means of grace, and especially our most powerful signs of grace, the sacraments? Are not the sacraments the church's most powerful missional tools? Why don't we use them as such?

An Unworthy Manner?

> Whoever, therefore, eats the bread or drinks the cup of the Lord in an unworthy manner will be answerable for the body and blood of the Lord (1 Corinthians 11:27).

Every now and then, someone will quote this verse to me as an admonition that welcoming sinners to the table will bring judgment upon us. Nothing could be further from the truth. Don't take this verse out of context and switch it around to mean something it doesn't. The whole letter of 1 Corinthians is meant to be a discourse to a church struggling with disunity. The people of the church in Corinth can't seem to get their act together. As a result, their community is fractured, as well as their worship. Look at the beginning of the passage. Read this verse within the context of the rest of the letter:

> When you come together, it is not really to eat the Lord's supper. For when the time comes to eat, each of you goes ahead with your own supper, and one goes hungry and another becomes drunk. What! Do you not have homes to eat and drink in? Or do you show contempt for the church of God and humiliate those who have nothing? What should I say to you? Should I commend you? In this matter I do not commend you! (1 Corinthians 11:20-22).

Paul isn't rebuking the church in Corinth because they welcome sinners to the table. On the contrary, Paul is rebuking the church for *not* including everyone. That is how they are participating in communion in an unworthy manner—by not actually practicing communion. How can communion be communion if only some are invited to the table? Therefore, it isn't heresy to practice the Lord's Supper every time we meet, and sharing in an open table is not an "unworthy manner." In fact, the very opposite is true. Those who share in communion once a season or once a month are the ones who should be rebuked. Those who exclude others from the table, and therefore exclude others from the kingdom of God, are the ones who actually practice heresy.

Sometimes I think that instead of doing its job living Christ's life out in the world, the church has decided to live the Pharisee's life while hiding away in dark places, allowing those who are "clean" to enter and keeping those who are "dirty" out. We forget that the requisites for entrance into the kingdom aren't about clean or dirty; it's all about surrender of self. Communion with God happens only by God's grace through surrender of self, not by knowing all the rules. We often fall into the trap laid down by our culture that upholds the winners and those who are deemed clean. The kingdom of God is the complete opposite. Jesus is for the losers of this world, for the wretched and broken. Jesus is for the dirty ones. For it's almost always the losers and the dirty ones who come to the table surrendered. Conversely, those who believe themselves to be clean, or who are tricked by the mask of superficial cleanliness, are those who see no need to surrender. They unfor-

DIRTY WORD

tunately find themselves alone and isolated as they stand in judgment of others.

Kisses from Heaven

It's been seven years now since my dad passed away. I'm talking about my adoptive dad. He was diagnosed with pancreatic cancer, and it was terminal. His painful stay at the hospital lasted three months, until he had finally had enough with the tests and all the crap that comes with staying at the hospital. As he lay there on the gurney, having his blood cleaned by the dialysis machine, he declared that he was ready to go home. It was a Thursday afternoon. The doctor told him that if he went home he would not survive the weekend. If he stayed at the hospital, he would last six more months. Dad opted for home. They rolled him into an ambulance, and we headed to the house for the most gut-wrenching weekend of our lives. The whole family was scared to death. Both my brother and sister were still in high school at the time. It was a very inconvenient time for my father to leave us.

When the ambulance rolled into the driveway of my parent's home in Cambridge Springs, Pennsylvania, the rain was coming down in sheets. We all scrambled into the house. My mother made room in the living room for his bed. My brothers and I held open the doors and made way for the medics, who pulled my dad from the ambulance and rolled him toward the house. They failed, however, to cover his face, so you can imagine what he looked like when he reached the living room. My father's face was soaked with rainwater. The dog, overjoyed to see dad, ran in and licked dad's hand. My mom went to the kitchen for a towel. When she returned and sat down beside him to wipe the rain from his face, my dad stopped her. "No, don't," he said. "The rain was like kisses from heaven. I think everything's going to be okay." And he smiled.

That phrase, "kisses from heaven," set the tone for the entire weekend, as my dad fell in and out of consciousness and then finally faded away on late Sunday afternoon. When it looked like he might breathe his last breath, the entire family gathered around his bed. My sister and I sang a song we wrote that weekend based on that phrase of promise, "kisses from heaven." When we were done, we moved, tear-filled, into singing "Because He Lives" by Bill Gaither. The words in that song's last verse say it all.

The promise of God's kisses upon our faces. The promise of the Risen Christ, here and now, alive and with us. This is the promise of assurance. The promise means that no matter what happens to us, God is with us, suffering with us, crying with us, struggling with us. It is that promise that overcomes fear and brings us the great gift of life. In Brennan Manning's captivating book *Abba's Child*, Brennan talks about how our identity is wrapped up in being "the beloved."

> God created us for union with Himself: This is the original purpose of our lives. And God is defined as love (1 John 4:16). Living in awareness of our belovedness is the axis around which the Christian life revolves. Being the beloved is our identity, the core of our existence. It is not merely a lofty thought, an inspiring idea, or one name among many. It is the name by which God knows us and the way He relates to us (*Abba's Child: The Cry of the Heart for Intimate Belonging* [Colorado Springs, CO: Navpress, 2002], 52).

Those "kisses from heaven" are small signs of our being beloved. Just like the rain, God covers us with love and grace. God beckons us out of our fear and into koinonia. As I watched my father, now dead, being taken out of the house to the waiting ambulance, my first thought was that this seemed so familiar to me. I had had that same feeling when I was so small that I can't clearly remember the event: the abandonment; the hurt; the overwhelming fear. I had had that same feeling when I was taken from my home and thrown into a foreign land. Here I was, fatherless again. Here I was afraid again. Then, for some reason, my thoughts moved to that moment when I was submerged in a German lake. I thought of a promise, a promise that I've always held dear:

> For the LORD your God is God of gods and LORD of lords, the great God, mighty and awesome, who is not partial and takes no bribe, who executes justice for the orphan and the widow, and who loves the strangers, providing them food and clothing. You shall also love the stranger, for you were strangers in the land of Egypt (Deut. 10:17-19).

I am the alien, orphan, and widow. Heck, I'm fatherless times two. That's me. I'm the outcast, the last, the loser. I am the unclean. I am the dirty. The good news is that God defends the cause of the fatherless, the loser, and the dirty. Those who have been counted out by everyone else are welcomed into the arms of an ever-loving Father. For us who are frightened, who shake with fear, God has something to offer. For us who are thirsty for assurance, for safety, and for refuge, Christ has a cup from which to drink. For us who are starving for love, for care, and for communion, Jesus has a loaf to eat. Appropriately enough, it's broken.

What Is It That We Offer?

Do we really need church? What does the church really have to offer? A big fancy building? Who cares about a building? Isn't God everywhere? Can't I have what I need, communion, right here in this coffee shop where I write? Does the church have cool praise and worship music? Look! I have better music on my iPhone! I play it while I go for a run through God's creation. The church has scripture readings and special liturgy? Wow. Guess what? I have access to thirty different translations of the Bible, including Greek, Hebrew and just about any other language at a touch of a button, right in my hand. And liturgy! I don't even know what a liturgy is! Do you have a twenty-minute sermon you want me to hear? I can download fifty better sermons, preached by the world's best preachers, right here, right now. You say you have fellowship? I can share in fellowship with friends I have made from across the globe. Don't you get it? I have in my life, in my hand, access to unlimited information, community, connections, and entertainment. I don't live in the Industrial Age anymore, where I need to come to church. I live in the Information Age. Tell me, please, what do you have in your fancy building that I can't get on my iPhone?

Here's the answer: A plate. A cup. A table. A gift. A body broken. Blood poured out.

The sacraments, the means of grace that we use to help us surrender our lives and connect with the inward grace of God—these are the wind in our sails. These are all we really have to offer this world. But they are all we need. The church needs to drop the heavy engines of buildings, liturgies, and cool fads. We need to hoist the sails and offer the world the gifts of God. I'm not the only person in this world who has been broken by divorce or family dysfunction. The truth is I am just one guy in a whole generation of people who are simply trying to survive. We need the church to become a bridge so that a whole generation of scared people can come to know the assuring love of God.

I've got a new means of grace for you. The next time it's pouring down rain outside, go out, lie down in the grass, and let the rain completely soak your face. Then remember these words: "Do not be afraid!"

Call it "kisses from heaven."

PART 5:
THE KINGDOM BELONGS TO THE REJECTS

Rejected

When I was in the ninth grade, I tried out for the school's baseball team. Of course, because my dad was in the Army, we had just moved into a new town yet again, and yet again I was the new kid. Although being the new kid can pretty much be hell, it can also be training for later in life. You have to get out of your shell, get to know people, or be very lonely. Therefore, motivated by loneliness, I was looking for something to be part of, somewhere to belong. Somehow, I can't remember how exactly, I ended up finding a seat in the cafeteria (which is the very worst part of being the new kid, right?) with a group of sports nuts. Every day at lunch these other boys would break open their baseball cards, make big trades, and talk about last night's game. Trying to find a place to fit in, I joined them.

As spring rolled around, it was time, evidently, to play baseball. The guys at the cafeteria table were abuzz with anticipation of the coming season. The homeruns hit. The strikeouts thrown. Although I have never been very athletic, I decided to pull my dad's old baseball glove from his footlocker and join my new friends at the baseball tryouts. Long story short, I didn't make the team. One sad afternoon, after falling all over myself on the baseball field, the coach called me into his office and gave me the bad news. Looking back, how anyone could have had the heart to cut a lonely, fragile, fourteen-year-old, new kid is beyond me. The next day when I sat down with the guys in the cafeteria, it was clear that I was no longer an insider. I was still welcome to sit at the table, and I wasn't completely ignored, but not being on the team made me the reject. I was a reject, perhaps not in their eyes, but definitely in my own. As the season went by, day after day, lunch after lunch, I heard the stories of wins and losses, of long bus rides, and of practical jokes. I tried to pretend that I wasn't jealous. I tried to pretend that I had other things, better things to do. But really, I was broken up inside. If only I was better at baseball, I thought to myself. If only I could run faster or throw farther or swing that bat better. Then I wouldn't be lonely anymore. I'd be part of the gang.

As the spring moved on, the team was really struggling. They were not winning any games, and as a result some of the students were quitting the team. One by one, players dropped off, and at each lunchtime conversation, I heard about how the team was shrinking. At one point, the team had been reduced down to just eleven players, and one of the guys at the table, very kindly and hopefully, said, "Hey, maybe the coach will ask Jim to be back on the team." I smiled and shrugged, but inside I wanted to explode. There was nothing I wanted in this world more than to be on that team. Who cares if it was a losing team? I wanted on.

A week went by, and I didn't get asked to be on the team, even as I tried to make myself more visible to the coach, walking by his office two or three times a day and running and playing my hardest in gym class, which the coach taught. Still, no call. Instead, I listened to the guys in the lunchroom talk about how they had lost the game the night before because they only had eight players. Eight players! Instead of inviting me or any other kid he had cut to return to the team, the coach had opted to field eight players. It was crushing. Was I that bad? Was a non-player actually better than I was? Was the team better off with a large gap on the field than having me standing in that gap with my dad's big glove and a dazed look on my face? Was I really that worthless? Was I to believe that no person at all had more value than me?

As a teenage, new kid trying to find a place to belong, this was disabling. The rejection was overwhelming, not the rejection that the coach had for me, but the rejection I had for myself. I hated myself. This hate manifested itself in some very self-destructive ways. I hid in my room and pretended to be someone else, someone I wasn't. My low self-esteem controlled my high-school years and has bled into the rest of my life, making it difficult for me to share real, authentic relationships with people. I think deep inside of me is a defense mechanism that goes off as I begin to make a new friend. It goes off, reminding me that if I'm not careful, I will be rejected yet again, and I will be hurt yet again, and so I keep people at arm's length. Don't get too close, Jim. You might regret it.

Forget That!

Whereas in the last chapter I focused on fear as the enemy, the big obstacle that leads us away from God's grace and assurance toward isolation, in this chapter I want to shine a spotlight on the alienating power of rejection. I suspect I am not the only one in the world who has had to deal with rejection. We all are subject to it. Not only do we find ourselves being rejected, we contribute to its power by buying into it, by playing the game with everyone else. We reject others, we reject ourselves, and we reject the God who created us. Just as we are all wired for communion with God, we are also wired to live in community and to be part of a family. Basically, we've been created with the *need* to belong. Belonging is as great a need as water. If we cannot find belonging, we die. Where fear is the enemy to communion, rejection is the enemy to belonging. Rejection is like a place that has no water; it is like a desert or barren wasteland. Rejection leaves us parched and dry as a bone.

Our whole culture is based on the value of rejection. It's as if our whole world never graduated from the seventh grade. We have television shows where the weakest link is rejected. We have a social and political scale that measures one's worth by what one looks like. In turn, we play into this value system by believing these lies. We are all guilty of judging people with just a glance, never bothering to get to know them inside.

One day I was crossing the street on the South Side as I waved at two of the guys from The Last Hope. They waved back, their chains jingling, their purple, spiked hair glistening in the sun. If you saw these guys coming toward you on the street, you might be inclined to run in the other direction. As I crossed and waved, the crossing guard, a nice middle-aged woman, noticed the guys sitting on the stoop of the tattoo shop and whispered to me, "Oh my, look at them. What a mess. I would never let my daughter go out with one of them." At which point, I could only reply, "Who? Dylan and Denman? You'd be lucky to have one of those guys as your son-in-law. Those guys might look rough on the outside, but they don't drink, smoke, steal, or even cuss. In fact, we're getting together later on for prayer. You're invited to join us." Of course, she wasn't interested in even talking with Dylan or Denman. She had already made up her mind about them based only on what they looked like. In her mind, she had taken out her rubber stamp and had stamped "REJECTED" on these guys without even bothering to give them a closer look. This crossing guard certainly isn't the only person on the planet who plays the rejection game. We all do it, every one of us.

The problem here is that if we are so quick to stamp "REJECTED" on others, how fast are we ready to stamp ourselves? See, you are a creation of God. You have been created in God's image. I've been created in God's image. When we reject others and reject ourselves, we in turn reject the one who made us. Rejection is the enemy of belonging. It draws us away from koinonia and into the darkness of alienation, the darkness of hell.

Now if Dylan and Denman had been dressed in polo shirts, with their hair nicely groomed and talking on their cell phones, the crossing guard would have given the boys high praise. Never mind the fact that they could have been mass murderers or child abusers. This lady could easily accept Dylan and Denman if they simply looked the part. This is where rejection really wields its power over us. More often than not, we look and act the way we do not based on grace or on who we are, but based on the fear of being rejected by others. Life just becomes one big game of acceptance or rejection. You look like this and you're in. You look like that and you're out. Blond hair, blue eyes, you're accepted. No hair, double chin, you're rejected. How awful! Is this really what life is all about? Are we all living in one big beauty contest?

In what is quickly becoming my favorite movie, *Little Miss Sunshine*, all of the members of this completely dysfunctional family try to grapple with the realities of a children's beauty pageant. In the movie, every single character is an utter loser by the world's standards. From the mother who's been divorced to the dad who's gone bankrupt, to the grandfather who does heroin to the uncle who's tried to commit suicide to the chubby little girl trying to win a beauty contest, everyone is what the world would label a loser or reject. Even the Volkswagen van that they have to push-start is a loser. My favorite line of the movie comes almost at the very end when Dwayne, who has spent most of the movie fulfilling his vow of silence, says, "Life is just one big beauty contest after another. [Forget] that."

Dwayne is right. Our culture, our society, has shackled us to its values. We have all bought into the lie that one's worth directly relates to one's looks, talents, or wealth. I'm with Dwayne—forget that. Life isn't meant to be lived like that at all. We all starve for acceptance, thirst for belonging, and desire a family. We want a place where we can find unconditional love and grace, where we can be ourselves and not hide behind the masks of superficialities and put-on personalities. This place should be the bridge. It should be the church. But it's not. The church has fallen into the same trap as the rest of our culture, and it finds every possible way to reject those who don't look right, or those who don't have much, and exalt those who do. Have you ever walked into a Christian bookstore and picked up a CD that didn't have a person with perfectly white teeth, perfectly groomed hair, and perfectly toned skin on the cover? Forget that!

Is this really Jesus' vision of the kingdom of God? I don't think so. The Jesus I read about in scripture is the Jesus who reaches out, puts his hand on the leper, and heals him. He is the Jesus who is born in an old stable and wanders the desert, homeless. He is the Jesus who makes friends with the prostitutes and tax collectors. He is the Jesus who hangs out with the dirty, rotten losers and rejects of this world. I don't think it's because Jesus is trying to "stick it to the man." I think Jesus hangs out with the rejected because he understands where to find true beauty.

I was in The Exchange not too long ago when a young, spiky-haired man behind the counter taught me a very important lesson in the most meaningless of gestures. The Exchange is one of those music stores where you can exchange your old music for new music. Because of their diverse clientele, their music selection is the best. Likewise, the music they play is always very loud and very eccentric. Walk into The Exchange at any given time, and you'll hear punk rock or country western or show tunes—they'll play anything. On this particular day when I was browsing the shelves, I think I might have heard the most horrible "music" in my life. I put "music" in quotes because I wonder if what I heard could be classified as such. It was sounds, strange sounds, smashed together. At one point there was grunting and what sounded like a toaster being beaten by a frying pan and then what sounded like a trash can being thrown down a flight of stairs. The "music" had no rhythm, really, or melody for that matter. It was loud, annoying, and awful. When I went to the counter to pay for my selections, I pointed to the ceiling and asked the kid behind the counter, "Who is this?" I'll never forget his reply. He looked at me with a big beaming smile and said, "Ed Melnick! Isn't it great?"

That instant, I wanted to say, "No. Turn that crap off. I can't think." Instead, I paused for a moment and realized that this kid loved it. This young guy thought it was beautiful. What I thought was complete trash, he found as treasure. Who's to say if the music I listen to is horrible and this music contained true beauty? It's true what they say, I guess; beauty really is in the eye of the beholder. The question is, what kind of beholder am I? Am I the kind of beholder who only finds beauty in the things that others have taught me is beautiful? From the moment we are born, we are taught what is good and what is bad. We've been taught to associate the color white with good and the color black with bad, for example. We've been trained to think that beautiful things are good, and ugly things are bad. Therefore, we have taught ourselves the crippling lie that our worth is based on our looks. Are we good or are we bad? Just look in the mirror to find out.

True beauty is not found in the mirror. True beauty is found somewhere else. We usually miss true beauty because we're too busy playing the rejection game, but Jesus didn't miss it. I think one of the reasons Jesus hung out with the losers of this world is that Jesus was able to see the beauty in people we overlook most of the time. I think Jesus is like the kid at The Exchange, who lives his life to the sounds of a completely different tune.

> And as he sat at dinner in Levi's house, many tax collectors and sinners were also sitting with Jesus and his disciples—for there were many who followed him. When the scribes and the Pharisees saw that he was eating with sinners and tax collectors, they said to his disciples, "Why does he eat with tax collectors and sinners?" When Jesus heard this, he said to them, "Those who are well have no need of a physician, but those who are sick, I have come to call not the righteous but sinners" (Mark 2:15-17).

This might sound really, really corny, but true beauty is not found on the outside. Yeah, I know, that's what your mom keeps telling you. But it's true! True beauty is only found on the inside, and this is what Jesus is saying in this passage. Jesus didn't come so we might have a new line of cosmetics that we could use to cover our own inadequacies and deficiencies and no longer experience rejection. That was what the Pharisees did. That was their game—mask wearing. No. Jesus did not come so we could look better. Jesus came to bring the antidote for rejection. The antidote isn't another coat of paint; the antidote is koinonia. It's connecting, belonging to the body of Christ. It is communion with others in the kingdom of God. Jesus came so that the kingdom of God would be near. By participating in that kingdom, we find acceptance and belonging just as we are. If *surrender* is the antidote, our escape hatch from *fear*, then *acceptance* is our answer to *rejection*.

How can we help to create a community of acceptance when we are so geared toward making instant judgments about people? How can we help to create authentic, intimate community? How can we be a bridge of grace and acceptance in a world so steeped in criticism and rejection? How can I even begin to train myself not to make snap judgments about people based on how they look? Is there any way to shape a faith community in such a way that anyone who connects with it feels loved and cared for?

I think the answer still seems to be the same. To practice koinonia we need to get dirty. And getting dirty means stepping into other people's dirt. To understand someone else's world, to understand someone's insides and not just their outsides, to see their inner beauty and, in turn, begin to train ourselves to accept people, we might have to immerse ourselves in other people's lives. We might have to surrender some time to people who are very different from us. If you're in community with people whose world is really your world, then have you really gotten dirty? Or are you just having your little "you have to look like me" clique? Maybe sharing in community with those who are just like you only reaffirms our twisted cultural values. If surrender is the antidote for fear, then seeking *uncommonality* is the solution to rejection, not commonality. Perhaps seeking uncommonality is the doorway to belonging. Think of it this way: if I think I'm experiencing belonging, but I look around the room and everyone looks exactly like I do (white and geeky), then perhaps I'm mistaking belonging with corporate mask-wearing. John Wesley called this "the love of self." In other words, if the only people you love or even associate with look like you, you really just love yourself. Jesus put it this way:

> "For if you love those how love you, what reward do you have? Do not even the tax collectors do the same? And if you greet only your brothers and sisters, what more are you doing than others? Do not even the Gentiles do the same?" (Matthew 5:46-47).

I think Jesus is saying, "Open your eyes and look around. Are you really sharing in authentic koinonia, or are you doing what everyone else does: hanging out with people who look and act just like you?" Look around: are we in a community based on grace and acceptance, or is this community based on a certain standard, a certain beauty contest, so to speak. Perhaps, to actually get dirty and begin to learn how to stop the rejection game, we have to share in koinonia with those who are completely different from us.

My wife Brenda, who is a United Methodist pastor as well, was recently appointed to a new church in a small mill town along the Allegheny River. Her experience has been similar to many other pastors who are newly appointed out of seminary. She has the daunting task of helping this small church of twenty-five people sustain itself. One Sunday, with all the passion and energy she could muster, she preached on the parable of the good Samaritan. Afterwards, as she stood in the back greeting people as they left, she noticed something going on outside. When she went to investigate, she found Bob, a local man, and his dog, Bobby, sitting on the front steps of the church. Much to her dismay, most of the congregation, being used to Bob and Bobby, were "passing by on the other side" as they made their way out of the church and into their cars. During a meeting the next evening, Brenda inquired about what the church could do for Bob and Bobby. One older woman groaned and rolled her eyes, "Oh, that's just Bob," she said. "He's harmless, but he'll have to get cleaned up if he's to be coming into *this* church."

I asked Brenda if she responded by quoting Dwayne from *Little Miss Sunshine*. She said *no*.

She's such a good pastor.

Uncommonality

We seem to put so much energy and concentration into finding commonality. And by commonality, I don't mean that we're always seeking harmony or unity. I mean we are prone to seeking out sameness, or people who conform to our little checklist of what a person should be. We go out of our way to make sure that those with whom we share everything surround us: same clothes, same color skin, same economic class, same values, same beliefs, same practice of those beliefs, etc. This isn't love; this is conformity. This is the pursuit of commonality, which you might think is what Christ is calling us to, but it's not. It is really a farce. We aren't called to find common ground with others. We're called to love even those with whom we share no common ground at all. I think this is exactly where Christ wants us to go—to places of uncommon ground. We need to be people who seek uncommonality.

The church should be the place where we experience uncommonality. The church should be the place where we learn not to make snap judgments about people. The church should essentially be uncommonality training. Instead, we do just the opposite. We take people and put them in little groups of commonality. The youth have youth group.

The singles have a singles' group. The men have the men's group. The women have the women's group. The divorced mothers have the divorced mothers' group. And on and on and on. Then we print our little brochure bragging that we've achieved full commonality. Everyone is cliqued up. Find your clique or find another church. Is this really the vision of the kingdom of God? Is the kingdom of God really meant to be broken up into commonality groups?

When I read the book of Acts, which is the story of the early church, I don't find any commonality groups. All I can find is story after story of uncommon people loving one another and trying to fulfill God's mission in this world. Look at who joins the Way: Simon the magician, an Ethiopian eunuch, and a Philippian jail guard, not to mention a Pharisee of the Pharisees. If in your mind you see the early church as a group of American white suburbanites, you better think again. These folks had very little in common at all. All they had was Jesus Christ. But that was enough to start a movement (or continue a movement, really) that changed the world. Look at Acts 2:44. It says, "All who believed were together and had all things in common . . . ." I'm sure none of us can really say what this looked like, but one thing I know for a fact: "all things in common" does not mean that they were all the same. Because who is this? Who are all these people who are sharing their possessions with each other? Look back at the beginning of Acts 2 and see:

> Now there were devout Jews from every nation under heaven living in Jerusalem. And at this sound the crowd gathered and was bewildered, because each one heard them speaking in the native language of each. Amazed and astonished, they asked, "Are not all these who are speaking Galileans? And how is it that we hear, each of us, in our own language? Parthians, Medes, Elemites, and residents of Mesopotamia, Judea and Cappadocia, Pontus and Asia, Phrygia and Pamphylia, Egypt and the parts of Libya belonging to Cyrene, and visitors from Rome, both Jews and proselytes, Cretans and Arabs—in our own languages we hear them speaking about God's deeds of power" (Acts 2:5-11).

Who was gathering every day for the sharing of the apostles' teaching, for fellowship, for the breaking of bread, and for prayer? Who had "all things in common?" These were people from across the known world. The people that had gathered there and in turn experienced the power of the Holy Spirit at Pentecost were people who were completely different from one another. These people dressed differently, acted differently, and spoke completely different languages. Yet, although they had little in common, the Holy Spirit gave them the only thing they needed to bind them together.

I believe this is one of the reasons the early church exploded across the region. When new people encountered this group of uncommon people and shared in koinonia, their hearts couldn't help breaking. They saw the kingdom of God, and they wanted to be part of it. Could you imagine what it must have been like to walk into this community? You would see something you never see. You would think you'd died and gone to heaven. And the truth is, you might not have died, but you would have gone to heaven—heaven on earth. Isn't that going to happen to all of us when we pass on and step into God's great banquet? Are we not going to see faces of uncommonality? And isn't that what we want here and now when we talk about the kingdom of God, heaven on earth? I've never gotten anywhere close to seeing what those folks saw on the day of Pentecost, but I have seen little bite-sized pieces. Something happens, the Holy Spirit moves within us, when we look around at the people gathered for koinonia and we see faces that do not look like our own.

At Hot Metal, where we worship in the round, it's not rare to look across the room and see a face looking back at you that is different— older or younger, of another race or another economic class, rich, or homeless. There, in a small, smelly cafeteria on the third floor of the Goodwill building on Pittsburgh's South Side, people of all different kinds have come, not because they seek the latest fad. A deep inner longing to be in community with those with whom we have nothing at all in common draws us. I think we long for this because when we stop and think about the reason we've gathered, it's certainly not because we all have the same interests, the same hobbies, or even the same worldview. We haven't gathered for the beauty contest. We've all gathered to worship the same God, the Risen Christ, and that's all we need. I don't know about you, but the thought of Mark, an older

Pittsburgh Steelers fan, standing next to Skull, a young guitar player for a punk-rock band, standing next to Gerald, a rapper and ex-drug dealer, standing next to Kathy, a caring, straight-laced mother of two who lives in the suburbs, standing next to Jason, a recovering alcoholic, standing next to Mike, who's six foot eight, standing next to Alberto, who delivers pizzas, owns a motorcycle, and was born in Mexico, all singing "I Love You, Lord"—brings me to my knees. When I think of how many times I've wept while witnessing the uncommon gathering at Hot Metal, I can only imagine what it must have been like for those first followers of the Way when they gathered in that place with people from around the world and found themselves all speaking the same language. I can't think of a modern equivalent. I guess it would be like being in JFK airport at rush hour, waiting for your plane with people from around the world, with people who have absolutely no commonality, and suddenly everyone begins to share "all things in common." That would be powerful. That kind of event would change your life and motivate you to experience it again and again and again.

I believe that experiencing holy moments of uncommonality does three things to us. First, it makes us hungry for more, and we begin to seek out community with those who are different from us. Before we know it, we find ourselves in the most unlikely of places, talking with and sharing with the most unlikely of people. It might be a bowling alley, a retirement home, or a roadside dive. It might be down the street, across the country, or down a dirt road of a third-world country. Seeing the real beauty within others makes us hungry for more uncommon connections. Second, I believe moments of uncommonality teach us the meaning of grace and unconditional love. They teach us not to make snap judgments about other people. We begin to learn by immersing ourselves in uncommonality. We learn not to reject those whom our culture might deem ugly, useless, or unworthy. This, in turn, teaches us not to reject ourselves. This is the very act of finding ourselves in Christ. The third thing I think happens to us when we experience communion in a diverse community is we see more clearly *missio dei* (God's mission) here on earth. Sharing a meal with a new friend in Cambodia, India, Chiapas, or Timbuktu opens our eyes to God's ways and how God intends for us to share in those ways. In other words, if the early church truly grew because of its willingness to share in koinonia with anyone and everyone, causing its movement to become contagious and spread in every direction, then how does the kingdom of God spread today? Answer: exactly the same way. The bad news is there is no magical program or special ministry package that comes with fancy brochures and a video that will help your church seek uncommonality. We simply become people who seek others who are different from us. We do it by getting ourselves dirty and immersing ourselves in dirty people's lives. These things can and will happen to us when we put ourselves in uncommon places with uncommon people. This is the awesome power of koinonia with the outcasts, the losers, and the Bobs and Bobbies of this world.

The funny thing is, when we seek uncommonality and we actually find ourselves sharing in koinonia with people with whom we thought we had nothing in common, we come to realize that we actually have plenty in common. Uncommonality is just a myth, really, just a fallacy. We all have enough in common as children of God to be able to connect with one another in a meaningful way. The Holy Spirit binds us, not common ground or uncommon ground. However, because of our self-centered bent toward people who only look and act like ourselves, we ought to be intentional about seeking relationships that will stretch us. It's almost like this: when we seek out uncommon friends, we get surprised by commonality. And it's a great blessing.

It is this reason that my favorite holiday is Halloween and not Christmas. Although the Christmas season is always a blessing, Christmas Day is anti-climatic, isn't it? On Christmas Day, we all celebrate by huddling together in our homes and opening a bunch of gifts we've gotten ourselves. Christmas is nice, but Halloween is a community event. Halloween, in my town anyway, is the opposite of Christmas Day, and I love it. Like so many other communities in America, it is Halloween night when all of the kids and families of the neighborhood dress up in fun costumes and go door-to-door for trick or treating. Instead of huddling in our homes, we're all on the street, meeting each other, connecting with our neighbors, maybe for the only time all year long, and we're sharing candy and conversation with one another. For me, Halloween night is a great community party, and although some

Christians shun Halloween, I always sense that the kingdom of God is near when I'm trick or treating with my kids.

Bible Fight Club

One Sunday after worship, Amanda and Eric approached me. Amanda is a twenty-something with a mix of blond, black, and red hair. Eric has a black and blue tint to his hair that I've always wanted and have never had the nerve to get. Both Eric and Amanda are eccentric, artsy, and love old monster movies and rock-n-roll. Eric and Amanda are the kind of people I want to be when I grow up. So, when they came to me on that Sunday morning with an idea, I listened.

"Pastor Jim," Amanda started, "We want to get involved in a Bible study. Is this church going to have any Bible studies?"

I quickly got defensive. That's what we pastors do when it is insinuated that we're not providing the right products. "We already have Bible studies going on right now," I replied. "We have a study on Monday night, a study about Ephesians on Wednesday, and a study on Romans on Saturday nights at the coffee shop."

Eric looked at me, politely, but pained, and said to me very gently and kindly, "Yeah, we went to those."

"It's just not what we're looking for, Pastor Jim," Amanda said.

"Well, what is it you're looking for? Maybe we can get something new going."

That's when Amanda got bold. I braced myself. "To be honest, Pastor Jim, I don't like those other studies because it's just a bunch of people sitting around nodding at one other. I mean, everyone is just agreeing with each other. I feel like we're being brain-washed or something."

"What are you suggesting?" I replied, kind of confused.

"I don't know. We want to be part of a Bible study where no one agrees."

"No one agrees?"

"Sure, why don't we have a study where everyone comes

and we fight?"

"Fight?"

"Yeah. We fight about the Bible and theology and stuff."

"Uh . . . All right."

And Bible Fight Club was born.

When we started Bible Fight Club, the purpose wasn't, and still isn't, discipleship. The club isn't meant to be a place where we grow in our faith, per se. The point to the gathering is not to worship, not to study scripture, and not to fellowship. The point to Bible Fight Club is to fight. It is a time for debate, a time for wrestling, and for doubting and questioning the things that we sometimes hold as gospel. Sometimes this even means *the* gospel. For our church, it has been a place where atheists, agnostics, believers, non-believers, and believers of other faiths can come and toss in their two cents. To make sure that the argument is valued and that people are valued as well, we made the following rules:

Bible Fight Club Rules:

1. **Respect**: this means we love and respect each other, but not necessarily each other's opinions. Also, respect the argument by being a good listener.

2. **Say Anything**: this means that there is no judging and no holding grudges. The tattoo shop basement is a safe place where anything can be said. This rule has made it possible for people to play devil's advocate—taking a side of an argument, they might not completely agree with just to see where the line of thinking goes.

3. **Fight**: this rule means that all those in attendance must participate. No one is allowed to come and observe. Observers and silent on-lookers skew the argument by inadvertently becoming a kind of jury that people try to convince.

4. **Get to the Point**: there are no speeches allowed. People are to make their point and shut up so that others can speak. Also, a good arguer listens as often as he or she speaks.

5. **Honor the Argument**: phrases like, "Well, it's all just a mystery" or "We'll never know the answer, so why bother arguing" do not honor the argument. Take a side and fight, no matter how mysterious you think the subject is.

6. **Admit When You've Been Hit**: At the end of the evening, we take time to talk about the argument. Everyone must share something that was said that made him or her think. Sometimes this might mean having some humility. But that's the point.

As the moderator, it has been interesting to see where certain arguments go. We have tackled such topics as hell, the devil, church and culture, politics, healing, money, angels, and on and on. We have people show up armed with books and commentaries. We have people show up who want to defend their territory. All different kinds of folks, with different backgrounds and faiths, have joined the argument. We've had Jews, Muslims, Buddhists and people who practice witchcraft. We've had Christians who would identify themselves as liberal and Christians who come from a more fundamentalist background. During one rather heated argument about the Trinity, one guy stood up, red-faced, threw his Bible on the ground in anger and cried out, "What is wrong with you people?! Aren't we all Christians here?!" At which point, three or four people shouted back at him: "No!" He slowly sat back down in his seat, scratching his hand and looking around the room suspiciously. He had come for a Bible study, not a fight.

My very favorite Bible Fight Club was the one in which we argued about the existence of ghosts. It was crazy. We actually found some professional ghost chasers who joined us for the fight. They brought a few pictures that kind of looked like there might be ghosts in them, and their personal testimony. What made the fight so interesting is where it led. Fighting about the existence of ghosts turned into an argument about the supernatural, which turned into a discussion about whether or not God answers prayer and heals people. The fight that evening was down-right hilarious and at the same time challenging. It did what it was meant to do. It made us think and connected us with one another.

Some might say this kind of study only helps to confuse people and doesn't send a clear message of what the gospel is. But I would say that Bible Fight Club has been a better forum for sharing the love of Christ than any other Bible study that I have ever attended. Many times, Bible studies can turn into indoctrination sessions, where the goal is to make everyone "be like us." Doesn't that kind of stuff turn everyone off? Because the Fight Club is more about valuing the fight than winning the fight, we all walk out invigorated and excited rather than demoralized. We have had many people return a week after a good fight and share how they did more research on the topic. We've had others say that the fight caused them actually to pick up the Bible and read it for the first time. Are we worshipping Buddha? No, Jesus is Lord. Do we compromise our faith by subscribing to some sort of watered-down relativism? No, Jesus is Lord. Are we encouraging people to think for themselves? Yes. Are we practicing the spiritual discipline of listening so that we earn the right to be heard? Yes. Are we creating a doorway through which people can come and experience the kingdom of God? Yes. We have had more people than I can count join us for worship on Sunday morning, where we preach the gospel, because they got to participate in a discussion on faith in the basement of a tattoo shop.

The most important part of the evening comes at the very end. Observing the last rule at the end of the fight, participants must share one thing that someone else said that was not in-line with their opinion and made them think. This has been a powerful time as we go around the room and honor the fight and the fighters. The act of admitting that someone else had a good point or a challenging argument is a gesture of humility. That small gesture can be the vehicle in which the group binds together. Suddenly, everyone is on the same playing field. We become one not because we all agreed, but because we all contributed to the argument. During this time of humility and encouragement, the Holy Spirit moves among us, and by the time we're done, we realize that although we're all coming from different points of view, we have actually shared in koinonia through the fight. Arguing over God and theology and the Bible doesn't have to be a bitter, hateful thing we try to avoid. Fighting over the Bible, struggling with the real questions of faith, can actually be a time of koinonia, binding ourselves to one another through our differing opinions. This is possible as long as we come to the fight, not ready to win the argument, but ready to value the argument. This is possible as long as we walk into the fight willing to listen, willing to acknowledge that we don't know everything, and willing to have humility.

The "One-up" Game

Humility is the key to enjoying community. Humility is how we come to form relationships that are intimate and genuine. Humility is how trust forms, how forgiveness happens, and how we find understanding. If communion occurs when we surrender ourselves to God, then authentic community forms when we humble ourselves before each other. The act of surrendering to God and the act of putting others before ourselves is essentially the same act. It is an act of surrender—surrendering our pride, our need to be first, our need to be right, or our need to be the center of attention. If rejection is the enemy, then we are saved from rejection by belonging to God's community, the kingdom of God, a kingdom that can only be experienced through Christ, the Humbled One. Was he not humbled, even to death—even death on a cross?

Sometimes, we as rejected people get things mixed up and, motivated by the hurt and brokenness we carry from being rejected, we try to create our own community. This is impossible and always fails. Only through Christ do we form genuine community. When we try to play God and create our own community, we set expectations upon it and others that can almost never be matched. This is not humility. This is community built on someone's arrogance. Living in Christian community means living in humility, thankfulness, and repentance. That's all we can really do. We can't control community. We can't make people be friends or love and care for each other. All we can do is, as is written in Micah 6:8, " . . . what does the LORD require of you but to do justice, and to love kindness, and to walk humbly with your God?" This means coming humbly to the cross and bowing down, handing our very lives over to the will of God. Dietrich Bonhoeffer has written *Life Together*, which, in my mind, is the definitive book on sharing in Christian community. This is how he puts it:

"God hates visionary dreaming; it makes the dreamer proud and pretentious. The man who fashions a visionary idea of community demands that it be realized by God, by others, and by himself. He enters the community of Christians with his demands, sets up his own laws, and judges the brethren and God Himself accordingly. He stands adamant, a living reproach to all others in the circle of brethren. He acts as if he is the creator of the Christian community, as if his dream binds men together. When things do not go his way, he calls the effort a failure. When his ideal picture is destroyed, he sees the community going to smash. So he becomes first a rejecter of his brethren, then a rejecter of God, and finally the despairing rejecter of himself" (Bonhoeffer, *Life Together* [San Francisco: Harper & Row, 1954], 7-28).

How do we conjure up authentic Christian community? We don't. Because frankly we can't. Really, we are not responsible for creating Christian community. It isn't up to the church to make people love each other, or even get along. As soon as we cast a vision of a Christian Utopia, we've condemned ourselves to endless frustration and disappointment. What we can do, however, is practice koinonia, which is completely different from casting a vision of community. Koinonia is the bottom-up approach to being the church. It is the way of the humble, the truth of the repentant, and the life of the thankful. Practicing koinonia happens when we simply humble ourselves before others. Again, we can't make other people be humble. All we can do is be humble ourselves. But humility is contagious. When people gather in humility and we bind together by the power of the Holy Spirit, then we enjoy authentic Christian community. But it is never formed by us; Christ always forms it.

One of the great barriers that we face in trying to enjoy authentic community is the One-up Game. I'm pretty sure you know what I mean by the One-up Game. It is that game we play with one another fueled by our constant need to find ways in which we're better than one another. There is a hilarious sketch series on Saturday Night Live that exemplifies the One-up Game. Penelope can never let anyone have a moment. If someone is going to Italy for two months, she's going for four months. If someone's cat has died, she has had a cat die that she's given birth to—and on and on. We laugh because we can see how ridiculous Penelope is behaving, always trying to one-up others, but the one-up game can be more subtle and sometimes not so funny. In some vain attempt to find value and worth for ourselves, we are always comparing ourselves to others. It is actually out of the fear we have of being rejected that we compare ourselves and subsequently try to one-up.

Ironically, when we play the One-up Game, we negate the possibility of enjoying authentic community and thereby miss finding the grace and acceptance we long for. Here's why: First, real community is never built on fear or rejection. Secondly, and most importantly, the fact that no one is better than anyone else makes being one-up an illusion and a lie. I don't care if we're rich, good looking, super smart, or super popular, it is a downright dirty lie to think we're better than anyone else. How can a real relationship be based on a lie? It can't. One-up isn't about communion; it's about self. It's about glorifying the self. One-up is anti-communion, which leads to death.

This becomes most destructive in the church, where we've managed to take the One-up Game to incredibly heinous extremes. Think about how many ways the church and the people of the church have used our presumed faith as a step-up, exalting ourselves above others. For over two hundred years now, the church of America has had a missional mind-set that has had the tendency to be one-up. We have gone into far-off countries, invaded ancient cultures, and insisted that they change to be like us. When we were in Chiapas, for example, we attended an evening church service in a building that looked very familiar and sang familiar songs accompanied by an organ. The people sat stoically, staring straight ahead. Afterwards, the people gathered outside of the church for ice cream and someone pulled out an old drum. That's when we sang, danced, laughed and had a great time. The kingdom was near. Too bad it had to happen outside the church. Someone, at some time, had come along and bullied these people into behaving "better," behaving like us.

> "Do nothing from selfish ambition or conceit, but in humility regard others as better than yourselves" (Philippians 2:3).

May I propose in the light of Philippians 2, that if we are sent to a people and we cannot "regard others better than ourselves," then perhaps we go in the name of ourselves and not in the name of Christ. Are we really missionaries, ambassadors of Christ, if we play one-up? I wonder if we're really ready for what it means to be followers of Christ. We might be ready to go to the streets of our dark world, but are we ready to consider others better than ourselves? We might be ready to go to the tattooed, the pierced, the drunk, and the addicted, but are we ready to consider them better than ourselves? We might be ready to go into the trailer parks, the city projects, and the neighborhoods on the wrong side of the tracks, but are we ready to consider the people who live there better than ourselves? Prostitutes, the homeless, the mentally unstable—better than us?

We have to. The moment we put ourselves one-up, we drop Jesus like an old newspaper, and we go for our own warped glory or demented need to be wanted. When we come together as people seeking our own glory, clamoring to be on top, we find ourselves thirsting for the very acceptance and grace we desperately need. But when we come together with the same humility that Jesus had, stepping down to be below others rather than stepping up, then community flourishes and, by the power of the Holy Spirit, love, grace, and acceptance fill us. Then we can avoid the rejections that constantly pursue us.

This all begins with humility, a stepping down. Following Jesus is actually the Stepping-down Game. I find it interesting sometimes to look up the origin of words in the dictionary, and I think it's important to note here that the root of the word *humility* is the Latin *humus*, which means "low to the earth." This is where we not only get our English words *humility* and *humble*, but also the words *humor* and *human*. Could it be that when we practice humility, step down "low to the earth," we're doing that which is most human? Is the One-up Game, therefore, an activity for non-humans like hard-hearted creatures, life-sucking zombies, or the walking dead? Could it be that when we share in humor, in a laugh or a joke, that we're actually connecting with one another on a most human level? Maybe. So, go ahead and joke around. It just might be a means of grace.

Backhand vs. Righteous Indignation

A few months ago, while the boys in the punk band The Last Hope were on tour, they found themselves in a situation where stepping down into humility became a bridge to the kingdom of God in a very real way. They were slated to do a show in a seedy bar in the middle of nowhere with two other bands. The first band to go on was a so-called "Christian punk band" called Righteous Indignation. The second band was called Backhand, and its members were anything but Christian. Backhand, as a matter of fact, liked to stick with songs about Satan, worshipping Satan, and all things related to Satan. And then there was The Last Hope, which is made up of six guys who are members of Hot Metal. As I've already said, although these guys look tough on the out-side, their hearts are like gold. And their faithfulness always amazes me as they try to live out the gospel in the midst of a very rough counter-culture.

As Righteous Indignation took the stage, The Last Hope guys knew they were in for a long night. Righteous Indignation thought of them-selves as being unashamed of the gospel, if you know what I mean. Their lyrics were overtly evangelistic, if not obnoxiously judgmental. Between each song, the band members took turns preaching to the small crowd of drunk people. Each one would chastise those at the bar who were drinking. "We used to live empty lives like yours," the lead singer decreed, "but since we met Jesus Christ, now we live right. And so should you." Then they would launch into a loud, screaming version of "God's Gonna Getcha" or something like that. Every word this group uttered and every song they sang had only one message, and although they intended it to be "Jesus is Lord," it wasn't. Instead, it was, "We are better than you because we are Christians." These kids saw being a Christian as being one-up, and they made every effort to propagate their superiority. As the guys from The Last Hope sat at their table with their forehands in their hands, wishing they could disappear, the guys in Backhand, who were sitting at the bar, got increasingly more agitated. By the time Righteous Indignation had finished playing, they were so lathered up they couldn't wait to get on stage.

Once Backhand got onto the stage and got their instruments plugged in, they were ready to go to war. And that's exactly what they did. The group launched into songs filled with hate and profanity, screaming and shouting with a fueled passion. Between each song, the guys in Backhand mocked Righteous Indignation and Christians in general. "This one goes out to all you self-righteous Christians out

DIRTY WORD

there," the lead singer squawked as they cranked out another tune about worshipping Satan. As Backhand's set drew on, things got even worse, and tensions ran high. While the guys in Righteous Indignation all left in disgust, the guys in The Last Hope were torn. Even though they were equally as insulted by Backhand's treatment of their beliefs, they decided to stick around, remain quiet, and see how they could be used.

Their faithfulness paid off. As Backhand wrapped up one of its more raucous songs, the bass player broke one of his strings. It was the perfect opportunity. Between the songs, as Backhand debated how to continue their set without a bass, Dylan, who plays the bass for The Last Hope, ran out to the trailer and returned with his own bass and handed it up to the Backhand bassist. The bassist, a little bit stunned, grabbed the bass with a grunted "thanks," plugged in, and the set continued. Every time I hear Dylan tell this story, I wish I could have experienced this moment. Can you imagine? Here's a punk-rock band singing songs about Satan with Dylan's bass, which is covered with all kinds of stickers lifting up Christ. That must have been hilarious. And meanwhile, outside in the parking lot, Righteous Indignation waited, hands over their ears, for the set to finish up so they could return.

The Last Hope ended the evening with what they said was their best show of the tour. Their passions were high, but they kept their anger to themselves. Afterwards, as the guys from Righteous Indignation angrily threw their stuff into their van and drove off in a huff, The Last Hope just hung out. They took time to help their new friends in Backhand break down their stuff and load up their trailer. The musicians in Backhand couldn't believe it, and when they were finished, the asked The Last Hope if they wanted to grab a beer. There was no evangelistic plan or overarching objective. The Last Hope simply sat and hung out with the guys from Backhand. They made friends. The boys in The Last Hope were as unashamed of the gospel as the guys in Righteous Indignation. It's not the meaning of unashamed where they would differ; it's their definition of the gospel. One band sees the gospel as a chance to be one-up; the other sees it as a way of life. The gospel is never lived out "one-up;" it is only lived as Christ lived: in humility.

The Communion Meal

It amazes me sometimes how the way we behave in church is completely different from the way we behave the rest of the week. For some reason, when we walk into a church, we become different people. All of the life is sucked out of us and we take on that "don't bother me, I'm trying to be holy'" look. Is church supposed to be a place where we go to pretend to be holy, or is it meant to be a celebration, a place to connect with the kingdom? We would never dream, for instance, of renting a movie, going over to a friend's house, sitting on the couch and watching the movie, and then getting up and walking out the door without saying a word. Why do we do this in church? We show up at eleven, sit down, listen to a sermon and maybe a bell choir, put some money in a plate, then get up and go home without saying a word to anyone beyond, "Good morning." What is that? Do we all really believe that having a relationship with God, or even practicing empty religion, is all about sitting in a big room with an organ for an hour on Sunday? I wonder if sometimes we go through the ritual of worship and the ritual of the Lord's Supper, but we never actually experience communion with Jesus Christ. I mean, aren't we the body of Christ? Aren't we Christ's representatives in the world? Is the Lord's Supper meant to be a solemn act between God and me alone? I don't think so. If it were, wouldn't we take communion by ourselves? No. It's meant to be shared when we are together because it binds us together. So, if communion is a binding act—binding us as a community—why would we make it so boring and empty of life?

This brings me to the key to sharing in authentic community: time. Building relationships that have depth just flat out takes time. You can't come together at eleven on a Sunday, leave at noon, say two words to one another, and expect to have authentic intimate community. It takes an investment of time in one another. People of other cultures understand this truth and therefore spend lots of time together, sharing a meal for example. If you've ever been to Germany, or many other countries like it, you know that once you sit down for dinner, your evening is over. For a rushed American, it seems to take forever. But for a German, it's all about taking time. In America, we rush through meals to get to the next big thing. In other cultures, the meal is the big thing. So it was with the early church. For those early followers of the Way, communion was rarely shared as we share it today, all by itself in a worship service and a liturgy. Many times, the church in Acts and beyond shared the bread and the cup before or after a meal. This is no accident. First, they were probably following Jesus' original intent, the bread and the cup almost an excuse to come together. It is the coming together that Jesus wanted to see happen. Secondly, they knew that if relationships were built and therefore the kingdom was built, then it was going to take some time. Church certainly wasn't eleven to noon on Sunday. It was a lifestyle, an ongoing event.

Are we patient enough in the church today to take time to share in a communion meal together? Or are we too busy? Do we have to go? Do we have a thing to go to?

Nothing compares to sitting around the dining room table and sharing a meal, a conversation, and a game of cards. It is where complete strangers become more than friends. It is around the table that we become family. As I was growing up, and especially when our family was living in Germany, we spent many evenings sitting around the dining room table playing Monopoly, Risk, or Crazy Eights. In my young adult years, since I lived so far away from home, I found a surrogate table at the Eddings' home. Jeff had grown up with the same dining-room-table ritual, where games were played, games that, many times, they had invented. An evening of cards at the Eddings house was a big event, very much like the piñata party I had experienced in Mexico. We were friends and family, sitting around the table joking, cussing, eating, and drinking. Other than my own house, I have never felt more at home than at Mr. and Mrs. E's house. One thing's for sure: there was always plenty to eat. Mrs. E always made sure you didn't go hungry.

On one particular evening, as we sat around shooting the breeze and throwing cards on the table, the conversation, for some odd reason, moved to spiritual gifts. In the middle of the discussion, Cathy (Mrs. E.) came into the dining room, oven mitt grasping a piping hot pan of brownies, or cookies, or something—I forget. But as she cut the dessert and distributed its delights around the table, she lamented how she had no idea what her spiritual gifts were. We just looked at her. It couldn't have been more obvious. But sometimes what is obvious to others we can't seem to see ourselves.

"Well, it's pretty obvious, isn't it? Mrs. E., one of your gifts is hospitality, that's for sure," I said.

"Hospitality? That's a gift?" she asked.

"Sure," I replied as I wolfed down a hot baked good. "The way you make everyone who comes to your home feel welcome. The way you never seem to have enough space around this table at Thanksgiving because you invite just about everyone you meet, even people you've never met before. The way you make us all feel like this home is our home. Think about it. Why is it that people who are here for the first time feel free to go to your refrigerator and make themselves a sandwich? You've been blessed with the great gift of hospitality, and in our world where people are lonely and searching, it probably is the most precious of all gifts. You could make a big impact on our fractured world with that gift."

Mrs. E. paused for a moment, smiled, and returned to the kitchen. For Cathy, it is pure joy for her to exercise her spiritual gift. And for Hot Metal, it has meant everything. Only about six months after our Bob Evans breakfast, Jeff and I decided to try doing a once-a-month worship service at our newly acquired Goodwill building space. We paid the rent out of our own pockets, called a few friends, and showed up on a Sunday afternoon with a couple of guitars, a Bible, and the communion elements. Our first service had just twenty participants. We'd probably still have twenty participants if it weren't for one additional thing: Mrs. E brought a small crock-pot filled with beef barbecue. From that first service until now, Mr. and Mrs. E. have shown up for worship with lunch for all, and it has been the key to our church's growth. Nothing compares to sitting down with someone and sharing lunch with them. It is the perfect way to get to know someone new and to get to know more intimately those you already know. It has been fun to watch people connect over a bowl of wedding soup, or a sloppy Joe or everyone's favorite—tacos. It has been equally fun to watch Mr. and Mrs. E. go from a small crock-pot to two crock-pots to a large roaster to four or five large roasters. They have gone from feeding twenty to feeding well over three hundred each and every Sunday. They do it all out of that same tiny kitchen where Mrs. E. has been working her magic for many, many years. God has taken Mrs. E.'s gift and has used it to help the lonely, the broken, and the rejected to find acceptance and healing in the kingdom of God.

We have found that the communion meal helps people connect with one another and share in koinonia, but there is a by-product of sharing in community through a meal that we, at first, didn't expect. We've always thought that it was the church's responsibility to cast the vision and reveal to everyone the needs of the world, creating ministries and programs to fill those needs. This isn't always the case. When people sit down, share a meal, and really take time to get to know one another, the needs of the world, the real needs are revealed. Our eyes are opened and we are moved to action, not because of some catchy cool ministry program, but because we come face to face with need. When Linda (whose roof is leaking and water is dripping into her bedroom) sits down with Dugan (who is a young engineer looking to use his gifts for God's glory), a roof somehow gets fixed. When Karen, who works at a daycare center, spending all day with children, sits down with Pam, who is new in town and looking for something to do, a night of karaoke bowling somehow happens. When Willy and Marie, who live under the Tenth Street Bridge and have been robbed multiple times, sit down with Kate, who's just returned from helping people on the Gulf Coast and wants to be a light for Christ, a ministry to the homeless is born. See, when the church hires program directors and such and tries to command ministry programs from the top down, then there is very little ownership, and the ministry runs more like a business or a ministry store. However, when the church creates a place where there is the possibility of authentic community, then the Holy Spirit moves. Instead of programs being created, people are actually loved and cared for. Isn't that really the goal?

> But you are a chosen race, a royal priesthood, a holy nation, God's own people, in order that you may proclaim the mighty acts of him who called you out of darkness into his marvelous light. Once you were not a people, but now you are God's people; once you had not received mercy, but now you have received mercy (1 Peter 2:9-10).

I used to read these two verses very differently than I do now that I have witnessed the fruit of practicing koinonia. I used to think that this meant we are all priests, individually. But that's not what the verse says. We read the scripture through the spectacles of modern individualism. Ambitious, self-promoting individualists like us didn't write these verses. People who lived in community wrote these verses. Now I see more clearly. I think the writer is telling us that we are "a royal priesthood," together. When people enter in and experience koinonia in our midst, the priesthood ministers to them. It is the body of Christ, working as one, that is the pastor, not you or me all alone.

The problem is rejection. The solution is not an expensive program. The solution is love and grace found in practicing koinonia. How does the church conjure up koinonia? We don't. We surrender ourselves, our time, our priorities, and our stuff to God and to one another. We live lives of humility, thanksgiving, and repentance. We practice hospitality. We gather around the table, welcoming all those who want to come, and we break bread together, beggars all. No games. No one-up. And we take time. Lots and lots of time. This means living a life, not centered on ourselves, but centered on serving and loving others. This means surrender. This means sacrifice. This means stepping down.

The Wonderful Life

Every year around Christmas time, our family, like almost every American family, watches the classic *It's a Wonderful Life*, where George Bailey gets to see what the world would be like without him. I always promise myself I won't cry. I've seen the dumb movie a million times, and the thing's pretty syrupy to begin with. I should be mature enough by now not to cry, I tell myself. It seems like every year we do the same thing. We mouth all of the lines that we know by heart, which is almost all of them, and we always shout at the television when George gets married and he's headed out of town on his honeymoon. We always yell, "Don't do it, George! Don't stop! Keep on going! Get out of town and live your life!" But George never listens to us. He always stops the taxi as he sees the crowd gathered around his Building Savings and Loan. He gets out, and he essentially gives up his wants and desires for the good of the people of Bedford Falls. Again and again, we yell at the television for George to wise up, and again and again, George doesn't listen, and he sticks around his hometown, caring for people. He pours out and pours out until it finally drives him to the edge. I always seem to hold the tears in when he encounters Clarence, his guardian angel, and as he sees the world without him, I'm unmoved. Even when George prays for his life back, and when he runs through town shouting, "Merry Christmas," I'm fine. When he runs into the house, finds his kids, and when his wife returns with half the town, I'm good. And when everyone in town is gathered in the house, and they're all singing "Hark the Herald Angels Sing," I think to myself, "Hey, I did it. I made it. I guess I'm not going to cry this year. All right."

Then the music stops, and I suddenly remember, "Oh, no. Not the brother. Not Harry. I forgot about the brother. Hold on. Hold on!" And Harry Bailey, George's brother, who George saved from drowning at the age of eight, returns. Harry Bailey, whom George let go ahead of him to college. Harry Bailey, who got to live, in a sense, George's dream life, raises the glass and says, "To my big brother, George Bailey. The richest man in town." Everyone cheers, and I'm a mess, tears streaming down my cheeks. That's when we realize that we've had things all backwards. George is the one who has it right. It's not about me; it's about others. It's about sacrificing me, and my stuff, and my plans, and even my dreams so that others may find the living waters of acceptance and grace only found in authentic community. It's about laying down my life for my brothers and sisters so that koinonia in Jesus Christ may defeat one of the most crippling demons in the world, the demon of rejection that rules our lives and drives us in to lonely, isolated places. The kingdom of God is near in Bedford Falls, not because George Bailey has a "Jesus Agenda," handing out tracts and preaching on the streets, but because George Bailey exemplifies what it means to live the gospel and to be a missionary in his little, boring town.

PART 6:
SHARING IN COMPASSION

Zombies!

One Sunday morning not too long ago, our small band of misfits—
some would call us a drama team—sat on the floor in a circle staring
at one another. The discussion during Tuesday night's creative arts
meeting had been lively, provocative, and quite meaningful. However,
the conversation never materialized into the formation of a drama that
we could use to proclaim the word during this particular Sunday worship. We, as an artistic team, have never had any high-falootin' expectations for our pieces. If we've come up with a drama that works and
proclaims the message, we give it try. If we have no ideas or only very
bad ideas, we don't do a drama. No big deal. We're always struggling
with the tension that exists between being honest and authentic, but at
the same time doing our best and creating quality dramas. On this particular Sunday, we had just about given up. When that happens, we
usually sit slightly deflated on the floor and discuss how the scripture
passage for that week relates to our lives.

The verse, if I remember correctly, was Philippians 3:10: "I want to know Christ and the power of his resurrection and the sharing of his sufferings by becoming like him in his death, if somehow I may attain the resurrection from the dead." As we shared, each of us expressed how we could relate to Paul, and we all, in different ways, wished that we had more situations in our lives where we could share in Christ's sufferings. We talked about all the ways our comforts and our luxuries get in the way of truly experiencing suffering. It seemed like we each had a story about how we had gone on a mission trip to a third-world country and had been surprised by joy. One young guy, Chris, shared how he had never seen such joy as he saw from the people he met in Central America. He commented that even though they had nothing, they had something we did not.

> "You know," Chris said, "I wish we could make a trade with the people I met. We could help them find a way to get clean water to their village, and in return they could teach us how to be human again."
>
> "What do you mean?" I prodded.
>
> "I mean, I came back from my trip changed by that joy I saw. Or at least I thought I was changed. Now, I don't know. It's like I've been bitten by the zombies of luxury and comfort, and now I feel like I'm just walking around like I was before. Hopeless, aimless, empty." Chris looked around the circle at the other faces, all of us knowing exactly how he felt. Then he smiled and cracked, "Back to the ol' pursuit of happiness."

Five minutes later, we had our drama.

I don't know if it was the most poignant drama we ever did, but it might have been the most pertinent. Chris and the gang came running into the sanctuary, yelling and screaming, knocking over chairs and tables, searching for a place to hide from the "zombies" that were slowly slouching toward them. The zombies were hilarious. The zombies of comfort, luxury, materialism, indifference, hopelessness, and the like, slobbered and drooled their way toward the cowering young people. Each zombie used its powers to draw the young people out of hiding. The zombie of materialism, for example, kept naming department stores in a low, growling, monotone voice, until one of the young ladies popped her head up and said, "You know, guys, this is kind of boring. I think I'm going to go shopping." The young lady wandered out from behind the table, much to the dismay of the others, was bitten by the zombie, quickly turned into a zombie herself and joined the mindless foot-draggers. There was a mix of laughter and knowing groans from the congregation. More than one person in the room could relate to being bitten by the zombies.

For some strange reason, we have all bought into the lie that to have meaning and purpose in our lives, and therefore have hope, we need to be comfortable, successful, and have our best life now. Unfortunately, nothing could be further from the truth. The things that we pursue—wealth, luxury, stuff—are actually obstacles that keep us from experiencing true joy. We think joy comes from having all the things that we desire and that we must avoid suffering at all costs. Suffering, we think, is what causes us to be in despair. This is not so. Look at Romans 5:3-5:

> "And not only that, but we also boast in our sufferings, knowing that suffering produces endurance, and endurance produces character, and character produces hope, and hope does not disappoint us, because God's love has been poured into our hearts through the Holy Spirit that has been given to us" (Romans 5:3-5).

We all want our lives to count. We all want our lives to matter somehow. That is why purpose and meaning are deep needs that must be fulfilled in our lives. We can pursue money, fame, material objects, notoriety, popularity, or power, but when it all comes down to it, those things are temporary and ultimately have no value. When we try to give our lives worth and meaning by going after these things, we find ourselves still longing, walking around like lifeless zombies. There really is only one thing that matters, one thing that really makes life worth living and gives meaning to our lives. There is only one thing that brings us hope, and that thing is love. How does one experience love? Through suffering with. Galatians 5:6 sums it up well: " . . . the only thing that counts is faith working through love." Everything else is vanity. Everything else leaves us zombie-fied.

As in the last two chapters, we're again going to wrestle with what it means to practice koinonia. In this chapter, we'll talk about what it means to share in koinonia with suffering and the importance this has in our lives. Two chapters ago, I showed how if one is to share in communion with God, one must surrender. The enemy was fear. In the last chapter, I proposed that if one is to share in authentic community with others, one must humble herself or himself. The enemy was rejection. In this chapter, I want to convey the importance of seeking out ways to "suffer with." The enemy in this chapter is hopelessness. Are fear, rejection, and hopelessness interconnected? Oh yes. Our faith isn't compartmentalized into little sections like this book is. With fear comes rejection, with hopelessness comes fear, with rejection comes hopelessness and on and on. Each works together to draw us away from an ever-loving, grace-filled God and into the dark hell of isolation and alienation.

La-Z-Boy Reclining

Years ago when I was still doing youth ministry, I had a brush with the reality of the hell of hopelessness in a most frightening way. A young girl named Jennie began coming to youth-group meetings after I had sent out thirty or forty handwritten notes to young people I found on an old church roster. Jennie was the only one to respond. While the church was located in the more affluent neighborhood of Oakmont, Jennie lived on the other side of the river in a small mill town, and, although at times she felt out of place, she became a youth-group regular. Jennie's life was a bit rougher than the other youth who attended. As a result, much of my time and many of my prayers went toward Jennie and her family. One evening during youth group, Jennie had a prayer request that went beyond her, which might have been a first and made me pay extra attention. There was a friend of hers, Lisa, who had stopped going to school. Jennie was concerned that her friend wouldn't graduate. As Jennie described the situation, it seemed to me that Lisa needed a good talking to by the most convincing person I could think of—me. I told Jennie that I would pay her friend a visit.

The next day at about two in the afternoon, I found myself on the front porch of a dilapidated, unkempt home. My heart broke. Old toys, used tires, and rusty bicycles were scattered across a little patch of land between the overgrown shrubs and the porch. It was clear that I was about to enter someone else's brokenness. I rang the doorbell and stood on the porch for what seemed like forever. I knew someone was home; I could hear people shouting at each other inside. I debated coming back another time, but I said a little prayer and knocked on the door again. There was shouting again, then:

"Who is it?"

I froze. I thought about running as fast as I could to my car, but I meekly answered, "It's Jim. I'm the new youth director at the church where Jennie . . . "

I was interrupted. "Door's open."

I turned the knob and slowly crept inside. It was like walking into a haunted house. I thought at any moment a guy with a hockey mask and a chainsaw was going to pop out. The living room was completely dark, as were the dining room and the kitchen. All the shades were drawn; all the lights were off. The only light in the house came from not one but two very large television sets. One TV took up almost the whole wall in the living room; the other took up almost a whole wall in the dining room. Trash was everywhere. Old newspapers, magazines, paper plates, and ashtrays were scattered throughout the house. But where there were elements of squalor, there were also elements of luxury. The house was nice and cool, almost frigid, because the central air conditioning was working overtime. There, sitting on a massive La-Z-Boy recliner was Lisa, cigarette in one hand and TV clicker in the other. She had a bag of chips and a can of coke sitting on the end table beside her, and she gazed at the TV like a mindless zombie. This girl was living the American dream! The television even had surround sound!

Without looking away from the television, she said in a monotone, almost ghostly voice, "Come on in." I navigated the room as if it were an obstacle course, climbing over all sorts of old, neglected pieces of nothing. When I got across the room and sat down on the only sliver of sofa left to sit on, I looked into the dining room and saw what I assumed was Lisa's mother, sitting in front of her own TV, puffing on her own cigarette. A fish tank, which hadn't been cleaned in years, gurgled behind her head and emanated a green glow. The whole scene was right out of some sort of horror movie. I still get the creeps just thinking back on it. I turned back to Lisa and tried to play cool youth pastor.

"So, hey, Lisa . . . Jennie was telling me that you're into art. That sounds cool. Really cool." Of course, Lisa just kept watching TV, a blank stare on her face. I scrambled for a moment as I tried to think of something to say, wondered why I had come, and what I could possibly do in this situation. As I thought through my line of discussion, I looked at Lisa more closely. Her hair was so black that it had no doubt been dyed. Her skin was so pale I wondered she had last been outside. Her fingernails were well-manicured and painted blood red.

"So, what are you watching?" I tried to find some conversation starter.

Lisa just grunted in response, totally immersed in the mindless television program that had her in a trance. I glanced into the dining room, hoping to get some help from her mother. Surely, her mother was concerned. There was nothing, just the ongoing drone of the other television in the background.

"Jennie told me that you've stopped going to school. Is that true?" I asked.

She finally glanced at me, annoyed. "I guess. Is that why you're here?"

"Don't you think maybe you should go?"

Lisa rolled her eyes, took a drag from her cigarette, smirked at me, and uttered the word that seems to be drilled into the heads of every teenager by our indifferent culture these days: "Whatever."

Whatever. Whatever. Whatever. Isn't that the mantra of so many Americans today, even those who identify themselves as Christians? Whatever? Who cares? What does it matter? What is the point to all of this? So many of us have been bitten by the zombies and life has been sucked out of us. Our motivation is gone, and the fire is extinguished. There is something about our comfortable, privileged lives that has put us to sleep. With so many luxuries, conveniences, and pleasures, what else can we really say but, "Whatever"? Isn't this what happened to the church in Laodicea? It's as if luxury acts as a wet blanket, putting out the fire of our faith. Look at the letter in Revelation 3:

"I know your works; you are neither cold nor hot. I wish that you were either cold or hot. So, because you are lukewarm, and neither cold nor hot, I am about to spit you out of my mouth. For you say, 'I am rich, I have prospered, and I need nothing.' You do not realize that you are wretched, pitiable, poor, blind, and naked" (Rev. 3:15-17).

Lisa shouldn't be sitting in a darkened living room at two in the afternoon watching TV and smoking cigarettes. Life is too short. It's easy to look at Lisa and shake our heads in disgust, but don't we all find ourselves in that same La-Z-Boy recliner? There are times when we can be just like Lisa. We simply give up. Our hearts become hard. We become indifferent, jaded to the needs of the world, to life altogether, and we decide to focus on our own comforts and desires. Sadly, at the same time, we abandon all hope and wander into the misery of our own personal, darkened living room.

When I think of the phrase "suffer with," I think of that day at Lisa's house. If hell is a place where there is no hope, I think I might have walked right into it. It was like being in the land of the living dead. When I finally finished my visit, I left the house like a wounded soldier and limped down the sidewalk holding my side, looking for a place to collapse. It was as if the same malaise had infected me that had paralyzed Lisa. I wandered onto a nearby soccer field, fell down on my knees, and cried. I'm still not sure whether my tears were tears of empathy or tears of conviction. Did I feel sorry for Lisa, or did I feel sorry for myself? Either way, I felt Lisa's pain, I had suffered with her, and it hurt. The alienation and isolation that I experienced for even a moment felt so cold, so dark, and so awful, it took me a while to recover. Maybe someone else might have seen it differently. Maybe someone else would have walked into that house, seen a lazy person wasting her life, and been unaffected. I don't know. For some reason, I felt this person's pain in a very palpable way, and I made a decision as I knelt on the grass: I'd work at finding a way to be a bridge of hope for Lisa.

Later that year, I got my chance to follow through on that promise. I had been planning a summer youth mission trip, and, a week before we were to leave, one of the youth decided to back out, leaving me with an empty seat. Lisa went with us on the mission trip that summer, and

God did something amazing inside of her. While most of our group painted on ladders in an elderly woman's kitchen, Lisa spent the whole mission trip pushing the woman around the house in her wheelchair, talking with her, caring for her, and, what else, watching TV with her. But this kind of TV watching was different. In a way, I believe that Lisa was practicing koinonia with that woman, sharing in her suffering. As a result, she experienced hope. By the end of the week, we saw Lisa smiling. As we drove home, she asked me when the next trip was. See, having compassion, or suffering with, isn't just about helping someone; it's more than that. Having compassion is about sharing in someone's suffering, and in turn sharing hope as well. In a bizarre way, when I connected with Lisa's suffering, and when Lisa connected with the elderly woman's suffering, we somehow connected with the suffering of Jesus, who is the source of all hope.

'Cuz or Cause

When I was a kid, my brother and I would do this thing we called "play outside." It was great. We'd play kick-the-can in the alley, hide-and-go-seek until after dark, and there would always be a pick-up game of ball. Sometimes we'd do something stupid, and we'd get in trouble. Whether it was throwing rocks at cars, climbing up on the garage roof, or stuffing a cat in a garbage can and rolling it down a hill, we did a bunch of stuff that just didn't make much sense. Whenever we were busted and had to give an answer as to why we did what we did, we always said the same thing, "Just 'cuz."

> Mom: Why did you moon the cops?
>
> Kids: I don't know. Just 'cuz.
>
> Dad: Why did you ride your bikes into the military training zone?
>
> Kids: Just 'cuz.
>
> Mom: Why did you paint the neighbor's dog?
>
> Kids: Just 'cuz.

Being a kid can sometimes be one big stupid mistake after another. When we're young, we do things *just 'cuz*. There are times when we do things that have no real purpose or meaning. But, life isn't meant to be lived from beginning to end *just 'cuz*. We have all been created to be part of something more than *just 'cuz*. Sadly, too many people, especially young people, walk through their lives just like Lisa, sitting around *just 'cuz*. Ask a random person on the street why he or she is alive, and you might get the same answer: *just 'cuz*. Why do you get up in the morning? Why do you go to work or school? *Just 'cuz. Just 'cuz.* Now, there's nothing wrong with *just 'cuz*. Some of the best moments in life have no rhyme or reason, but there has to be a deeper purpose for our lives than *just 'cuz*.

Strangely enough, there's another word spelled exactly the same as *'cuz* (cause), but with a completely opposite meaning. That word is *cause* (cawze). *Cause* is completely different from *cuz*. Cause is the motivation. *Cause* is the reason. *Cause* is the goal and the purpose. It's also the journey. *Cause* can be like a fire in the bones; no matter how much you try to hold it in, it wants to punch out of you. A cause is a reason to get up in the morning. A cause is a reason to live. Sometimes we get involved in something, and we completely forget why we're doing it. This happens all the time in church. You get people who are completely hateful to one another, ask them why they come, and you'll probably get *just cuz*. Even when we start out living for a cause, it can quickly turn into *just 'cuz*.

A fellow United Methodist pastor, Craig Forsythe, is appointed to a local church in our conference, but he is also one of the brave few who serve as chaplains in the United States Armed Services. I see Craig every now and then, usually at our annual conference. When I do, he is dressed proudly in his Army issued BDUs. They called them fatigues when my dad served in the army, but now they call them BDUs (Battle Dress Uniform). The last time I saw Craig, I noticed something interesting about his uniform as we talked. All of the emblems that adorn his BDUs were attached with Velcro. The cloth placards that bore his name, rank, and company were velcroed on his uniform. Even the honors he had received, even the American flag, were attached with Velcro.

"Craig," I said, "What the heck? What's with the Velcro?"

"It's simple," he said. "In case I get captured by the enemy, I can just rip off my identity, and no one knows who I am."

Then I noticed the cross of Christ, pinned to his chest.

"What about that? Does that come off?"

"No, no," he replied. "That stays. That stays. We don't use Velcro with the cross. It's on there no matter what."

I was amazed. In a world where most people prize their identity, here is Craig. In a world where most people would never dream of parting with their name, their rank, their associations, or their accolades, here is Craig. In a world where most people are attached to the cross of Christ with Velcro, quickly removing it whenever it becomes inconvenient or dangerous, here is Craig. Talk about being motivated by a cause! Craig knows what his cause is—his cause is the cross of Christ. Craig isn't going back to active duty in a few months "just 'cuz." Craig goes for the cause. Despite the danger it puts him in, he has it pinned permanently upon his chest.

For many Christians, the cause of Christ is an empty phrase that has more political meaning than anything else. Ask any Christian what his or her cause is, and you might get the proverbial, "My cause is the cause of Christ." But what does that mean? Is the cause of Christ really our cause that we've slapped Jesus' name on to help our cause to succeed? Is the cause of Christ to display a cross in our front lawn and vote for a certain candidate? Or does the cause of Christ have deeper meaning? Is the cause of Christ really the cause of the cross? And is the cause of Christ really the cause of hope, which comes from going to the cross ourselves and suffering with others? This is why Craig is going back to active duty. His cause isn't to be a walking billboard for Jesus. He intends to be an agent of hope in a part of the world that really needs hope right now. He goes as an ambassador of hope to people in what might be considered a hopeless situation. And how will he fulfill this cause? By having compassion, which means "to suffer with."

And that's the difference between 'cuz and cause. 'Cuz is about me. Cause is about others. 'Cuz is about indifference. Cause is about caring. 'Cuz is about meaninglessness. Cause is about hope. 'Cuz is about being comfortable and safe. Cause is about suffering with. Cause can get a bit dangerous. *'Cuz* is about whatever. *Cause* is about everything and anything that really has a worth at all.

What is the cause of Christ? Is it not to save the world? That's his name right? The name *Jesus* actually means "God saves." Jesus is the Savior. But is that the end of his identity? No. Remember, he has another name, *Emmanuel,* which means "God with us." And this *God saves* who is *God with us* endured the cross in what we call the Passion, which means "the suffering." Could it be that the cause of Christ is to save the world by suffering with us? If our cause is Jesus' cause, then does it not make sense that our mission is to live Christ's life and to suffer with others? Could it be that this is how we find salvation? Could it be that this is how we overcome the hell of hopelessness? Could it be that this is how we find the kingdom of heaven, here and now, by suffering with? Is this why all Paul wanted in Philippians 3:10 was "to know Christ's sufferings" because it is through Christ's sufferings that we find heaven?

When we suffer with others, we practice koinonia, and therefore connecting with God, which brings hope. What does it mean, to "suffering with others"? What does it mean to have compassion? Although I do not claim to be a man who lives a life of compassion 24/7, I believe it means more than simply feeling sorry for others, having sympathy, or helping someone. Certainly, there is nothing wrong with having sympathy or helping people, but I think that having compassion means more. In Octavia Butler's book, *Parable of the Sower,* the main character, Lauren Olamina, suffers from a futuristic disease called Hyperempathy syndrome, where she is able to feel other people's pain. If someone else is punched, she feels it. If someone else is bleeding, she bleeds. If someone else is shot, she staggers to the ground. Butler's book, of course, is science fiction, but do you wonder what the world would be like if we really could feel each other's pain? How would we treat each other? How quickly would we rush to someone's aid? How much closer would we be to one another?

I believe that we practice koinonia when we actually connect with one another's pain. We share in compassion when we share our own suffering with someone else's suffering. Sometimes when we have sympathy or we lend a helping hand, we do so from a one-up position. Helping people out of arrogance is not compassion. Writing a check after watching a moving video is not compassion. It's nice, but it's not "suffering with." Telling people how they can fix their problems is not compassion. When we come together in humility and share our brokenness with one another, when we connect our suffering with other's suffering, then we come from a bottom-up position, which actually brings real hope. That's compassion.

When I was a youth pastor, we would participate in the Thirty Hour Famine each year as a way of raising funds for the hungry around the world. It is a good program run by World Vision, and it helps young people connect with the suffering of others by going without food for thirty hours. Every year, we would gather at the church for a lock-in, play some games, and learn about the injustices that were occurring around the world. On one such evening, we played a game in which youth got into small groups and created their own country. Once each group had a name, flag, and a national anthem, we divided the world's resources among the groups. The outcome was quite interesting. Just as in the real world, some of the countries ended up with great wealth, while other countries came out with nothing. For fun, we added the specter of nuclear weapons in the form of a Nerf football, which went to the wealthiest country. Once we passed out all of the resources and wealth and nuclear weapons, the groups worked together to solve the problem of poverty and injustice before time ran out and those in the poorer countries died of malnutrition and disease. I will never forget what happened next. The young people in the wealthiest country felt pretty good about themselves; they were real jerks, actually. They laughed and made fun of those in the countries that ended up with nothing. Once they had had their laughs, and time was running out, they decided to help by sharing their wealth and resources with the other countries, but they did it in a most creative, or maybe uncreative, way. The kids delivered food, water, and shelter by dropping it onto the other groups from their Nerf ball. As the youth from the rich country ran around the room, laughing, dropping water bottles and plastic donuts from their nuclear weapon, the kids in the poorer countries began to reject the gifts, throwing the shared supplies back at them.

As I watched the chaos, I couldn't help thinking about what it really means to have compassion. Do we really have compassion, or do we help people the way these youth were helping? Do we still hold a conquering and controlling view of compassion, left over from colonialism? We will help you, but on our terms? Or do we humbly step into other people's suffering from the position of our own suffering? Dropping water out of a nuclear warhead is not compassion. Dropping food out of a nuclear warhead is not compassion. Dropping Jesus out of a nuclear warhead is not compassion. Jesus never comes from the top-down. He always comes from the bottom-up. Jesus saves. Not the Jesus we've created in our own image to bully, conquer, and control people. But Jesus, the God who suffers with us, saves. It is by connecting our suffering with others rather than dropping Jesus on others that we truly practice koinonia. Then, we connect with the cross. Then, the kingdom of God is near.

The Curse of Luxury

I discovered something interesting about people while serving in youth ministry. In my quest to help young people grow in their faith, I became frustrated because kids, for the most part, were indifferent and blasé about Jesus. No matter how wonderful a program or event we put on, kids were unresponsive. However, I always looked forward to that annual event when, for one week at least, the Holy Spirit moved and youths' faith exploded. That one week out of the year was the week during the summer when we went on the mission trip. Every year we piled the youth group into the church van and traveled to West Virginia. As young people encountered other people's hurt, their cynical hearts melted, and God had room to work. During those trips my own heart melted. At the end of the week, we all stood and shared how important the trip was to our faith and how we would see the world with new eyes. What I discovered was that, although these young people lived in the luxurious bubble of suburban America and had everything they could ever want and need and more, there was something they deeply desired, something we all desire: suffering with.

We are all just like Lisa, whether we sit in the dark in our living room watching television, or we sit in a church pew staring at the ceiling counting ceiling tiles. We all are starving for hope, and though we think we might find it in material possessions or our luxuries, we actually find hope when we connect our brokenness with other's brokenness. This is why luxury can be a doorway to hopelessness rather than the kingdom of God. We have a need for our lives to have purpose and meaning. Instead of filling that need with that which is the most meaningful, we try to bring fulfillment to our lives with stuff.

Just as fear can be the enemy of communion and rejection the enemy of community, luxury can be the enemy of compassion, and therefore the enemy of hope as well.

Need:	Curse:
Communion	Fear
Community	Rejection
Compassion	Luxury

This is why the mission trips were always so powerful for the youth. We were, for at least a week, forcibly removed from our luxuries. We slept on the floor, ate small meals, took cold showers, and worked our tails off. As a result, we were freed to experience the blessing of suffering with others. The blessing of suffering with was so much better than any luxury we had back home that many times we would talk about dreading our return home. We knew that the flame of our faith, which had burst to life under the fuel of compassion, would certainly go dim once again under the wet blanket of luxury. It is this revelation that finally made me ask: if luxury is a barrier to experiencing compassion, and therefore a barrier to experiencing the hope of Christ the Sufferer, then why can't we remove ourselves from luxury and make church a mission trip all year long? Why does the mission trip have to be just for one week during the summer? Why can't church be a mission trip? Isn't that really what church is supposed to be? We need church to be a place that pulls us away from luxuries and compels us toward compassion. Unfortunately, church is often the place where, as we drive through the parking lot and see the nice cars, then walk through the marble hallways, enjoying the fancy mood lighting and sipping a tasty latte, we are actually pulled away from compassion and compelled toward luxury.

How in the world, in our culture of luxury and comfort, do we create a bridge to the God of hope by helping people share in compassion?

In our society, the mere suggestion is complete lunacy. Why would people put themselves in a situation where they had to suffer with someone else, or share their sufferings with someone else? Yet, this is exactly what a faith community should be. I believe this is one of the main reasons why people get involved in our faith community. Although we don't have any special lights, projection screens, or even clean floors, there is something about a faith community that shares its sufferings with one another that helps people feel safe and welcome. Remember, the church isn't a store, and we're not about filling seats with people. We're about helping people find belonging in the kingdom of God. How does this happen? Not through luxury, but by suffering with.

Up until we started Hot Metal, I had not really experienced belonging through suffering with. In fact, if you would have approached me with the idea that suffering with was a key to sharing in communion with God and others, I would have told you that you were nuts. We are taught, not only by our culture, but also by our seminary training, to cover over our hurts and to keep our pain to ourselves. We've been taught to keep church nice, clean, and tidy. Church has to be slick. But in the past few years, as our faith community has blossomed, I've come to feel a deep sense of community and belonging, mostly because others know me and my brokenness, and I know theirs.

One Sunday morning, a guy named Eric approached me after worship and wondered if he could talk with me some time. Later that week, we sat down at the local Starbucks, drank coffee, and Eric shared some of his brokenness with me. As he shared, quite openly and candidly, I felt a bit uncomfortable at first. I almost felt as if I were being set up on *Candid Camera*. To my surprise, Eric's childhood experiences were very similar to mine. As a result, Eric had some brokenness that was very similar to mine. As Eric told me of his experiences, I was moved to tears. Somehow, some way, by the power of the Spirit, we connected to the cross of Christ while connecting with each other's hurt over a cup of coffee. To me, this was a moment of holiness. To me, this was a moment of sanctification. Eric and I have become close friends, and I've gone with him to a few AA meetings. We have found belonging, not through some religious affiliation or through our luxury, but through the connection we shared with the cross through our suffering with one another. As with many other guys in our faith community, we've been willing, with grace, to step into each other's crap. This act of stepping in each other's crap builds real community, and real compassion happens.

I had an older pastor come to me not too long ago, looking for some imagery for a brochure he was designing. He had a great idea for a new program he was cooking up, and he wanted to convey the idea in a fancy brochure. The idea was that church was like a plant. For the plant to grow, it needed to be in fertile ground. I said, "How about a picture of a pile of poop?" Of course, he looked at me as if I had two heads. "No, no," he said, "it needs to be an image that conveys life, like a seed or a vine or fruit, or something." "What's more fertile than poop?" I pushed him. "Don't the best plants grow in manure? Don't farmers cover their fields with crap so something good will grow?" But it was out of the question. There was no way he was going to associate his new ministry idea with a pile of crap. He was completely offended and disappointed that I didn't have any good ideas for him. Well, let me tell you something. I dare say that ministry almost always happens in the crap of life. You can put up as many chandeliers and fancy paintings as you want, and your luxurious palace of a church building might bring in some audience members and some big bucks in the offering plate. However, real spiritual growth doesn't happen in the squeaky-clean confines of luxury. Real spiritual growth happens in the smelly piles of manure. It happens when we dare to get dirty and walk through each other's crap.

Hold Your Nose, This Stuff Might Stink

If hell is hopelessness and Jesus Christ, the Sufferer, is our hope, then our mission is to live Christ's life and to suffer with others. What does this mean for our ecclesiology? How does the church suffer with others, and how do we create a space that encourages and empowers people to share in compassion? Sharing our brokenness with one another isn't only counter-cultural; it's completely alien to the church life that we have known. We've been taught to be silent in church, to sit, listen, and not to make waves by dumping our problems on each other. What is more, the church has perpetuated the myth that it is the pastor's job to do the caring and compassion while everyone else watches and then analyzes his or her performance. In many ways, pastors are the guilty parties here, because they sometimes fly around like super-pastors, doing all the work and not letting anyone else participate because they're unqualified. When we were down in Biloxi, Mississippi after Katrina hit, we met a young pastor who had a pick-up truck, trunk of tools, and a group of youth. The young pastor had a lot of energy and was certainly helping people out, but every time we saw his group, he was up on a ladder working his tail off, and the rest of his group was sitting on the ground watching. This is a shame because when a pastor does all of the caring, it robs the group of the opportunity of actually being the body of Christ, participating in the mission of God, and experiencing the hope that suffering with brings. Instead of being a pastor-centered church, how can we become the body of Christ? How do we help people participate in the kingdom of God through being in koinonia with suffering? How do we help people to act rather than just watch?

I don't think there are any hard, fast rules or "how tos" when it comes to getting people involved in compassion. It probably, and most importantly, comes from a missional mindset that is already instilled in the DNA of the church. If most of the people in the faith community understand that church is a 24/7 mission trip, you're already on your way. It's really a change of assumptions rather than a list of steps. However, I do think there are three common means to sharing in authentic compassion: listening and seeing, letting others in, and becoming last. Just as the means of grace work to help us connect with God, these means can help us engage in compassion. Listening and seeing. Letting others in. Becoming last. All three are insanely difficult, at times exhausting, but eternally rewarding. None of these sound like any fun, do they? Know why? Because these three things aren't about me- they require self-denial and sacrifice. This might not sound like what you sign up for when you decide to follow Jesus Christ, but it is. And it is good.

The first one, listening to and seeing others, might be the simplest but most selfless thing we can do. You know, your ear might be the most precious gift that you can give someone else. Actually seeing clearly someone's suffering is all that compassion needs to take place. In a world where it's all about me—my ideas, my website, my product, and

Sharing in Koinonia—Compassion

Listening and seeing

Letting others in

Becoming last

my thing—how precious is it to find someone who will sit, take time out, and listen, I mean really listen? It is rare. If you've ever sat down with someone and tried to listen without thinking about what you were going to say, what advice you could give, or what response you will make, you know how hard it is. Listening is the art of valuing someone else's words, thoughts, ideas, worries, and concerns above your own. Listening might be the simplest way to consider others better than ourselves. Personally, I'm no good at it, which is my loss, really. I usually justify myself by saying that I'm introverted, but the truth is I'm so selfish. My wife Brenda, on the other hand, not only has a gift for listening and valuing others, but also she has the uncanny knack of bumping into people who are desperate to dump their hurts on someone. And she always seems ready to let them. I was amazed just a few days ago when we got on an airplane and sat down next to a woman who evidently wanted to talk. Of course, I rolled my eyes and buried myself in my newspaper. But Brenda just sat and listened. She didn't pretend to listen, which is easy to detect, but she really listened to this woman. On and on this woman talked, for almost all of the three-hour plane ride. I would have exploded. But not Brenda. As we walked through the terminal, instead of complaining about the woman, she chastised me for missing an opportunity to receive the gift of this woman's interesting life. Brenda wondered at her story, her struggles, and all of the places life had taken her. Brenda could have easily tuned the lady out, put on her headphones, or buried her face in a magazine like I did, but instead she saw the value of listening, not only for the woman's sake, but for her own as well. Both women were blessed as one shared and the other listened.

The second part of listening and seeing is really just listening with our eyes. When our eyes fall upon the overlooked, hurting person that no one else sees, we're actually moving toward compassion. This might sound like a no-brainer, but how often do we avoid seeing the hurts, pains, and brokenness that is everywhere around us? How often do we drive through neighborhoods with our eyes open to the poverty that is so close to us? How often do we put ourselves in places where our eyes see the suffering of others? Our luxurious culture makes it easier and easier for us to avoid seeing the real suffering that is all around us. This is part of our goal with our Saturday afternoon homeless ministry—helping people to see. We go out to the streets, partly to fill stomachs with food, but also to expose ourselves to other people's suffering, for our sakes and for the sake of the homeless. We need to see as much as they need to be seen.

Are there ways that the church can facilitate listening and seeing so that compassion reigns? Yes and no. On one hand, there is no way to program listening; people listen to each other or they don't. We can't make people see the suffering of this world. On the other hand, the church can provide a venue or a space where listening can happen. Also, the church can put itself in a place where it can't help seeing. Just about every Sunday I am amazed at how much time people take for one another at Hot Metal. Though our service ends and lunch begins at about 12:30 pm, many parishioners sit down and listen until 2:30-3:00 pm. Often, we have to kick people out, even on Sunday afternoons in the fall when the Steelers are playing! Of course, some folks rush out before lunch; we don't force people to stick around. But we've created a space where listening can take place. By positioning our faith community in an urban setting—in bars, coffee shops, tattoo shops, and on the streets—we can't help seeing suffering every day. I know not every church has the benefit of being on the streets of the city, but no matter where your church is located, it is not far from suffering. Is it possible that your faith community has been avoiding actually seeing the suffering, intentionally or unintentionally? Is there a nearby neighborhood that people consider the wrong side of the tracks? Is there a place that you avoid? Putting yourself and your faith community in a place where you're forced to see the suffering in this dark world and taking time to listen when you'd much rather be doing something else are the keys to sharing in koinonia with Christ's sufferings. There is no special DVD, PowerPoint, or forty-day program. There is simply listening and seeing.

The second key to sharing in compassion is a willingness to let other people into our own brokenness. This isn't easy. Opening up and sharing our brokenness with other people can be quite difficult. As hard as it is to step into someone else's pain, to listen and to see others, it is equally hard to let someone else step into our pain, to let others listen and see our real selves. This is how we suffer *with*—we expose our own suffering. We have to be willing to let other people in. We have to be willing to let other people suffer with us. We need to surrender our pride, admit we have hurt, and let others step into it. However, this is tough. Often, it can be infinitely easier to help than to be helped. If that is the case, however, then wouldn't the willingness to let others know our hurt be a selfless, Christ-like act? Conversely, when we cover over our own dirt and pretend that we don't stink ourselves, are we not building up barriers that keep people from knowing our brokenness and negating the opportunity to share in compassion, thereby alienating and isolating ourselves?

If there is any group of people better at covering over their brokenness than church people, I haven't found them. We are so good at hiding, aren't we? We're so good at pretending that we have it all together, that everything's fine. Somehow, I think we've bought into the myth that our brokenness is the result of our faithlessness. As a result, we gather for church, big fake smiles on our faces, and sometimes we even gather to help others, but we very rarely share in one another's brokenness. It might be our pride. Perhaps we're ashamed. Whatever the case, we rip ourselves off from the blessing of sharing in compassion with one another when we pretend that everything's fine. How can the church become a place where people feel safe to open up their hurts with one another? Again, there is no recipe. But I believe it starts with the pastors. If the pastors are willing to lay their sufferings down before God and all those gathered, then the rest of the fellowship has a better chance of becoming a place where grace reigns and people feel free to let others in.

Lastly, if the church is to share in koinonia with those who suffer, if we are to share in koinonia with the last, the least, and the lost, then we need to become the last, the least, and the lost. Don't worry, this shouldn't be very difficult because we already are the last, the least, and the lost. If somehow we believe that we are the first, the best, and the discovered, then we're really buying into a lie, a cheesy façade. We need to step out from behind that façade and into the lives of the suffering. If we want to reach out to the poor, then we ourselves have to be poor. We have to live among the poor. If we want to reach out to the broken, then we ourselves have to live with the broken. If we want to reach the lost, then we ourselves have to get lost. This really is what it means to follow Jesus Christ.

Listening. Sharing our brokenness. Being the last, the least, and the lost. This is suffering with. This is compassion. "Where is the charity?" you might ask. Where is the help? Where is the benevolence? Don't worry; it'll happen. For when we finally place ourselves in the midst of real suffering and brokenness and not just watch a TV show about it, it cannot help compelling us to do something. When we truly listen, we cannot help responding. When we genuinely open ourselves up to others, we cannot help connecting, in deep meaningful ways, and in turn, responding. When we put ourselves last, become least, and get lost, we cannot help becoming vessels in which God can pour grace, love, and power and really deliver what we all need—hope.

When I think about how hard it is follow Christ in our world today, I think about Joshua's dilemma. He was the leader of a people who had to make some tough choices. They liked to follow the Lord when it was convenient for them, but when the going got tough, they turned to other gods that they still worshiped. Finally, Joshua had enough of their two-timing disloyalty, and he makes this speech in Joshua 24:14-15:

> "Now therefore revere the LORD and serve him in sincerity and in faithfulness; put away the gods that your ancestors served beyond the River and in Egypt, and serve the LORD. Now if you are unwilling to serve the LORD, choose this day whom you will serve, whether the gods your ancestors served in the region beyond the River or the gods of the Amorites in whose land you are living; but as for me and my household, we will serve the LORD" (Joshua 24:14-15).

Perhaps the same charge should be posed to us, the church in America. Perhaps we should take a long, hard look at what it really means to follow Jesus Christ, the Sufferer, and then decide. If serving the Lord seems undesirable, if suffering with seems too much to stomach, then let's be honest and admit it. If we are bowing down to the idols of wealth and luxury, then let us stop pretending that we are Christians, and let's give the terms back to those who actually live Christ's life. But if we choose to echo Joshua's passionate plea, "as for me and my household, we will serve the LORD," then let us carry through on that declaration and be willing to sit and listen, to see others' suffering, genuinely to care for others, to let other people into our own hurt, and to go to the last, the least, and the lost by becoming the last, the least, and the lost. If this sounds impossible, it pretty much is. Unfortunately, the alternative is to live life, sitting on the Lay-Z-Boy recliner, as a hopeless zombie.

Norman Rockwell

On the wall in my office, I have a framed poster-size replica of the Norman Rockwell mosaic that graces a wall, floor to ceiling, in the United Nations building in New York City. Every day as I walk into my office, the diverse faces that look back at me in that tiled mosaic greet me. There are faces from around the world in that picture. There is a little girl from Ireland, an old man from India, a young boy from Japan, and a mother from Ethiopia. Every now and then, I pause and take it in for a moment, pondering their charge to me that appears in gold letters near the bottom: "Do unto others as you would have them do onto you." How painful it is sometimes, to do unto others as I would have them do to me. As I think of how I would like others to treat me, it convicts me. How often do I expect others to treat me like a rock star or a prince, but when it comes to my treating others, I expect them to make do with my half-hearted efforts. And that's when it comes to dealing with my friends and family, who aren't in the mosaic! The people in the mosaic are different from me. They are from far-off places, with completely different customs, practices, and worldviews. How will I ever find the capacity to "do onto others" on a global scale? How will I ever find the courage to stand up to injustice? How will I ever find the means to join the fight against poverty and world hunger? I think the only answer is, get up and go to those places where there is injustice, hunger, and extreme poverty. Listen and see, and, in response, act with compassion. Suffer with them. There is a serious choice we have here. But as I reflect on the mosaic, I would much rather be found in the mosaic, surrounded by those many different faces, than surrounded by La-Z-Boy recliners, big screen TVs, surround sound, and central air.

PART 7:
LETTING THE DIRT
HIT THE FAN

Derek's Father Abraham

Whenever someone asks for my two cents on the old traditional versus contemporary worship conflict, I always like to tell the story of how Derek did the call to worship at Hot Metal one Sunday.

Derek, who had been in an "on fire for Jesus" kind of season, approached Jeff and me that morning and asked if he could share a Psalm at the top of the service. He held up the Bible, turned to the spot where he wanted to read, and told us how moved he had been by this particular piece of scripture that week.

Let me describe Derek to you for a moment. He almost always dresses in black and usually wears the latest punk-rock group on his chest. He's covered with tattoos, and he has big gauges in his ears. And you can usually hear Derek coming before you see him because his chains jingle when he walks. He's the most lovable guy in the world. People around the world love him, but if you didn't know him, he might intimidate you. He comes across as a tough guy, but for those who know him, he's a teddy bear.

When we began the service, Derek rose, jingled to the center of the worship area, and with that same Bible in hand, he read the Psalm. When he had finished, he looked up from the book with that mischievous grin on his face he sometimes has. "And now," he announced, "if everyone will get on their feet, I want to do something I haven't done since I was a kid." I tensed and braced myself for what was about to transpire. "No, no," I thought, "this isn't happening. What should I do? Should I do something? Should I take control?"

But I didn't do anything. I stood there in disbelief as Derek raised an arm in the air, began waving it like a giant bird, and sang:

Father Abraham had many sons,
Many sons had Father Abraham.
I am one of them and so are you
So, let's just praise the Lord! Right Arm!
Left Arm! Right Foot! Left Foot! Chin up! Turn around!

I will never forget the morning Derek led the Hot Metal throng in a rousing rendition of "Father Abraham," his big arms flapping, his black, spiky hair bouncing, his chains a-jingling—it was quite a scene. By the end of it, I was in tears, and I know I wasn't the only one. Derek's rough exterior could not contain his child-like love for God and for life, and it moved us all. "Father Abraham" reminded us that we're really all just kids. We could have broken bread the moment the song was over and all gone home.

There is only one thing more hilariously inspiring than that story, and that is the look on people's faces after I tell it, especially at a church conference or workshop. After people ask me for my wisdoms on the subject of traditional vs. contemporary worship and I tell them about Derek and "Father Abraham," they aren't sure what to make of it. I mean, none of it fits into our little box that we've put church into. Not only does Derek himself break the mold, but the idea that "Father Abraham" would move people to tears just doesn't compute. The fact is, God doesn't care about traditional worship or contemporary worship. In fact, one could argue that despite what the hymn-makers say and the worship-music industry (which, by the way, is making serious money) would lead us to believe, we have not been created solely for the purpose of standing in a big, dimly-lit room with a whole bunch of people singing "Shine Jesus Shine." And if I get to heaven and all I see is a group of self-righteous people standing with their eyes closed singing "I Could Sing of Your Love Forever," I'll ask Saint Peter at the Pearly Gates to pull the switch and send me straight into the abyss. Worship isn't about traditional songs, contemporary songs, or any songs at all. The real reason we are called to gather is to share in koinonia. Is it possible to share in koinonia through music? Sure, music can be a powerful tool, but it isn't the reason we gather. The reason we gather for worship is to be in communion with God, with one another, with suffering, and with the Word. See, we think we need worship to entertain us because our consumer-pleasing culture tells us so. The truth is we don't need an entertaining, senses-pleasing worship service. What we need is koinonia. We haven't been created to desire a good worship service; we've been created for authentic, intimate relationships with God and others.

So many churchgoers are actually churchhoppers. They hop from church to church, looking for that cool experience that will give them the best show. Worship isn't meant to be a show. And it's not meant to be the center of all church life. A faith community needs to center on the mission, living Christ's life. The worship gathering is the place where we come and give our thanks to God for sustaining us through that mission.

Worship isn't the place where we come to be entertained, or where our warped cultural values are reinforced. Worship is where the exhausted missionaries gather to connect with God, give God thanks, and find strength enough to go out and share in compassion some more. Worship isn't about us. It isn't about what I can get. Worship isn't a product at all. Worship is the gathering of Jesus followers, sharing in koinonia, and being broken apart like bread. It is when we connect with God and connect with God's Word. Then our identity is made known, and we are freed from the lies and the deceptions that this world feeds us.

Identity and Truth

In the three preceding chapters, I have tried to outline the deep meaning of koinonia with God, others, and with suffering. I have also tried to convey the spiritual importance each one has in our lives. Fear, rejection, and hopelessness grab onto us and drag us into hell, which is alienation and isolation from God and others. Sharing in communion with God by surrendering our lives, sharing in community with others by humbling ourselves, and sharing in suffering are thresholds into the kingdom of God as revealed through Jesus' life, death, and resurrection. In this chapter, I want to talk about the importance of sharing in koinonia with the Word of God.

What is the Word of God? Sure, the Word of God is scripture. It's the Bible, but I think it goes beyond that. Wasn't the Word around before the books of the Bible were even written, much less organized and canonized by the church? I'm not sure the Word can be defined completely with words, strangely enough, but I define the Word as God's love made known to us, God's grace revealed to us, and God's salvation given for us. It is the gospel, the good news of the kingdom of God. It is God's great story, where God redeems this broken world. Also, in John 1:14 it says, "The Word became flesh and lived among us." This means that Jesus Christ himself is the Word. What in the world does that mean? In addition, if we, His followers, are the body of Christ, then we are the Word, by the power of the Spirit. In a less theological terminology, the Word is the testimony of God and the testimony of God's people as both journey together through all of history and through this very moment. It's God's story and our story woven into this wonderful tapestry we call life. The Word is the truth, and the truth sets us free, mostly because the truth is so closely related to our identity.

In the movie *The Lion King*, Simba runs away because he believes he's responsible for his father's death. After playing in the jungle for some time and living for himself with no worries, the ghost of his father, manifested in the clouds, confronts him. Mufassa wants to know why Simba has forgotten him.

> Simba replies, "Father, I haven't forgotten you."
> Then Mufassa answers, "Simba, you have forgotten who you are and therefore have forgotten me."

We can all relate to that line. Many times, the different messages and voices that shout to us to go this way and that confuse us in this whirlwind of a world. We forget who God is, and therefore we forget who we are. We get spun around and turned upside-down to the point that we can't tell which way is up. In a way, we lose ourselves when we slap on a mask, and we become someone else. It is a terrible feeling not to know who you are, to forget your identity. In an effort to pursue the things of this world—money, power, fame—we get confused as to who we really are, and we put on the masks of superficiality. When we do, we find ourselves starving for the truth, longing for the steady footing of reality, and needing to know the truth. We need others to know who we really are. In a way, this is another aspect of hell, to be lost and not to know who we truly are. To lose our identity—this is hell, isn't it? This is why there is such a close link between the truth and our identity. The truth actually reminds us who we are.

The Word of God is the truth, and being in koinonia with that truth helps us to understand who we are and fulfills our need for identity. The Modern Age has turned scripture into the "rules," an uninspiring list of dos and don'ts, but the truth goes deeper than just rules. The scriptures are actually the means by which we find the truth, but they are not the truth in itself. In other words, we don't find the truth in the Bible; we find the truth *through* the Bible. Scripture is more than a list of rules. The words act as lenses, as spectacles, through which we look and see God more clearly. The Bible is like a pair of eyeglasses or maybe even binoculars that we peer through, and although the image is blurry, we get a better view of God. Therefore, the Word of God helps us to see who God is and then understand who we are. The truth of the Bible centers more on identity, knowing God and knowing ourselves in the light of God, than on rules. The Pharisees fell into this trap. They took the law and made it into an empty list. They made the list the truth rather than using the words to see the truth. Perhaps this is why Jesus refers to them as blind men.

In the movie *The Matrix*, Keanu Reeves's character, Neo, wakes up in a futuristic cocoon to find that everything he's known has been a fabrication. He sits up in the pod and pulls the wires from his body that had been filling his mind with a false world, a computer generated, fake existence known as the Matrix. He's been sleeping, and he didn't even

The Enemies	Salvation	Means
Fear	Assurance	Koinonia with God through Christ
Rejection	Belonging	Koinonia with others through Christ
Hopelessness	Meaning	Koinonia with suffering Christ
Superficiality	Truth	Koinonia with the Word, who is Christ

realize it. When he finally wakes up and experiences the truth, he also discovers who he really is. This is how superficialities can become such awful enemies. Hell is similar to living in the Matrix, where everything seems fine but actually isn't real at all. This is the power of the truth; it opens our eyes to what is real. Connecting with the Word of God, sharing in koinonia with the truth, is like waking up and discovering what is real and realizing that you've been lied to and that the world that you've been living in is a fraud. Our job, as followers of the Way, is to help other people see the truth and get unplugged from the superficialities that lull us to sleep.

As I shared before, my mother's second husband adopted me when I was a child. When dad adopted me, my world completely changed; my identity changed in more ways than one. First, I took my new father's name, and that has been who I am ever since. Second, the adoption gave me the right to be part of the family, to share in the family's home, and to have a piece of my father's inheritance. Third, it granted me the awesome blessing of sitting at my father's table every evening and to be loved and cared for by him. Being adopted meant I took my father's name, became part of the family, and determined who I am. Being adopted by my dad is and was the truth that changed my identity and made me who I am. I am my father's son, through the adoption.

This is reality. This is the message of the truth. This is the message of all of scripture. God through Christ has adopted all of us. God has determined who we are by the adoption. It is our identity; we are children of God. When my father adopted me, he went to the courthouse and paid the three-hundred-dollar fee. When God adopted all of us, welcomed us into the family, and granted us rights at the table, God paid a lot more. God gave us everything. God's only begotten Son—that was the adoption fee.

Mephibosheth is an obscure Old Testament character. He is Jonathan's son, and I identity with him more than any other character in scripture. In the story, which you'll find in 2 Samuel 9, King David is looking for someone in the house of Saul whom he can bless. The only one left is Mephibosheth, who, the scripture say, is crippled in both feet. When King David comes to Mephibosheth and tells him that he wants to restore his life, Mephibosheth bows down and says to King David: "What is your servant, that you should look upon a dead dog such as I?" (2 Samuel 9:8). Although Mephibosheth was a dead dog, crippled in both feet, with no assets or value of any kind, King David raised him up, and every day of his life, he ate at the King's table.

This is how scripture becomes a lens to the truth. This story isn't just about Mephibosheth and King David; this story is about God and me. This story is about God and you. This story conveys a deep truth that doesn't give us rules to follow. It shakes up our worldview, determines our identity, and reminds us who we truly are. We are all "dead dogs" whom God has redeemed and has invited to sit at God's table to eat. This is why we gather for worship services, not to be entertained, but to see clearly, through the Word of God, who God really is and who we really are. We don't desire cool music and a clever drama; what we desire is identity. Being in koinonia with the Word fills that desire and carves out who we are. This is why Jesus taught in parables. He wasn't doing stand-up comedy. He taught in parables so the listener would connect with the truth rather than simply be entertained by it. So often, it seems we walk into worship, sit, critique, go through the motions, and then walk out completely unsatisfied. This is because instead of throwing down our masks and our superficialities, we actually slap on a few more. Sharing in koinonia with the Word should have the opposite effect. We should wander into worship, and the masks we wear to cover our real selves should melt away as we connect in a real way to God's Word.

What does this all mean in terms of what the church's mission is and how we execute that mission? What does it mean to be in koinonia with the Word of God? Remember Dale's Cone of Learning? Do we simply read the Word of God, or are we helping people experience the Word of God? If we need to help people connect with the Word, how do we do it? How do we help people participate in the Word of God? How do we help people discover the truth, who God really is and who they really are, not by telling them, but by showing them and helping them experience it?

Connecting to Truth through Story

The great philosopher Aristotle said that we get to truth using the four wisdoms: science, philosophy, religion, and art. These are the vehicles we use to help explain and to answer the deep questions of life. Who are we? Who is God? Are we all alone? Where did we come from? We answer these big question taking bits and pieces from the four of the wisdoms. With our civilization, just like all of the civilizations in history, we don't use just one of the wisdoms. We are always pushing back and forth, using all four at once. However, there have been, at different points in history, periods where one of the wisdoms takes the lead and we emphasize one over the others. In Medieval times, for example, truth was explained more through religion, not just in the West, but also around the world, from Angkor Wat to the Mayan Peninsula. In the Modern Age, science has taken the lead role. In the Classical period, philosophy had the most weight.

Where do we find people today? Where are we searching for the answers to the big questions? Are we packed into large cathedrals? When we want to know truth, do we ask the Pope or even a pastor? Does research fascinating people of our generation? Can we be found in the laboratory? Do people of our day sit around quoting the great philosophers? Who, besides philosophy majors, ever even picks up a philosophy book? Let's face it: no one. We don't live in a world where we use science, or religion, or philosophy to find truth. The main vehicle we use today, in the Post-Modern world, is art. More specifically, it is the art of story. Whether we like it or not, people of our culture have come to explain life through story. Look at where we gather—the movie theatre, the bookstore, and in front of the television, or YouTube. We can't get enough stories; they've become our bread. We can't wait for another story to break out in the world, so it can nourish us. That's why we have twenty-four-hour news channels like CNN. We can't wait for the next story to break so we can eat it. "What's the story?" we cry out. "What's going on? I need to know! Feed me!" We feed on stories like this because we use them to define who we are, as individual, as sub-cultures, as a country, as a generation, and as a people of faith on the journey searching for God.

We cannot underestimate the power of stories. These stories connect us with some sort of truth. Now, is the truth that we're connecting with *the* truth, or is it just a fallacy that we proclaim as the truth? This, of course, is where the church's role as the proclaimer of the truth needs to step up and help people connect with God through the Word. One thing cannot be denied or avoided: the church must find ways of helping people connect with the Word of God through the power of story.

Stories don't just entertain us. A story fills our minds and spirits with imagery so we can vicariously participate in the events, experiences, and feelings that take place in the story. Sharing in a story is sharing in koinonia with the people and the events in the story, no matter who they are or when they happened. A good story doesn't just change our minds or our opinions on a certain topic, as arguments are meant to do. You can't argue someone into the kingdom. A story works to change our whole outlook, worldview, and our assumptions. A story can make us laugh, make us cry, or make us angry to the point of motivating us to do something. A good story moves us in a way that changes us completely. This is why Plato said that the most dangerous people in town were the storytellers. The storytellers had the power to sway not only a person's opinions, but also to steer the opinions and worldviews of society as a whole.

Stories have this power to help us see and feel what the characters in the story see and feel. In a way, we put ourselves into the shoes of the characters in the story. Whether it is a fictional story or a story from real life, we can't help connecting ourselves vicariously to the events. Sharing in the story of the parable of the prodigal son helps us to be in koinonia with the characters and situations in that story. In addition, when I realize that I am actually the prodigal son, it moves and changes me. The same goes for any other story we find in scripture. I am Zaccheaus. You are Peter. I am the woman at the well. You are the lost sheep. I am the widow who gives her last two coins. You are the good Samaritan. Sharing in koinonia with the Word connects these stories, parables, and poems in a way that touches us and helps us see the true character of God.

For the church today, this means we need to embrace the art of story so people can connect with the Word of God. We need to push religiosity, scientific analysis, and philosophy to the back of the line and emphasize the art of story. For the church this is really bad news, and it is really good news. It's bad news in that the church must change its modern methodologies and mindsets when it comes to proclaiming the Word. It's bad news for the pulpit, the homiletics class, and the old models of worship. The good news is that the Bible *is* a piece of art, or pieces of art. Heck: it's a whole art museum! The Bible is made up of poems, verse, wonderful stories, parables, and metaphors. It is one big story made up of thousands of stories of all shapes and sizes. And they're almost entirely stories about people struggling in their search for God. Scripture isn't just a proof of God that we bash people over the heads with. It is a piece of living, breathing art in which we can share in koinonia and in some way, by the power of the Spirit, find the truth and, in turn, find identity.

The Family Album

Our family has an album with page after page of different kinds of entries about our lives together. In the album, there are pages of pictures, either photographed and drawn, or painted pictures. There are also pages with letters, stories, and documents such as report cards and birth certificates. Everyone in the family has had a hand in creating the family album. I have some entries and Brenda has some entries, as well as Carly and Daniel, our children. One of my favorite pages has two entries, one side done by Daniel and the other side done by me. On my side there are a number of pictures of our trip to the beach, including a picture of Daniel and me throwing a Frisbee. In the picture, which is a photograph, I am very small and Daniel is much larger because I am quite a distance from the camera and he is standing right in front of it. On Daniel's side, there is a story that he wrote about our trip to the beach and a picture he drew with crayon that depicts a similar scene— him and his dad playing Frisbee. Daniel's picture is very different from the photograph, but it tells the same story. In Daniel's version, he is much smaller, and I am as big as a house. Both versions are true, but true in different ways. In the photograph, the truth is actual. We played Frisbee, but Daniel's version isn't untrue; to him, I am as big as a house.

This is how we should approach scripture. The Bible is like a big family album, with page after page of a variety of entries by a variety of contributors and perspectives. Are there contradictions at times? It would seem so . . . but not really. The truth is the truth: God loves us and wants to be in communion with us. In our family album, is it really important whether Daniel and I are throwing a Frisbee or a football? Or is it more important that we are together and we love each other? This is the Word of God; it's the truth, but it is true in a deeper way than just static truth. This truth is alive, and by the power of the Spirit, it's a piece of art that melds us into itself and into God as it shapes who we are.

F-Bomb Sunday

How do we utilize the power of story? How can the church be a bridge to Jesus Christ by helping people participate with the Word of God and share in koinonia? Well, to begin with, we don't add a couple of stories to our sermons and call it a day. Our sermons aren't story; the whole worship gathering is a story with whole bunches of little stories. Just as the church is mission, the church is also story. Collectively, we are God's furtherance of the great story, and individually we are little stories of God's grace. Remember Acts 2: "They devoted themselves to the apostles' teachings . . . ." What was that? What do you think that translated into? What else could it have looked like but everyone gathering around the apostles and listening to their stories about Jesus? Most certainly, they added to these stories as others began to have experiences in their faith, just as we have experience in our journeys of faith that turn into inspiring stories.

There are many different ways to utilize the power of story to proclaim the gospel. Many churches use videos and pictures, which are good. However, sometimes I think that anything projected on a screen comes off as flat and dead, no matter how good it is. When worship presents a story live, something happens that makes the moment a one-of-a-kind moment. This makes the moment raw and compelling. When we connect to a live story, it raises our emotions, and we might even tingle or our hearts might race because we're unsure what might happen next. Anything that we witness first-hand is always going to be more visceral and more captivating than anything on a screen.

A great example is what our church has come to call F-Bomb Sunday. As you might have already guessed, we had something unexpected happen that Sunday. The scripture verse we were using that morning was Luke 10:38-42 where Jesus scolds Martha saying, "Martha, Martha, you are worried and distracted by many things; there is need of only one thing. Mary has chosen the better part, which will not be taken from her" (Luke 10:41-42). Our idea for the drama was for Jesus to scold some young people who in the congregation the same way Jesus scolded Martha. Of course, the people being scolded knew what was going on because they were part of the drama. Jeff was playing Jesus, and after the scripture was read, he walked through the congregation. When he came to one of the young people, he scolded him saying, "Jonathan, Jonathan, you are so worried . . .," and Jonathan stood up and talked about his worries, sharing with the congregation the story behind his anxiousness. Most, if not all of the stories, were real, so this drama was less of a drama and more of a time of testimony-sharing or confession.

Earlier that morning, a guest missionary had shown up. She was traveling through town trying to raise money as she shared her testimony. She wanted to participate in some way in our worship. We explained to her the idea for our drama, and she agreed to be one of the actors. When Jeff as Jesus scolded her with the same line as he scolded all the others, this young missionary got up and shared the stories of her experience as a missionary in Ireland. In the midst of describing the behavior of the children she worked with, she dropped the F-Bomb. "It's so hard," she said, "to do ministry in a country where seven or eight-year-old kids greet you with the finger and a big F-you."

The amazing thing was that the moment she said it, there was little to no reaction from our congregation. There was no gasp, no one walked out offended, and, in a weird twist of fate, we had two first-time visitors that Sunday. Tom and Jean Cox eventually decided that Hot Metal would be their church. They take great pride in telling people that F-Bomb Sunday was their first Sunday at Hot Metal.

The point I'm trying to make is that we don't really need to use movie clips or videos to utilize story in our faith communities. The stories are all around us, and they all can connect to God's Word if we give them a chance. Often, when we use multi-media, we rob the body of Christ of the opportunity to do its own storytelling. If koinonia means "to participate with," then shouldn't we try to get people involved in the proclamation of the Word instead of letting them watch? Setting people in front of a television screen is the work of a lousy babysitter, not the job of the church that is trying to manifest the kingdom of God.

Just as we want to help people experience communion with God, participate in community, and share in each other's sufferings, we also want to empower people in the proclamation of the Word of God. If you haven't noticed, the average attention span is shrinking. Why go on and on boring people to death when you can involve people in the preaching? I don't mean individuals preaching; I mean the body of Christ preaching together. Instead of one priest doing the sermon, let's get the royal priesthood to preach the Word. I will refer you back to Dale's Cone of Learning one more time. How much of a twenty-minute sermon is the average person going to digest? The answer is less than ten per cent, and that's if you're good! But what happens when you involve people in preaching the sermon, in a drama, or in a stylistic testimony like the "Martha, Martha" example above? How much of that do people digest? A lot more. The people who actually present the drama will directly experience the Word of God, and in some cases put it to memory. Those who watch the drama see the Word of God played out. The Word of God is *shown* to us through a drama instead of *told* to us. Showing is much more powerful than telling, every time. And the power of a group of people working together to share the Message cannot be overstated. You risk experiencing an F-Bomb Sunday, but even that can be redeemed.

One Sunday, we did a drama called *Gird Your Loins*, where Derek played a young adult who walked through life with his pants down. Of course, he did it with discretion. Derek wore a pair of pajamas to cover his skin. Nevertheless, his pants were on the floor. We used the metaphor of the pants around his ankles to describe what life is like when you pursue the trappings of this world and become spiritually empty. Derek took water to those who were thirsty, but he repeatedly failed because his water pitcher was bone dry and his pants were wadded up around his ankles. It was a hilarious drama to watch as Derek tried to navigate from person to person, shuffling across the stage with his pants down, filling thirsty people's cups with nothing. When the drama concluded and we moved to a time of prayer, a young woman raised her hand, and with tears in her eyes said, "Please pray for me. I've been walking through life with my pants down too."

If I had tried to convey the same idea in the midst of a long, tired sermon, it would not have been as moving. Somehow, this young woman connected with Derek's character in a profound way. If the Word of God is like bread, as in "give us this day our daily bread," then a good drama can be like the yeast.

Creative Arts Meetings

From the very beginning, our intention was to involve as many people as possible in Sunday morning worship. More specifically, we wanted to have a drama that proclaimed God's Word in a provocative way each week, and we wanted to empower others to be part of that proclamation. Therefore, even before we had weekly worship gatherings, we had creative arts meetings. We used the term *creative arts* mostly because church dramas are notorious for being awful, and we wanted to distance ourselves from that. We took the task of proclaiming God's Word very seriously, and we still do.

As a result, our creative arts meetings are very prayerful. We take time to read the coming week's passage a number of times, from a number of different translations. We research the original meanings of words and original translations. We crack open a commentary to get a deeper understanding of what the passage means, and then we open it up for discussion. Our discussions, which are always quite fascinating, have four levels. First, we discuss what the passage means theologically. What does the passage tell us about God's character? The second thing we do is talk about what the passage means on a macro-scale. What does this Word mean for the world of the writer? What does it mean for our world? What does it mean for Pittsburgh or our region? What does it mean for the church? What does it mean for our specific faith community? Third, we share what the Word means for us as individuals. How does the scripture reach you? What are you going through in your life that this preaches to? How does this Word apply to how you live?

Finally, when we have wrestled through all of these questions, we begin the work of putting together a drama or some sort of creative expression that will proclaim the Word that has been birthed out of the Bible and out of our discussion. This time of discussion has been priceless, and many people come to the creative arts meeting because they like the Bible study part of it. They don't intend to be in the drama. This last question we wrestle with, "how does this message get proclaimed," is sometimes the most difficult. It can be hard, after digesting so much information and sharing so much discussion, to come up with one overarching idea. Our group has come to trust one another, and we've come to learn how to give and take, which has been crucial.

Our group has also learned from experience. From both our successes and our failures, we've begun to catch onto what makes a good drama. Here are some of the tips that we've stumbled onto:

1. Honesty always trumps cleverness.

Sometimes, because it's called creative arts, we think we have to put on our creativity masks and see how clever we can be. This almost never works. We have found that what works better than being clever is being honest. I can remember one particular night when the meeting turned into a "let's see who can be the most creative'" contest. The wild ideas were flying. By the time we were done one-upping each other with our cleverness, we had plans to build a large set and purchase several cases of 3D glasses for the congregation to wear during the drama! We started to make a to-do list. That's when someone asked, "Wait a minute. What's the point of this drama again? I'm confused." We all looked at each other and laughed because we realized we'd gone off the deep end. After a moment of silence and prayer, one young artist, Caitlin, quietly shared how difficult the given verse was for her to apply to her life because she struggled with anxiety stemming from a low self-esteem. When she had finished her story, there was another pause and then someone in the group said to her, "You know, I think everyone feels that way, really. Are you willing to share that on Sunday morning, Caitlin? That would be powerful." Caitlin agreed, and instead of building a complex set and ordering 3D glasses, Caitlin honestly shared from her heart. Our clever ideas would never have been as powerful as Caitlin's honesty was. The congregation connected to Caitlin's life through her story, and then they connected to God's story.

2. The questions are more important than the answers.

This one sometimes makes people uncomfortable, but we've found that the best dramas are the ones that raise questions rather than give out pat answers. Just as in our philosophy around Bible Fight Club, it's not necessarily the answers that draw us closer to God. More often than not, the questions push us further in our faith. The risk is that the questions can sometimes cause us to doubt. But isn't doubt really the "ants in the pants" of faith? If you never itch, would you scratch? If you were never thirsty would you drink? We try to put together dramas that cause people to thirst, which will hopefully cause them to seek out water.

Being a community of faith isn't about force-feeding each other all the answers. It's not about gathering for Bible studies and nodding at one another in agreement. The life of a community of faith is a life of questioning together, of conflict, and of conversation. It's about journeying together, struggling together over the mysteries of life and faith. A good drama can play a role in this process by throwing gas on the fire and by bringing up the questions that the church doesn't want to ask. In *Pandora's Lunch Box*, a drama we wrote about hell, a construction worker engages in numerous discussions and arguments about hell during his lunch break. The opinions come from all different directions with a number of people with different perspectives. The play is a bit risky because we ultimately ask the tough questions: is there a hell and, if there is a hell, what and where is it, and how do we escape it?

People who have hated this drama hated it because we didn't present the "truth" as they saw it. Sometimes when people get red in the face and begins pounding their fists on the table and shouting words like "absolute truth" and "God's Word" and "inerrancy of scripture," what they're really saying is, "I'm right and everyone else is wrong." Those kinds of folks hate this drama because it doesn't validate their opinions. Those who have connected with this drama have connected with it because they relate to Howard, the construction worker who is trying to figure out what he believes about hell and is getting messages and opinions from all different directions. As Howard wrestles with the tough questions he faces, we in the congregation share in koinonia with him and struggle with the questions as well. Posing the tough questions can be challenging, but I believe the wrestling draws us closer to God. Conversely, laying down pat answers and then making people feel like they aren't allowed to doubt draws people away from God.

3. Trust the Holy Spirit shellac.

When we first began this church-planting journey, we obsessed with being "excellent" and we committed a lot of energy and time to making the dramas well-polished and slick. We wanted the dramas to be like shiny and sparkly diamonds. What we've learned, however, is that, more often than not, a choppy, unrehearsed, lump of coal of a drama can be just as powerful. In fact, in the same vein as "God uses our honesty," the messy dramas are more powerful than the slick ones. We've come to call this phenomenon, "The Holy Spirit Shellac." God shellacs our meager efforts with the Holy Spirit and touches the eyes, the ears, and the hearts of those who witness the drama, despite its shortcomings.

When I was in college, I attended a church that was the hip and cool, upcoming church with all the young people. The music was always excellent, the preaching was always excellent, and the church activities were always excellent. One Sunday morning, a young woman got up to sing a song as a special music offering. As she began to sing, it was clear that she wasn't very good. Her voice was gravelly and the notes were flat. I cringed; the whole congregation cringed. At one point, the woman's voice cracked, and she stopped singing as the music kept playing. Not knowing what to do, she began singing again, but because the music kept going, she wasn't even in sync with it. It was awful, and she knew it. Finally, as her last real option, she stopped singing and asked the musicians to stop playing. There was silence. The woman bravely stood on stage, tears welling up in her eyes, as the congregation stared back at her. I couldn't breathe, as I felt so panicked for her. I tried to use telepathy, "Get off the stage. Go! Run!" But she didn't. She stood her ground and very softy said, "I'm really sorry. I've never done this before. I just wanted to sing this song because it means so much to me. I've been in the hospital for the last few weeks, and it's been the promise of this song that has carried me through." She shared her whole experience of being sick and how her illness had caused her to struggle in her faith. Then, instead of singing the song, she read to us the words:

> When peace like a river attendeth my way,
> When sorrows like sea billows roll,
> Whatever my lot thou hast taught me to say,
> It is well, it is well with my soul.

When she had finished reading the words of the song, she said a short prayer of thanksgiving and slowly made her way off the stage and back to her seat. She didn't seem to care what anyone else thought. She just wanted to express her honest love for God. As she sat down and the preacher got up to preach, I looked around the room—there wasn't a dry eye in the house. This woman had brought us all to our knees with her song that she couldn't sing. The Holy Spirit shellac had covered her.

In Spirit and Truth

The thing that moved us to tears that day wasn't the woman's voice or even her message. It was the fact that she was herself. She was real. She was able to get up on a stage, a place where most people hide themselves behind a mask, and she was completely honest. She was true. We connected with that truth, and that truth connected us with God. When we finally become the kind of followers of Christ who value honesty over polish, questions over answers, and Holy Spirit power over the power of our own abilities, we will begin to be the kind of church where people of the twenty-first century can find truth. We've become so accustomed to finding truth through proofs and explanations that we've fallen asleep and have, in many ways, become irrelevant. As a result, the church has ironically become a place where truth isn't easily found. We have great, old creeds in dusty old hymnals but no connections, experiences, or stories that reflect those creeds. For the postmodern person, the channels of truth are art and story, personal relationships, and experience. For many of us, who are not quite living completely in the postmodern world, this is alien. For others of us, who have already left modernity behind, it is second nature. No matter where you are, the fact remains that in order to communicate truth in the not-so-distant future, the church must embrace art, story, and personal relationships. To do this effectively, we've got to cut the crap and get real.

I wonder if this is what Jesus means in John 4 when he says, "God is spirit, and those who worship him must worship in spirit and truth" (John 4:24). God is being, existence, and truth. For us to be in koinonia with that truth, and therefore exist as well, we must approach God with complete honesty and transparency. Perhaps the kind of people that God is looking for are those who are simply and honestly themselves.

As you already know, one of our core values at Hot Metal is participation. We make it a priority to get people involved in our community. As a result, we try to include as many people as possible in our Sunday worship. This has led us to have multiple worship bands that rotate, rather than one fixed band. The upside is we get people involved, and everyone who wants a chance gets a chance. The downside is that the bands are not as prepared as we might wish. On one particular Sunday morning, we had a band that was a bit out of sorts. The guitar was out of tune, there was some serious feedback, you couldn't hear the words, and on and on. But we all sang and worshipped and moved on. No big wup. Later that week, however I received a call from a mother who had dragged her teenage kids down to Hot Metal in order to get them excited about church again. Her kids had been bored with church, and she thought that good ol' trip to Hot Metal would perk them right up.

"Pastor Jim, I wanted to let you know that I brought my kids to church on Sunday and . . ."

"Oh, no," I interrupted. "I'm so sorry. Maybe next time . . ."

"No. wait," she interrupted right back. "Wait 'til you hear this. When the service was over and we got into to the car to head for home, I asked them what they thought. They said they loved it!"

"Oh, come on!" I said.

"I know, that's what I said too," the mother replied. "The music was out of tune and you couldn't hear anything." But they said to me, "Don't you get it, Mom? It was so real. It was like sitting in on a garage-band rehearsal. It was awesome. Where else could you experience something like that?"

The mother and I were both stunned. Maybe it's a generation gap, I don't know, but quality was not as big a concern for these kids as honesty. It seems they would much rather have something that is true than good. And this band that played on Sunday morning, although a bit out of tune, was dripping with authenticity. Perhaps their worship was closer to spirit and truth than I first thought.

On another occasion, during a group discussion, I posed this question, "Have you ever felt that you were really worshipping God in spirit and truth?" After a contemplative moment, a brilliant, life-loving young adult named Emma spoke up.

"I was on one of those youth retreats with my youth group when I was in high school," she said. "They crowded us all into this room lit with candles and with mood music playing. As the band began to play the usual praise and worship songs, their eyes squinted shut, as if they were in great pain as they played. I guess we were all supposed to join them. As I looked around at my follow students, their eyes squinted shut. I suddenly felt completely manipulated. The candles, the music the dim lighting, the words, and the pictures on the big screen were not doing it for me. So, I escaped. I slipped out as if I had to use the restroom and fled down a long corridor. At the end of the hall was a small Sunday school classroom. The room was ugly. The walls hadn't been painted in years. The floor was dirty. The lighting was that ugly florescent lighting that makes everything look depressing. But I sat down on the

DIRTY WORD

floor and I prayed. And you know what? God spoke to me. I had the most wonderful prayer time of my life on that classroom floor. It was one of those moments I remember whenever I'm struggling with doubt. You know, all those other kids had a great time singing in the other room, but I met God on the floor of an ugly Sunday school classroom. Sometimes I think we get all worked up with how things look."

And then Emma finished her story with a sentence that has stuck with me and has changed the way I think about how we do church. She smiled a sly smile and said:

"You know, God can be found in the florescent lighting, too."

Wow. What a statement. It might sound a little stupid for me to repeat it. I mean, of course God can be found everywhere. But as churches try to find all the high-tech ways to draw in young adults, this young adult is saying that God can be found in the florescent lighting, too. Imagine what the church would look like if a whole generation of people were to say, "We don't care about stained-glass windows, PowerPoint slideshows, or cool videos." Imagine what the church would look like if people said, "I just want to connect with God and with others. I just want to worship in spirit and truth. I just want koinonia. And that can happen anywhere. Even in the most unholy looking of places. Even without cool mood lighting!"

Just like everything else in this book, the ways of God and the kingdom of God are completely opposite to the ways of the world. God works through our weaknesses, through our brokenness, through the songs we sing out of tune, through the ugly florescent lighting to bring us the good news of redemption. The Word of God, the language of the kingdom of God, is lewd and offensive, dirty and grimy. Worshipping in spirit and truth isn't about presenting an entertaining show. It's about letting the mud hit the fan and letting it splatter wherever the Holy Spirit wills it to splatter.

PART 8:
DIRTY DEEDS DONE DIRT CHEAP

The Parable of the Town with the Bottomless Pits

As young Justin, a skinny neighborhood kid with long, unkempt hair, and holey blue jeans approached old first church, the oldest, biggest church in town, with a crowbar in his hand, it certainly caught people's attention. The whole city block was in a stir. The church doors swung open, and three little old church ladies in a panic scrambled down the front steps as they ran toward the young man.

> "Now, hold it right there, young man. Hold it right there. Just what do you think you're doing?" The women created a wall with their bodies, quickly cutting him off from his intended target.
>
> Justin, with a mischievous grin and a gleam in his eye, looked up at the towering steeple. "I've got an idea."
>
> "Oh, no. Oh, no, you don't." One of the women, her eyes

dancing fearfully between the crowbar and the old church steeple, belched out, "Over our dead bodies!"

"Look around you," pleaded Justin. "Look what has happened. Look what's become of us. We have no choice now. This has to be done. I'm sorry."

The women paused for a moment and looked away from Justin and down the hill into the town that once was so beautiful, so lively. They knew this day would come; they just didn't think it would come so soon. They had lived in the little town all of their lives. This is all they had ever known. They had gone to this church every Sunday morning. They could remember a time when everyone in town knew each other, when everyone knew each other's names, and when everyone in town gathered on Sunday morning in the old first church for worship. The good old days, they called them. The gigantic sanctuary would be packed to the gills each week. People were connected. And, best of all, you could walk from block to block throughout the whole town without difficulty, without having to risk your life.

That was before the gaps.

Now, things were different. The town had changed dramatically since the gaps began to open up and the town's foundations began to give way. That was twenty years ago. The streets were long gone now. All that remained were the bottomless pits that sank between the blocks. You could literally walk to the edge of the sidewalk and look straight down into darkness. Through years of mine subsidence or earthquakes or sinkholes or who knows what, the city streets had sunk deep into the earth, creating a town that was now fractured and completely disconnected. It was like Venice, only without the water. Every block had become its own isolated island. Most people had made the best of it, creating makeshift bridges and funky-looking catapults out of whatever they could find. But because of a lack of resources, the bridges were dangerous and only used in real emergencies. Therefore, people seldom came out of their homes. The people of the town seldom interacted with one another at all, and no one knew anyone anymore. This led to fear, which led to violence. The women had taken refuge in the big, now empty church. It was all they had ever known. It was safe. It was their hiding place.

And now it was under attack.

Justin, now joined by a few of his friends, armed with a ladder, climbed up the side of the enormous dinosaur and began ripping off pieces of the ancient steeple and throwing them to the ground. The women below, at the sight of the first piece of church falling to the ground, gasped, grabbed their chests, and almost fell over dead. Once they had recovered from the initial shock, they ran around screaming and hollering, completely freaking out. One of them was on the phone to the proper authorities. Unfortunately for them, when local officials finally made their way to the scene, catapulting themselves from far across town, they saw what the young people were doing, rolled up their sleeves, and joined in the project. Throughout the day, more and more help arrived, and more and more pieces of steeple, pipe organ, and pews were pulled from the behemoth and taken to the edge of the sidewalk. By the time the sun began to set, a brand new bridge had been erected across the gap that divided the church with the rest of the town. The bridge, which looked like a piece of modern art, had pews for its beams, organ pipes for its arches, pieces of steeple for its railings, and old wooden doors for a deck. As much as it was beautiful, it was also safe and functional. The church that people used to walk into had now become a bridge that people walked on.

As night fell, people from all over gathered to celebrate on the bridge. Lovers held hands and dreamed of life together on the bridge, children raced up and down its deck giggling and laughing, people who hadn't seen each other in years were reunited, and the young men who had taken the risk to make the bridge possible hung out on its railings, watching the moon rise and smoking their pipes. Even the church-women, who had finally calmed down, and given into change, made a delicious pot of pork barbecue for the folks who had worked so hard. It was one of the best parties ever.

The next morning, Sunday morning, everyone gathered at the church once again with a new sense of joy and purpose. For the churchwomen, it was just like the old days. As they watched all of the people of the town pour into the church, they confessed that they were glad that the bridge had been built. As Justin and his friends walked up the front steps of the church, they were greeted with plenty of hugs, thank yous, and apologies from the church ladies. Although the church had lost a few pieces here and there, it was a small price to pay to see life in the church once again. "We'll get those things replaced," they thought to themselves. Everything had turned out fine. The church was packed. The women couldn't wait until it was time to take the offering. This was going to be a good Sunday. It was happily ever after . . .

. . . Until about 11:30 am, when it was about time to take the offering. For once the people of the city had broken bread , said a little prayer, and were about to pass the plates, they all pulled out their crowbars and went back to work, prying out pieces of church. In the midst of the chaos, one of the churchwomen, completely stunned, stopped Justin and the other young men and women that they had thanked earlier and said, "What are you doing? What's going on? The work was done. It was over. The bridge was complete."

"Look at this place," Justin said. "It's absolutely huge. Do you realize how many bridges we can make out of this place?"

"Isn't it wonderful?" chimed another. "Do you realize there is enough here to connect the whole town?"

The churchwomen's mouths dropped open. One of them almost fell over dead—again. They were not quite sure what to do or say. They just stood there, staring in disbelief at the young people as their precious church came deconstructing around them. Just then, a group of young women approached the older ladies with a bouquet of flowers in hand.

"Sorry to interrupt," one of the girls said as she handed over the flowers. "We just wanted to say thank you for sacrificing so much for the rest of us. No one in this town will ever be isolated again, thanks to the church."

By the end of the month, the whole church had been torn down, and a bridge had been built across every gap in town. The town that once had been known as the town of the bottomless pits was now known as the city of bridges.

Building New Bridges like Nehemiah

Now, of course I in no way mean to endorse the dismantling of old churches so their pieces can be turned into bridges. That would be stupid. The story is a parable, a metaphor. I have nothing against old churches at all, they're beautiful, but they do tend to be quite empty, don't they? What I mean to say is we live in a world very similar to the one in the story. We live in the world of the bottomless pit, where giant chasms divide us. We might not be separated physically, but something has happened in our world, and gaps have opened up. We find ourselves alienated from one another, divided by these gaps. Many people find themselves on their own islands, isolated from everyone else. They need bridges built that will connect them with God and connect them with community. To do this, we need to find ways to take pieces from the store-style church and use them to create new bridges.

There is a model of good bridge-building in scripture, but it doesn't come from a bridge builder, it comes from a wall builder. In the book of Nehemiah, there is a story of a guy who sees the suffering of others, has compassion, and acts to make things right. Nehemiah has a vision of rebuilding the walls of Jerusalem, not for his own glory, but for the welfare of others. Nehemiah's story is inspiring because he is an unlikely hero, a simple cupbearer to the king. He is a hero, not because of his heroic actions, but because of his heart.

> They replied, "The survivors there in the province who escaped captivity are in great trouble and shame; the wall of Jerusalem is broken down, and its gates have been destroyed by fire." When I heard these words, I sat down and wept and mourned for days, fasting and praying before the God of heaven (Nehemiah 1:3-4).

What's clear to me, through these verses, is that Nehemiah was a sensitive, humble man whose heart broke at the same things that break God's heart. If we want to build bridges, our hearts need to break. Then we need to respond as Nehemiah did. Nehemiah got down on his knees and prayed. He prayed for forgiveness and guidance. Then, Nehemiah did three things that led to the rebuilding of the wall. First, he saw a big problem. The city of Jerusalem was in shambles, and people were suffering and in poverty. Second, he saw clearly the solution to the problem. The city wall needed to be rebuilt, not just to make it look good, but to provide protection, jobs, commerce, identity, and hope. The third thing Nehemiah did, even though he was just the cupbearer to the king, was to put together a plan. When the king finally asked what was bothering Nehemiah, he told the king the burden that he had on his heart for the city of Jerusalem. The king asked him what he needed to get the job done, and Nehemiah was ready with an answer. He was able to tell the king that he needed letters to the governors of the regions, letters that would give him permission to get supplies, and on and on. Nehemiah wasn't simply a guy who complained about a problem; he was also a man on a mission, a man who had a plan to make things better.

Just like Jerusalem in Nehemiah's day, we have big problems, and they don't revolve around church attendance. We live in a world with deep chasms stemming from poverty, racism, sexism, and technological advances that leave us disconnected from one another. Just like Nehemiah, we need to diagnose the real problem. In addition, while the church today might want to blame the government, Hollywood, or one political agenda or the other political agenda, the truth remains that fear, rejection, luxury, and superficialities cause the gaps. We've become more and more isolated and alienated from one another to the point that we don't want to come out of our homes or step out of our own little worlds to help somebody.

Just like Nehemiah's vision of the walls being rebuilt around the city, we need to embrace a real solution to our gap problem. If the real problem is luxury, why would we try to solve the problem by building a brand-new fancy, building? If the real problem is rejection, why would we try to solve the problem by demanding that people conform? What is the best way to solve the gap problem? Build bridges. Nehemiah saw the need for a wall, and he built a wall; we see a need for bridges, so let's build bridges. And by bridges, I don't mean new mega-churches. That's the last thing we need. We need small, intimate faith communities where people can find family.

Didn't John Wesley essentially do the same thing? In 1729, Wesley found himself in a world where there was much suffering, poverty, and spiritual malaise. At the same time, he encountered a church, the Anglican Church, that was irrelevant, irresponsible, and ineffective in engaging the real problems that Wesley saw on the streets. In response to what John diagnosed as a serious problem in the world around him, he and his buddies formed what folks called "the holy club." It was a group of followers who gathered for prayer and fasting and dedicated themselves to doing acts of compassion. What was it that made Wesley's group such an influential force? Did they come up with some new answer or some new idea? No. The answers and the ideas were from the first-century church. See, Wesley's core values really didn't change at all. However, he changed the way he practiced those values so that his group could be a bridge to God. And it worked.

Just like Nehemiah's plan to rebuild the wall, and Wesley's plan to form a holy club, we need to have an idea about how we can build bridges in our world today. Our dilemma is very similar to the townspeople in the bottomless-pit story; we have ideas, but we don't have many resources. Or do we? The fact is, the church has abundant resources, but is the church ready to part with those resources so that it can become a bridge? In the story of Nehemiah, he had to face a local bully, Sanballat, who wanted to run Nehemiah and his crew out of town because they were horning in on his territory. In a similar way, will the church become its own Sanballat, or will the church respond to the real problem and willingly begin prying the pews out its sanctuaries?

It is tempting to follow the ways of this world and pursue the idol called "big." After struggling early on, Hot Metal began to grow in number. At first, this was a great blessing. Over the next two years, fifty turned into a one hundred, and one hundred and fifty turned into two hundred. It seemed that every week we had to find some more chairs from some place. But when three hundred pushed toward four hundred, and there was standing room only, our faith community began to suffer. Hot Metal Bridge was a faith community that was growing very rapidly. In any other church, this would not be a problem. Certainly, another church would gladly welcome a big crowd. Other church leaders around the region and around the country took notice, and we were lifted up as a model of what could be. This, unfortunately, is the power of numbers in the church today. (Our skill as a pastor, and therefore our worth, is measured by how many people are coming, which is an idol that needs to be thrown to the ground and crushed.)

However, the problem isn't church attendance. It goes much deeper. We have gaps in our world, and people have gaps in their lives. We live lives of hell. We live in alienation and isolation from God and one another, brought on by our tendency to give glory to fear, rejection, luxury, and superficiality. The problem is anti-communion. The problem is selfishness, and not just in our culture, but in the church! The problem is that the gaps have invaded our churches, and the one presence that could make a difference in this world doesn't because it has lost its relevancy. A wet blanket has been thrown over the church, extinguishing its fire and leaving the people of our culture without any bridges.

Church attendance is just another idol, another wet blanket. Moreover, when it comes to the missional church, growing numbers aren't always a good thing. Missional churches like Hot Metal have a mission centered on building intimate relationships. The growth actually threatened to hurt the communal depth and richness that had been its beauty. The growth was actually killing our mission rather than enhancing it. Anthropological studies have shown that human beings cannot relate intimately to more than 150 people. Once a group of people, like a faith community, grows beyond 150, its social dynamic changes, usually for the worse. How can intimacy thrive in a room with four hundred people in it? How can a person connect and be real? With so many people, it is so easy to overlook someone. It is so easy for someone to slip underneath the radar. People in our world, although they might enjoy slipping under the radar, really need to be connected with God and others. That's the point of church: to connect with the King, not to build the biggest castle.

In *The Tipping Point*, Malcolm Gladwell shows us the importance of what has been discovered through the research of Robin Dunbar, a British anthropologist. Through her work, she has found that human beings have the brain capacity to have authentic relationships with roughly 150 people.

> "The figure of 150 seems to represent the maximum number of individuals with whom we can have a genuinely social relationship that goes with knowing who they are and how they relate to us. Putting it another way, it's the number of people you would not feel embarrassed about joining uninvited for a drink if you happened to bump into them in a bar" (Malcolm Gladwell, *The Tipping Point* [New York: Time Warner Book Group, 2000], 179).

This research shows the need for smaller, more intimate faith communities rather than big mega-churches. How is it possible for people who have a 150 person social capacity to relate on a real level with hundreds or thousands of people? The answer is we can't, and that's one of the attractions of the mega-churches—we can show up and hide. As a result, does the average mega-churchgoer really experience koinonia, or is the mega-church another "store-like" experience that reinforces the worldly values of materialism and luxury?

For a bigger church trying to pay its mortgage and sustain its big programs and salaries, growth is necessary. More people have to come, and more money needs to fill the offering plate. But is this really what God desires? Is this what we need from church? For the emerging missional church trying to practice koinonia and build authentic, intimate relationships, growth over two hundred is not a good thing. We began to sense this ourselves. We realized that if Hot Metal Bridge were to become yet another mega-church, then we would have failed to accomplish our mission. Our mission wasn't to create the next big thing; our mission was to live out Jesus' teachings. Our large numbers began to hinder rather than help. After some prayer and reflection, we decided that the solution to the growth problem was not to build a big building or start a second service, or even birth another church. All of those solutions seemed to dilute intimacy and were all about being "big" rather than kingdom. The solution, as we accessed it, was to "sneeze" out into multiple local communities so that everyone could experience true intimacy and communion. Therefore, we began what we called The Sneeze Project. Through this plan, we hoped to empower other leaders with a similar vision of the kingdom of God to build bridges in other parts of the city. In other words, we approached our church with crowbars in hand.

You might be wondering why we decided to use the imagery of a sneeze. Frost and Hirsch, in their book, *The Shaping of Things To Come*, discuss the way in which churches will be birthed in the future:

"We need to find the appropriate mechanism of organic multiplication. We need to locate the strategic medium into which we "sneeze" our message so that it can do what all great idea viruses are made to do—spread like mad" (Michael Frost & Alan Hirsch, *The Shaping of Things to Come:*

Innovation and mission for the 21st Century Church [Jointly Published by Hendrickson Publishers and Strand Publishers 2003], 215).

A sneeze is a perfect way to describe what the church needs to do to build new bridges. A sneeze is messy. A sneeze is chaotic and uncontrollable. There is no rhyme, reason, or order to a sneeze. And yet, a sneeze can be the most effective way to infect a large number of people with a virus in a very short period of time. A sneeze can be the catalyst that starts an epidemic. The emerging missional church operates like a sneeze. The new church of the early twenty-first century will not be birthed like babies or planted like trees in an orchard. Rather, the kingdom of God will be spread like a cold. Growing emerging churches will sneeze out into multiple local communities at once, helping large numbers of young adults connect intimately and communally with God.

Our idea, which was probably a bit over-ambitious at the time, was to create a number of small groups in different communities that would simply practice missional koinonia. Beyond that, there was no plan. The group would go and do whatever the Spirit led them to do. If the Holy Spirit led the group to open a coffee shop, they did that. If the Spirit moved the group to be a bridge to the homeless, they did that. If the Spirit worked in the group to bring about a worship gathering, they did that. Our vision was kind of an anti-vision, really, a non-vision, where we would practice koinonia and let God work. We figured that it worked on the South Side, so why wouldn't it work everywhere else?

Similar to Nehemiah's identification of a problem, a solution, and a plan, we created The Sneeze Project in response to the problem of the gaps in our world today. Our solution was to pull apart the pieces of our church and build new bridges elsewhere by sneezing out into all kinds of other places. All we needed was a plan, and we already had one. It was the plan from Acts 2:42: practice missional koinonia, share in communion, community, compassion, and in the Word of God, and see what happens. We weren't interested in starting new churches; we were captivated by the prospect of being part of an epidemic of bridges.

DIRTY WORD

Catalyst, Missio Dei, and the Oakland Teahouse

Catalyst

Tom and Jean Cox, the same Tom and Jean who began participating in Hot Metal on F-Bomb Sunday, decided that they would step out in faith and becoming sneezers. You have to know Tom and Jean to understand what this meant. Tom and Jean don't seem to do anything halfway. Within two weeks of their decision, they had purchased a home in the eclectic Pittsburgh neighborhood of Lawrenceville. And not just any home—a building that had been used as the home of the local Polish Club, complete with serving bar and beer tap. They chose Lawrenceville because of its large population of artists and people living in poverty. It seemed like a good place, not for a church, but for a bridge to the kingdom.

What God has done with their mustard-seed offering of faith is anything short of amazing. In just a year's time, they have made themselves fixtures in the community. Instead of moving into town, creating a cool worship service, putting up a sign, passing out flyers, and doing a big mailing, Tom and Jean simply got involved in what other groups were doing. Imagine how many friends they made when they volunteered for the local Art all Night celebration. They hang out at the coffee shops and local diners just getting to know people, not so that they can get them to come to a thing, but because that's what you do when you're building bridges.

There is a three-story building where the art shows are held in Lawrenceville. The building was an abandoned public school that was recently renovated. The small faith community that is beginning to grow in the The Polish Club living room hopes to use the facility one day. As Tom was driving over Fortieth-Street Bridge heading home one evening, he noticed a word carved into the stone at the very top of the building: Catalyst. The faith community has taken on this word as their identity. The group sees itself as a catalyst for the kingdom of God, which is neat imagery, because isn't that our role as the body of Christ, to be catalysts for the kingdom?

Missio Dei

Across the city, in a neighborhood called Brighton Heights, another young couple, Matt and Tracy, rented a small apartment and set up shop as missionaries to the aching community. Matt and Tracy have brought people together through a weekly soup night at their house and by getting involved in the life of the neighborhood. Matt, who is a recent seminary graduate, could easily find a well-paying "call" in a suburban church somewhere. Instead, he opted to get a part-time job at the Vault, a little coffee shop down the street from their home. Through the soup nights and connecting with people in the coffee shop, Matt has been able to create a bridge in a place that desperately needed one. Matt and Tracy, who have dreamed about doing foreign missions, find themselves doing foreign missions closer to home.

Matt, Tracy, and their crew call the blossoming faith community "Missio Dei," which in Latin means "the mission of God" or "the sending of God." This name really fits what they are doing through the Sneeze. Through their gatherings, worship, and activities, they have been proclaiming an understanding of mission as being derived from the very nature of God. The missionary initiative comes from God alone; we have nothing to do with any of it. Missio Dei correctly emphasizes that God is the initiator of God's mission to redeem the world. God sent Jesus for this purpose, and God sends us into the world with the message of the kingdom of God for this purpose. God is a missionary God—Jesus has been sent, and we, the body of Christ, are sent. It is not the Church that has a mission of salvation to fulfill in the world; it is the mission of the Son and the Spirit through the Father that includes the church. There is Church because there is mission, not vice versa. The Church must not think its role is identical to the missio Dei; the Church is participating in, or sharing in koinonia with, the mission of God. God is using Matt and Tracy, not to put up a new show, but to bring hope to a community that needs it.

The Oakland Teahouse

When Justin first got involved with the Sneeze Project, he was a college student at the University of Pittsburgh where, in an effort to give other students a recreational alternative to binge drinking, he gathered hundreds of students together every Monday night for four square. Do you know four square? It's that game you played on the school playground as a kid, with the big red playground ball. It might sound ridiculous, but Justin's use of four square has a way of drawing people together to enjoy koinonia. Every Monday, Justin and his team of volunteers drew dozens of four-square quadrants in chalk on the sidewalk in the middle of the Quad and gathered students up for four square. But not just for four square. This group also spent time in prayer, took time to worship and to fellowship, and they planned mission activities such as gathering health kits for people who needed them on the Gulf Coast. Odd as it may seem, this passionate group of young people who gathered to bounce a rubber ball at one another did so with a purpose, and that purpose turned four square into ministry. They did more praying, connecting, and sharing in compassion in a week than some churches do all year! All through four square!

When Justin heard of our church's plan to Sneeze out, he was ready to jump in with his heart and with his ideas. Just like Nehemiah, Justin saw a big problem, devised a solution, and came up with a plan. Justin, who saw a need at his university for late-night activities on the weekends that did not include getting blitzed, decided to create a missional faith community that began at midnight on Friday night and went deep into Saturday morning. The group calls their missional community the Oakland Teahouse. The Oakland Teahouse is simply a place where students gather to sip tea, share in the scripture, share in deep, meaningful discussion, and pray for one another. When 2:00 am finally rolls around, they hit the streets of Oakland, armed with bottled water and loaves of bread donated by Panera Bread. They hang out on the corner, handing out bread and water, making new friends. Their goal isn't to convert people. They've simply found joy in serving. The group involved in the Oakland Teahouse shares in communion, in community, in God's Word, and in compassion. It all sounds like church to me.

All three Sneeze communities have begun to grow just as steadily and substantially as Hot Metal, both numerically and spiritually. But more importantly, people and the spirit have created these groups where there weren't bridges before, using bits and pieces of our faith community. The kingdom of God is breaking out in an old Polish Club in Lawrenceville, in a little coffee shop in Brighton Heights, and on the streets of Oakland in the middle of the night.

Can the church of the early twenty-first century make the transition from store to bridge so that people experience the kingdom of God? If the church insists on holding onto all of its stuff, the answer is *no*. But if the church is willing to shed its baggage like a camel going through the eye of a needle, then the answer is *yes*. In a world where churches are desperately trying to keep their attendance growing, our church decided to send people away. What's the risk? Is the risk that everyone leaves and we don't have a church anymore? What kind of risk is that in the light of the kingdom? None. Because if our church is left with nothing, that means bridges have been built somewhere else. And if our mission is the mission of God, which is to be sent out, then we will have done what we were created to do.

Incidentally, we've been working together on The Sneeze Project for a year. With these three small faith communities beginning to form, the total cost so far is about three thousand dollars. Practicing missional koinonia, especially on the streets of the city where the rent is zero dollars, is relatively inexpensive. Doesn't this make the possibilities limitless? It makes me wonder where else we can build bridges. What does it look like to build a bridge within all of the subcultures around us? What does it look like to build a bridge within a group of young skaters? Or within a group of businessmen and women gathered on their lunch breaks? I've heard of a small group of Jesus followers who gather each week on the city bus, ride it for a full circuit, pray together, pray for the neighborhoods they pass, and pray for those regulars and those irregulars that frequent the bus. Their cause is the cause of Christ, simply being ambassadors of grace, love, and compassion on the city bus. The group has become a bridge to Jesus at a whopping $2.50 per person!

A New Model for Creating New Bridges

When it comes to creating new bridges, what does it really matter what shape they take as long as they bridge the gap and lead to Christ? Who really cares how the bridge is built? One thing I have noticed about our current models of church planting is that we usually come into a new community or neighborhood with the colonial, conquering mindset. Whether it is the Mother/Daughter model, where an existing mother church plants a new daughter church in a new area, or whether it is the "parachute" model where a denominational committee drops a church planter into a community, the models that seem to reflect the industrial age. Usually a mother church, or church planter, will come into town with an existing vision, an existing, pre-determined plan, and begin doing worship with a pre-formed style. It's almost like McDonald's setting up shop on the strip. In the existing church planting models, the new church's ecclesiology is already predetermined before anyone meets a person from the community. This seems strange to me, and although wildly successful, I wonder if this model of church planting reaches everyone, or just those who like eating at McDonald's, i.e., like that brand of church? I wonder if these current church planting models will continue to work in the future, or if we need to rethink how we go about bridge-building.

Mother Church/Daughter Church

What if, instead of rolling into a new community with a set vision, plan, and worship style, the church sent a group of people who would, if they didn't live in the community already, move there and begin practicing koinonia? The group would gather to pray, break bread, share in the scriptures, and share in each other's sufferings. That's it. No other agenda, no other plan. As new people began to connect, and a new faith community was born organically, or virally, the visions, plans, and worship style would develop. What if we gathered for community and let the vision come from the people seeing the needs of the community? What if we suffer with each other and let the Holy Spirit motivate our actions? What if we share in communion with the Word, and let it fall into people's lives like seeds into fertile soil? What if we step back from doing God's work and let God work?

Where the old style of church planting is intentional and controlled, this style of planting is chaotic and open to wherever the Spirit leads. Is it organized? Kind of. Is it structured? Not really. Is it effective in building big mega-churches? No. Is it effective in solving the overall problem of the gaps by creating bridges to Jesus Christ? You betcha. The group of Jesus followers simply practices the ways of Christ and then lets the Holy Spirit move in their midst. It's like throwing spaghetti at the wall and seeing what sticks and what doesn't. It's like going back to the beginning and starting from scratch. When our

The Sneeze Model

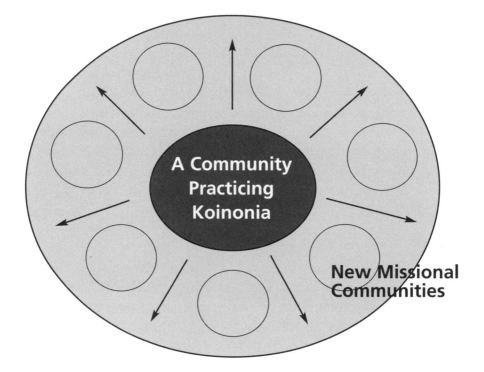

Sneeze group began meeting, its members came together to practice koinonia and to discern where the Holy Spirit would have us go and what we were to do. Because of the missional question of "where are we to be sent," the group had a spiritual edge that was intense, an edge, I noticed, that is sometimes missing in small groups or cell groups.

I attended a gathering with a group of fellow pastors the other day. We were doing the "go around the room and share what's going on" thing. One of the pastors stood up, looking burned-out and disheveled, as if he'd just been chased by a pack of wild dogs.

He stood and asked for prayer for his upcoming fall programming. "This will be our church's third attempt at doing small-group ministry," he said. "Please pray for me. The last time we tried small-group ministry, it just about split the church in half." My heart broke for the poor pastor and the victims he was about to torture with another church program. So many times we try to control our church's spirituality, and we try to force people to grow in Christ, or else. Our tactics can become Frankensteinian, forcing people to gather in a group for mandatory navel-gazing. How is this church? We can't force people into groups and make them love each other. This is why small-group ministry is another one of those Frankenstein-monster ministries that some expert put together with clever charts and conned us all into implementing in our churches. The result is just more of the same dirt.

Practicing missional koinonia is simply the same small-group ministry, but without the charts and circles and schemes, without the conquering and controlling mentality, and without the navel-gazing. Missional koinonia is gathering "in" with a focus on the "out." And, conversely, missional koinonia is pushing "out" with a focus on the "in." I know this might not make logical sense, but this is how we grow in Christ. We need to think missions when we gather inwardly and discipleship when we push outwardly. This is what missional koinonia is and what The Sneeze Project was designed to help people do. Moreover, isn't this exactly like John Wesley's holy club, which gathered to practice koinonia and inadvertently started a people movement that has changed the world?

What if there were a way to take pieces from the old store-style churches and create new bridges, as John Wesley did with the formation of his holy club, and as these sneezers have done with the Sneeze Project? What would that look like? What if that way was centered on practicing missional koinonia? Could this be possible everywhere? What would this look like? Could an old store-style church rip a group out of itself, a group of willing participants, and send them down the street to the local laundromat to do their laundry and to practice koinonia? What would be the outcome? Would the outcome even matter? What if a whole district of churches gathered a group together to practice koinonia? What kinds of resources would that group have available to them when the Spirit began to move and ideas started flowing and needs began to rise? If each district in a particular conference had a group participating in this kind of new bridge-building, what could be possible?

I'll tell you what they'd be: limitless.

One thing is for sure, instead of having one new store-style church planted every five to ten years in our conferences or presbyteries, we would have five to ten new bridges built every year, and at a cost, mind you, of surprisingly much, much less.

Connected Like a Web

One of the dangers of all this is dismantling the store-style church just to build more store-style churches rather than bridges. We could very easily tear down one store just to put up another. Usually a church is planted with this model in mind: first, we'll come up with a vision, a blueprint of the building, if you will. Next, we put together the strategy for getting the thing built—who's going to lay the foundation, who's doing the plumbing, etc. Then, we form the frame by giving the church "structure." This plan may work for building store-style churches, but it doesn't work for building bridge-style churches. The image of a web is a better way to describe how bridge-churches, based on koinonia, are formed and are connected.

Every September since our faith community began, we've pulled our leaders together and have said, "Okay, let's create some structure," and every year we've created some sort of chart or graph with circles and squares and lines and arrows. And every year we've failed to create "structure." Yet, despite our failings at putting together a cohesive structure, ministry expands and people receive care. This makes me wonder: does structure really exist? Or is structure just a myth? I think sometimes we seek structure so we can say we have control of things and so we can prove we have our heads and hands around what's going on in our churches. The fact of the matter is we have no control and our hands are around nothing—God is in control. Many times, when we try to put structure to our koinonia, we actually kill it. I wonder if we really need structure. I wonder if all we need is koinonia and accountability. Look at scripture: does Paul prescribe a certain structure for the church to maintain? Or does he prescribe accountability? Is it possible that the structure we create weighs the church down like a ship stuck in the sand? Could it be that we don't really need it, that it diverts our attention away from the things that really matter? Could we very easily throw these structures overboard and never even miss them? Is there a way to replace the structures of the store-style church with a simple web of accountability that works for the bridge-style church?

I'm sure it raises questions in your mind, such as, "How does the pastor get paid?" and "Where's the accountability?" While my idealistic side says that the kingdom of God isn't dependent upon salaries, I also know from experience that faith communities need good leadership. Pastors and community leaders can be like rivets in the bridge. When they pop out, the bridge can collapse. Likewise, when there is little to no accountability, a church can run amuck with strange teachings and un-Christ-like behavior. Accountability is a huge part of being a follower of Christ, both for individuals and for the community. However, pastors' salaries and a good accountability system are not dependent upon the vision, strategy, and structure model. In fact, money that we waste on dysfunctional systems and structures could help pay for the salaries of missionary bridge-builders and strong webs of accountability.

When we were on our mission trip to Chiapas, Mexico, we met a pastor named Pablo who was an inspiration to us all. Pablo, who had gone to seminary in southern Mexico, was a pastor to no fewer than a dozen churches. His role as the ordained minister was to train and empower deacons, who acted on his behalf for the community. He also provided spiritual guidance and leadership. Was Pablo paid? Sure. Was there accountability? Yes. The small bridge-churches that Pablo served were all connected like a web to one another. If this sounds like the old circuit-rider model from the early nineteenth century, it is. But when you're starting from the beginning, that's where you go for pointers—the beginning. Certainly, the church is older than two hundred years, but the Protestant church in America, as well as all of its missional endeavors around the world, was born during the Second Great Awakening (1800-1830). We might not want to duplicate their methodologies of tent evangelism and Sunday school classes, but the role of the circuit rider, in terms of accountability, might be very similar in the small bridge-style churches that are to come.

Fear of Failure

This is how our Sneeze Project has developed over the past year. We have not known what we were doing or what to expect. There hasn't been a vision, a strategy, or a structure, only koinonia. It has been kind of like jumping out of a plane. None of us has known where we were going to land. Our adventure has been like cutting a trail through the jungle. Sometimes you end up at a dead end, and you have to go back. It has been like I said, like throwing spaghetti at the wall. While some of the leadings, to Lawrenceville, to Brighton Heights, and to Oakland, have stuck to the wall, other leadings that we had toward other communities really did not. We don't know why and we don't really care. Did we *fail* in those other communities? We don't know. Who cares? I wonder, in the light of the kingdom of God, what *failure* means?

As a way of drawing guys together, we like to get together every now and then and play Risk. It's the perfect game for men—you win by wiping your fellow players off the face of the earth. One evening it was my turn, and a young player was trying to bait me into attacking. "Come on," he said. "The game's called Risk, not Pansies!" Now, of course, the church isn't in the business of attacking or conquering anyone, but at times I wish I could scream, "It's called following Jesus, not Pansies!"

It seems at times that the church is so afraid of failing that it never takes any risks. Let me say that again: it seems the church is *afraid* of *failing* so we never take *risks*. In the kingdom of God, not only is there no reason to fear, because we have victory even in death, but our failings are actually God's strength, which God uses to do God's work. Therefore, there are no real risks in the kingdom of God. Now, in terms of the cultural values we hold dear, there are plenty of risks. Failure, in worldly terms, means that you have no worth as a person and therefore deserve rejection. If the church holds this value, then there are plenty of risks. Failure in our society is a curse worse than death, but in the kingdom of God, it is just another way that the Holy Spirit moves to draw people in.

If Nehemiah had been afraid of failure, then a wall would never have been built. If John Wesley had been worried about rocking the boat, a movement would never have started. Being a follower of Christ means being people who are ready to take risks and who are ready to put it all on the line for the cause. By "all," I mean all of those things that we hold so dear: our pews, our organs, our buildings, and our stuff. We need to be ready to surrender to God what belongs to God already, get in the boat, and head out to the deep water. If we are afraid of the deep water, afraid that we might fail (and as a result look bad), then new endeavors will never get off the ground, and new bridges will never be built.

PART 9:
PUT ON YOUR PANTS!

Late Nights and Comic Books

When I was a kid, all I wanted to be when I grew up was the Amazing Spiderman. Every night, when the rest of the family had gone to bed, I could be found lying in my own bed, my desk lamp on, reading the latest adventures of Peter Parker, the Spectacular Spiderman. That's what I wanted. That's what I dreamed about. To be a hero like this spunky, wisecracking wall-crawler who leapt from the pages into my heart. To me, Peter was (and is) the greatest of all the superheroes. Sure, Batman looks cool and has a bunch of gadgets, but where's the heart? Where's the desperation? Clearly, anyone who lives in a mansion and drives a cool car has very little desperation. Look at Spidey. He can't even pay his rent! Then there's Superman. To me, he isn't even a real hero. I mean, where's the risk? Where's the vulnerability? I'm sorry, but heroes don't live in safe, secure mansions, and they aren't invincible. In fact, heroes are the exact opposite. Heroes live on the edge of danger, at the gates of hell, and are ready to be crushed at any given moment.

How we define a hero isn't based on superpowers or super gadgets. We define a hero by heart, sacrifice, and principle. We define a hero by courage in the face of all the risks and perils. A hero is vulnerable and weak. And that's Peter Parker. Peter doesn't live in a mansion. He has a one-room apartment. Peter isn't invincible; he has many weaknesses, both physical and emotional.

That's why I love him. That's why I want to be Spiderman when I grow up. Despite all the risks and all the hazards, he puts his life on the line for the cause. Parker lays it all down, not because he wants to be a hero, but because of his Uncle Ben's words, "Remember, with great power comes great responsibility." These words keep him going.

My favorite of the three Spiderman movies is the second one, Spiderman II, where Spiderman takes on Dr. Octopus. This is the episode where Peter Parker burns out and decides that the responsibilities of being a hero are too much. Spiderman decides to quit. Peter throws his costume in the dumpster and gets back to living life for himself. At first, Parker is on top of the world. He blossoms in his newfound freedom until he begins to see the consequences of his selfishness. In the a scene toward the end of the movie, Peter has a conversation with his Aunt May, where she reminds him what a real hero is:

> "Too few characters are out there, flying around like that, saving old girls like me," she says to Peter while she packs up her belongings. "Lord knows, kids like Henry here need a hero. Courageous, self-sacrificing people, setting an example for all of us. Everyone loves a hero. People line up for them. Cheer them. Scream their names. And years later they'll tell how they stood in line in the rain for hours just to get a glimpse of the one who taught them how to hold on just a second longer. I believe there is a hero in all of us. Who keeps us honest. Gives us strength. Makes us noble. And finally allows us to die with pride. Even though sometimes we have to be steady and give up the thing we want the most. Even our dreams. Spiderman did that for Henry, and he wonders where he's gone. He needs him" (Aunt May, Spiderman II).

I think Aunt May hits the nail on the head as she reminds us what a real hero is. Sometimes we get confused. We think of a hero as someone who is strong, fast, forceful, and who has the power to save the world. If that is our definition, then there is but one hero, and that is Christ. But, as Aunt May says, heroes are courageous and self-sacrificing. This is what makes a hero a hero. Heroes are people who are ready to surrender. Heroes consider others better than they consider themselves. Heroes are ready to care and to suffer with. Heroes are ready to stand up for the truth. Heroes are ready to lay down their lives, ready to risk everything, for the cause. Heroes don't think of themselves as cowards do. The act of self-denial actually makes someone brave. If this is our definition of a hero, then not only is Christ the ultimate hero, but he is the very model of the hero God intends us to be. Each of us has the potential to be a hero. Each of us has this Divine Call: Hero. God is calling us to be heroes.

We All Want to be Big Rock Stars

Everyone wants to be a hero, though, right? I mean, who doesn't? Bravery is a part of who we are as followers of Christ and as people of this country. It's in our DNA, right? Or it used to be anyway. In our national anthem, we all sing, ". . . o'er the land of the free and the home of the brave." I really don't mean to be blasphemous, but I wonder if this is still true. Is America still the "home of the brave?" The home of the heroes? Or do we live in the home of the "me" now? The home of the cowards? The home of self-centered rock stars?

We all want to be heroes, but we all don't share the same definition of what a hero really is. When some people say "hero," they actually mean "rock star." There is a popular song called "Rock Star" by the band Nickelback. The song is about how we all want to be big rock stars, rock-and-roll heroes. Whether the songwriter is being serious or making a prophetic statement about our culture, I am unsure. Either way, the song is right on. It seems that we've all given up on being heroes and have given ourselves over to the draw of being rock stars. The song pretty much paints a picture of the lifestyle we all strive for: a life filled with plenty of money, plenty of stuff, plenty of sex, plenty of screaming fans, and plenty of drugs. I was listening to the song the other day as I drove through a section of our city that poverty has devastated. The singer belted out the lines of the song, which reinforced the theme of self-gratification, as I passed gutted-out homes, graffiti -covered dumpsters, and schools with bars on their windows. It was a stark contrast. How can we all be lusting after fame, fortune, and wealth in a world so desperate for heroes? This world doesn't need any more people who dream of being rock stars. We need people who dream of being heroes. We need people who are willing to go without, to surrender, to sacrifice, and to wash feet.

I almost laughed when I heard the rock-star song on the radio while I was on vacation in one of America's southern states. I'm still unsure why, but the radio station down there decided that the word *drugs* was a bad word, and so it was bleeped out of the song. As we drove along, I smiled and looked over at my wife and said, "If they're going to bleep out the word *drugs*, why don't they just bleep out the whole song? Who are they trying to fool?"

Somebody somewhere is missing the point. The point seems to be that it's okay to be a greedy, self-centered, anorexic, over-sexed jerk, but, "Say no to drugs, kids!" Are drugs bad? Sure, but they are a symptom of larger problems. Just censoring a single word from a rock-star song isn't going to solve it. The larger problems in our culture actually stem from our desire to be self-centered rock stars to begin with. We need bridges, and rock stars or people who want to be rock stars don't build them. The people who censor rock songs don't build them. Heroes build them. People who are willing to lie down and become a bridge build them. People who choose to surrender their lives to be part of the solution, rather than laying their lives down before the idol of rock stardom and being part of the problem, build bridges.

In the early days of the Hot Metal adventure, Jeff and I had a phrase we used as a kind of rally call to one another. When the going got rough, we would say, "Come on. Put on your pants!" What we meant was, "Let's get serious about this. If we're going to do this, let's do it. I mean, really do it." In poker terms, you'd say "all in." So many of us don't know what that means. We live in so much luxury that we have been walking around aimlessly with our pants down. We dream of being heroes but settle for the pursuit of rock-stardom, which we never achieve either. Come on, stop living for yourself, put on your pants, and let's go. No more fussing. No more complaining. No more me time. Let's throw down our idols and let's go where Jesus would go. Let's get dirty. Put on your pants.

What does it really mean to be a hero? What does it mean to be a pastor or a leader of a missional faith community, a builder of a new bridge? I don't think there is a particular model, but I do think heroes have distinctive qualities. Heroes, for example, are unselfish, giving up what they want for the benefit of others. Heroes don't give up. Heroes see beauty in what others see as dirty. Heroes step down. Heroes stand up for the cause. Heroes speak up when there is injustice. And heroes don't flinch in the face of persecution.

One Sunday morning, Adrienne approached us with a petition. A local radio station called "The X" had erected a large billboard near her home on the South Side. The billboard depicted an almost naked woman. Disgusted, Adrienne had begun a petition to get the radio station to take down its advertisement and put up something more discreet. As we signed her petition, we were unaware that she had already called the local news and had set up a time for them to come down to the South Side and get some footage. When she finally told us that the news crews were coming, and that she had told them that we would talk with them, it was too late to turn back. It was time to put on our pants and speak out against the inappropriate image.

The next evening, Jeff ended up on the local evening news, standing in front of the billboard and talking about the petition. Jeff didn't get high and mighty, but he suggested that the billboard was inappropriate for a neighborhood that was trying to be family friendly. It was one of those slow news days, and the story was pretty tame. It seemed harmless. The next morning, however, we received a number of phone calls from people in our community telling us that "The X" was ripping us apart. We turned on the radio and listened as the morning DJs spent most of the morning finding every way to make fun of us. The DJs mocked, roasted, and slandered us across the airwaves that morning. And this continued deep into the afternoon and the next day. And the next. We were called names and accused of being a cult and completely humiliated on a radio station that is popular with our target audience—young adults. We were pretty much dragged through the mud for taking a stand for what we believed was right.

Now, we've been featured in a number of different news outlets, including the Pittsburgh *Post-Gazette*, the *Wall Street Journal*, and the

Today Show. However, those articles and features never amounted to anything when it came to people connecting with our faith community. Nothing prepared us for the power of persecution. After a week of being taunted and ridiculed on the radio, our worship gathering reached maximum capacity. It was painful to be made fun of publicly as we were that week. But you can make fun of me like that every week if it means it will create bridges and people will connect with God who might have never connected with God before.

In Jeremiah 20, we find the ultimate hero. Jeremiah, by the way, is a complete failure. If he were to apply for a ministry position in any church, he'd probably not get the job. Jeremiah is a loser. He has a word that no one wants to hear. As a result, he was beaten, imprisoned, mocked, and belittled. But Jeremiah is my hero because of these words:

> O Lord, you have enticed me, and I was enticed; you have overpowered me, and you have prevailed. I have become a laughingstock all day long; everyone mocks me. For whenever I speak, I must cry out, I must shout, "Violence and destruction!" For the word of the Lord has become for me a reproach and derision all day long. If I say, "I will not mention him or speak any more in his name," then within me there is something like a burning fire shut up in my bones; I am weary with holding it in, and I cannot (Jeremiah 20:7-9).

Jeremiah's cry is the cry of a hero. It is clear: this man has surrendered his life into the hands of the Father. Although following the Lord means he has to suffer, he surrenders willingly, knowing that he has no choice. Being a hero means being a failure, a broken, empty jar that God can fill with grace, love, and power to bring about hope.

In talking with the young adults who are part of our community, I have noticed that many of them are paralyzed by life. With so many choices and so many expectations, they freeze and don't do anything at all. I think part of the problem is that our culture demands that we do something "big" with our lives. In the face of that expectation of big, we go into a coma. There is a strong undercurrent in our culture, which makes its way into church, that pulls us into thinking that we have to change the world somehow. This expectation leaves many young people who want to follow Christ trying to figure out how they can be a disciple of Jesus, the sufferer, and a big rock star at the same time. The result is an epidemic of Christian rock stars. Instead of finding places to serve, these Christian rock stars will only serve when the work is cool or sexy, or they get to climb up on the roof and take their shirt off. Or when there's a camera around. Instead of being honest about their struggles, , they push their dirty laundry under their beds and pretend that they have it all together. Instead of running toward the cross, they run away from the cross, all the while talking about their plans to change the world. We need less Christian rock stars and more heroes, people willing to surrender and sacrifice so that the kingdom of God will be near.

Christian Rock Stars	Heroes
Seek self glorification, use Jesus to get it	Seek Jesus' glorification, humble self
Do not want to die to self	Will lay down life for others
Seek notoriety	Seek Christ, who made himself nothing
Serve if its "cool and sexy"	Serve when no one is looking
Have it all together	Broken, and honest about it too
Squeaky clean	Piles of dirty laundry
Afraid, running away from the cross	Afraid, but running toward the cross
Want to do something "BIG" with their lives	Seek small acts of love
Want to help the poor	ARE poor
Want to reach the last, the least, and the lost	ARE the last, the least and the lost
Worship when it's their turn to lead music	Setting up chairs is their act of worship
Want to change the world	Want to wash a foot
Take	Sacrifice

I believe that we are at a crucial point in church history. There is a great conflict going on, and we need losers like Jeremiah to stand in the fray and be torn to shreds. The outcome of this conflict will affect the future of the church. The conflict is within the church and between those who call themselves Christians. The conflict is between those who are surrendered and those who use fear as a weapon. It is between those who humble themselves and wash feet and those who use rejection to conquer and control. It is between those who share in compassion and those who guard their luxury. It is between those who pursue the truth, the Word of God, and those who hide behind the fake veneer of superficialities and disillusion. It is obvious who will win and who will lose this conflict. The winners will take the spoils—the beautiful buildings, the large endowments, and the places of position and power. The losers will quietly go their own way, back into the catacombs from which they came. They will go back underground, to the tattoo-shop basements and dark, dirty holes of this world where they share little pieces of body and little drops of blood with one another, and they sing quiet hymns of praise. We need heroes who are ready to go and lose that battle for the sake of the kingdom of God, ready to be losers for Christ, and for the sake of those who do not yet know of the awesome love and grace of Jesus.

When I think of a sacrificial hero, I think of my mother. She has sacrificed a lot for me and my brothers and sister. Many times, she has gone without so that we could have. Sometimes the sacrifice has been very small, like taking time off to watch our kids. Other times, she has made great sacrifices that have taken my breath away. One such time happened in my early twenties. My wife and I met in college, and when we were finished with school, we wanted to get married. We felt strongly that we were meant to be together, and we wanted to begin our lives together as husband and wife. At the time, however, we had very little money, and I had no way of purchasing an engagement ring. Without any hesitation, my mother pulled me aside and gave me her own wedding ring to give to my future bride. It was an awesome gesture and one that has become one of those big life lessons for me. Sometimes, for others to be bound together, precious things must be sacrificed. Perhaps this is a parable for the church today. If we are to build a bridge for the next generation to walk on so that they can find koinonia with God and the kingdom of God, then the church might have to sacrifice its most precious belongings. I guess that's the real definition of sacrifice: to make something sacred by giving it away. When my mother gave away her most prized possession, she made that ring even more sacred. Now, my wife wears it as a symbol of our covenant as husband and wife, but someday Brenda plans to hand that ring down to the next generation so that another marriage can be blessed. This makes the ring's symbolic significance even more meaningful. Are there precious things that the church has that if they were given away they would become even more meaningful?

Heroes in Training

While we were away on one of our mission trips, I had a young man named Jack approach me with a question that still has me a little bit stumped. Jack pulled me aside late one night and said, "Pastor Jim, I think God is calling me into the ministry."

Now Jack had just read a book about another young man who had given away everything and had gone to live in war-torn Iraq for a while. The book had inspired young Jack to live with that kind of radical faith. He had also witnessed missionaries working happily in another country where they had almost nothing. For me to tell Jack that the path to ministry was to go to college and then make his way through seminary seemed ludicrous.

Just a few days earlier, I had sat with Jeff in a coffee shop as he looked over his ordination exam evaluations.

"You're not going to believe this," he said. "I got a 'satisfactory' on the parking-lot question."

"There was a parking-lot question?" I asked.

"Yeah," he said. "There was this whole issue about a church parking lot, and you had to tell how you would have responded."

"But we don't have a parking lot," I said.

"I know," he said.

"We don't even have a building."

"I know," he said.

"So, what does it matter if you got a 'satisfactory' on the parking-lot question? What's that going to matter once we're gathering in the catacombs?"

"My point exactly," he said, shaking his head.

So, here I have young Jack asking me about his call into ministry and my friend Jeff, who has already helped build a bridge, going through the process that seems to have no bearing on anything except church parking lots. What am I supposed to do? What do I say to Jack? What Jack really needs is "hero training," and all I can offer him is parking-lot maintenance preparation. "Get ready, Jack! There's a church parking lot with your name on it! Come on!" In a world that is quickly changing, with huge gaps that need bridging, and a church that is floundering in irrelevancy, why would we need one more parking-lot guy? We don't need more people who can maintain parking lots; we need people who know how to use crowbars! How can we train others (and ourselves, for that matter) to be heroes in a world where churches and seminaries are more concerned about their luxurious parking lots than sharing in compassion? The problem is systemic. The church is a store where we get our spiritual goods and services, so our seminaries are places that train the store clerks, the salespeople, the CEOs, and the parking-lot managers. If we're going to build more bridges, we need places that train heroes.

Our response to Jack's need was to create a kind of apprenticeship program. We call it the Hot Metal Apprenticeship Program. The idea was to help young people find their place on the bridge or learn how to build new bridges. The Apprenticeship isn't some wimpy Bible study or small-group thing. This program is intense and requires an application process and a hefty time commitment. This is how we outlined the program:

Hot Metal Apprenticeship Program

A Nine-Month Experience

Hot Metal Apprenticeship Program is an opportunity for a group of missional leaders to come together, work as a team in ministry, and learn from one another in order that we may:

- develop missional leadership;
- wrestle with and discover what it might mean to do ministry in

the twenty-first century;

- do theological reflection in a missional context;
- be challenged in ministry;
- have a deeper knowledge of scripture;
- exercise and discover spiritual gifts;
- take time to discern God's call;
- be part of God's mission, both locally and globally.

Vision:

To develop missional leadership within ourselves, both individually and communally, so that we might engage more effectively with this strange, new, postmodern world that is longing to be in relationship with Christ and participate in the kingdom of God.

Mission:

We will develop missional leadership through theological reflection, leadership development, missional ministry training, spiritual-gift development, and by being involved in mission, both locally and globally.

Tasks:

Theological Reflection: participants will meet weekly for theological reflection and interaction. Each month we will study in-depth an assigned book and a book from scripture. As a response to the research, participants will work together on a project based on their studies and their interactions with one another.

Leadership Development: each participant will take on (choose) a new leadership role within the church or within one of our Sneeze Project new church plants, leading a study group or small mentoring group of some type. Participants will take time each week to discuss and reflect on the challenges of being a missional leader in today's world. The group will also participate together in a retreat in the fall.

Missional Ministry Training: the group will set up a missional challenge and to work toward meeting that challenge during the year. The challenge could be as small as creating a service project, or as large as creating a new ministry to the poor. The group will work as a team to fulfill their challenge.

Spiritual-Gift Development: Hot Metal and Sneeze Project leaders will give apprentices opportunities to exercise their spiritual gifts.

Apprentices will be called upon to do such things as lead prayer in worship, lead music, do informal counseling and/or preach in different settings throughout the city. We will also take time, individually and as a group, to discern God's call in our lives.

Local & Global Missions: An effort will be made to deepen our understanding of local and global missions in the twenty-first century. The group will work together on one local mission ministry that they choose as a group. The group will plan and lead a mission trip to Chiapas, Mexico.

Schedule:

This program will begin the first week of Sept. and end in the last week of April.

Sep: Church History
> Shelley, Bruce. *Church History in Plain Language*. Nashville: Thomas Nelson, 1996.
> The Gospel of Matthew.

Oct: The Missio Dei (God's Mission)
> Claiborne, Shane. *The Irresistible Revolution: Living as an Ordinary Radical*. Grand Rapids: Zondervan, 2006.
> The Gospel of Mark.
> Retreat.

Nov: The Kingdom of God
> McClaren, Brian. *The Secret Message of Jesus: Uncovering the Truth that Could Change Everything*. Nashville: Thomas Nelson, 2007.
> The Gospel of Luke.

Dec: Spiritual Care
> Foster, Richard. *The Celebration of Discipline: The Path to Spiritual Growth*. San Francisco: HarperOne, 1988.
> The Gospel of John.

Jan: Christian Community
> Neibuhr, H. Richard. *Christ and Culture*. San Francisco: Harper and Row, 1956.

Bonhoeffer, Dietrich. *Life Together*. San Francisco: HarperOne, 1978.

Philippians, Ephesians, Galatians, Colossians.

Feb: Missiology

Michael Frost & Alan Hirsch. *The Shaping of Things to Come: Innovation and Mission for the 21st Century Church*. Peabody, Massachusetts: Hendrickson, 2003.

The Book of Acts.

Mar: Leadership

Purves, Andrew. *The Crucifixion of Ministry: Surrendering Our Ambitions to the Service of Christ*. Nottingham, IVP Books, 2007.

Romans.

Apr: Global Concerns

Haugen, Gary. *The Good News About Injustice: A Witness of Courage in a Hurting World*: Nottingham, IVP Books, 1999.

1 and 2 Corinthians.

May: The Mexico Trip

Thurman, Howard. *Jesus and the Disinherited*. Boston: Beacon Press, 1996.

Apprentices: This apprenticeship is not for the faint of heart. It will be a serious, intense program that will take up some of your time, energy, and devotion. Each participant must apply to the program by filling out an application. Space is limited; up to twenty-four people will be accepted. Each participant will be asked to be in covenant relationship with everyone else in the apprentice group. Apprentices must keep up with reading assignments from the books and from scripture. Attendance at a weekly group gathering is required. Apprentices who regularly miss gatherings and/or consistently do not complete assignments will be asked to remove themselves from the program.

Who should apply? We are looking for people who are hungry to follow Christ in revolutionary and radical ways. No special gift or calling is required, simply a heart willing to go where Jesus leads. This apprenticeship program is by no means an attempt to replace formal education. It is an effort to give participants a taste of what ministry might be like in the not-so-distant future as the church begins to redefine itself for the twenty-first century.

The Pastor of the Twenty-first Century

What are we training people to do? What is the job description of a surrendered, self-sacrificing hero? The image that we think of when we think of an emerging church leader is blue jeans, cool hair cut, a soul patch, and a Mac. These, hopefully, are not the only characteristics of the pastor of the twenty-first century. We also have the reputation for sitting around in coffee shops, shooting the breeze, and preaching a gospel that's free of morals. This is myth. Or it should be. The pastors of the future, our future heroes, need to be people who bear witness to Jesus Christ and the kingdom of God, encourage obedience to God's Word, gather people, and send them as one.

Bearing Witness to Christ

We cannot change people. Only God changes people. However, God calls us to be agents of change. We do that by bearing witness to Christ and by pointing to him at all times. This is really all we have the power to do. We are never to point to ourselves or to our agenda. When we see Jesus, we need to point to him. When we see the kingdom of God breaking into this dark world, we need to point to it. Bridge builders of the future will find themselves being prophetic voices in a corrupt culture that needs to be slapped up side the head. Heroes sometimes do some serious head-slapping. And, like many prophets, such as Elijah and his confrontation with the four hundred prophets of Baal on the mountaintop, a hero might sometimes find himself or herself outnumbered. Nevertheless, this world needs heroes, not rock stars. We need pastors who are willing, in the face of all adversity and persecution, to stand up against injustice and oppression.

Encourage Obedience

If the ship is ever going to get unstuck, someone is going to have to hoist the sails of communion. God calls us to be people who encourage others to connect with God. Our job is to encourage others to surrender, to humble themselves, and serve. We encourage people to share in compassion and to connect with the truth, which is God's Word. Our job is really to help people connect with the way, the truth, and the life. When we let people embrace fear, rejection, luxury, or superficiality, we let them cover themselves with a wet blanket that extinguishes the fire of their faith. Likewise, when we condone sinful behavior, be it selfishness, greediness, or sexual sin, we turn a blind eye to that same wet blanket. Heroes throw gas on the flames, not wet blankets.

Sent as One

We need to remember that we can't save the world. It isn't the job of the pastor to do all of the work of the church. Actually, one of the hardest jobs of a hero is to step down and let someone else be the hero. We are leaders who lead by empowering others and getting others involved in the mission. We are the body of Christ, sent as one. The pastor of the twenty-first century is the kid on the playground who makes sure everyone is invited to play. No one is left sitting in the school cafeteria alone.

Are You Guys Really the Pastors?

When Dietrich Bonhoeffer was just twenty-seven years old, he was exiled to London for his terrible preaching abilities. When the young pastor was brought before his authorities for an evaluation of his ministry work at his new pastorate, he was told that his preaching style was too demanding. His message was too depressing. Later in the meeting, when Dietrich brought up the terrible changes that were occurring throughout Germany, the church leaders gave Dietrich the same proposal they were giving all their pastors—a strategy for accommodating Hitler and his fascist platform. Bonhoeffer couldn't believe his ears and pretty much said, "You've got to be kidding." In response to Bonhoeffer's resistance, the church authorities told him that no church in Germany would want him as a pastor. Dietrich had a choice: soften his convictions or take a low-paying job in London. He took the job in London. Of course, Bonhoeffer eventually returned to Germany, helped form an underground seminary, plotted to assassinate Hitler, and was finally martyred in a German concentration camp.

Now, we all laud Bonhoeffer as a great hero of the faith, but at the time, I wonder how many faithful churchgoers criticized him? How often did other Christians say "Come on, Dude. Lighten up a little bit. Don't you think you're being a little extreme?"

Extreme times call for extreme measures. And extreme measures call for extreme leaders.

I can remember at the beginning of our very first Hot Metal Worship gathering, Jeff and I got up to pray and to introduce ourselves. When we said that we were pastors Jim and Jeff, there was a hearty laugh from all twenty of those who had gathered. "Pastors? You guys? You've got to be kidding." And the laughs haven't really stopped. There isn't a week that goes by when we don't have someone who approaches one of us and says, "Are you guys really the pastors?" I wonder if we live in the kind of times that require the kind of leadership that makes people say, "Are you guys really the pastors?" If rules are to be broken, we need rule-breakers. If questions are to be asked, we need prophetic voices. If bridges are to be built, we need people with crowbars.

Simply saying something is wrong is not enough. What if Nehemiah had seen the broken walls of Jerusalem and had just shrugged his shoulders? What if John Wesley had seen the indifference and mediocrity in the church of his day and had just pretended it wasn't there? What if Bonhoeffer had seen the great evil sweeping across Germany and decided he was too tired or to inexperienced to do anything about it? We live in a world that is so fragmented and among people who are so isolated from one another. We live in a cursed world where the church reinforces those curses, using fear and rejection to alienate and divide. What will we do? Will we shrug our shoulders, pretend its not happening, and decide we're too tired or too inexperienced?

No. By the grace of God, we will put our pants on and build the bridges the world needs.

Fire

There have been two moments in my life where I have sensed God might be trying to tell me something. The first I shared at the beginning of this book, the vision of Jeff and me running across the railroad bridge. The second event happened on a snow-covered hill in Ligonier, Pennsylvania. It was February 18, 1996. Again, it was another one of those moments that has been so influential to my living that I remember the exact day and time. I had gone up to Ligonier Camp to be the guest speaker at a youth event. When I arrived at the youth camp, the youth hadn't gotten there yet, so I was the only person on the hill. It was like walking into a ghost town. Even though it was dark and the snow was falling heavily, I decided to walk around a little. Brenda and I had worked together as camp counselors on that same hill seven years earlier, so the place has rich memories for me. As I walked through the snow, I could see in my mind's eye the activities of summer camp. Kids were running and laughing as the wind blew through the leaf-covered trees. I stood for a moment, took a breath, and listened. I guess I was praying; I don't know. But something happened. Again, I didn't hear the voice of God, but there was a distinct moment of God's presence. God was near.

"FIRE."

That's what I heard. "FIRE." On that snowy evening, alone on that hill, I heard the word "FIRE." For me, the word has taken on many meanings, from my connection to the all-consuming Fire, to an image that helps me understand how the Spirit moves, to how I describe my vocation. A fire can take on many forms and has many uses. A fire can inspire like a lit candle. A wildfire can spread like an epidemic. A fire can protect, cleanse, and comfort. A fire, in many ways, is like the church, God's people gathered. A fire is like koinonia, that vulgar, offensive word that, when the wet blankets of fear, rejection, luxury, and superficiality are pulled off it, can and will explode across this country and across this world. It will run into the dark and violent places of our world and set them ablaze with the love of God that is found *only* in koinonia.

Way back, when we were still trying to build the bridge of Hot Metal and we were seeking help from the Presbytery or the Methodist conference, we went to visit some "denominational authorities," if you know what I mean. As we gave our presentation, which was most of the stuff you've just read in this book, they sat staring at their laptop computer screens. One leader sat and played solitaire as we talked. They weren't sure what to make of us, and there was no fire in that room that day. Our vision was not embraced by that group. Later that week, one of the tattoo artists asked us when we were going to get our first tattoos. As a way of avoiding the painful-looking ordeal of getting a tattoo, we pledged that when Jeff and I were both "official" pastors of the

Hot Metal community, we'd get tattoos together. We kind of smiled, knowing that the chances of this happening were slim to none. Later that year, our conference got a new bishop, who exhibited all of the qualities of a great hero. Once he caught word of the way our church was creating a bridge to the broken and hurting, there were soon two official pastors.

When we finally wandered down to the tattoo shop, and I sat down in the chair on that fateful day, the tattoo artist asked me what I wanted on my arm. I only said one word in reply, "FIRE."

★★★★★★

"Would someone please save me from this bull#@%?"

That's the line that went screaming through my head. God's been faithful. God's answered my prayer. God has rescued me from church and has thrown me into the fire of koinonia. I am thankful.

I hate church. I really do. It's become a wet blanket.

But I love the fire of the kingdom of God. It is a dirty word that needs to be uttered more often. It needs to be on the tips of our tongues. May its vulgarity set this world ablaze.

Blessing:

Therefore, since we are surrounded by so great
a cloud of witnesses,
let us also lay aside every weight and the sin
that clings so closely,
and let us run with perseverance the race that is set before us,
looking to Jesus the pioneer and perfecter of our faith,
who, for the sake of the joy that was set
before him endured the cross,
disregarding it's shame,
and has taken his seat at the right hand of the throne of God.
Consider him who endured such hostility
against himself from sinners,
so that you may not grow weary or lose heart
(Hebrews 12:1-3).